Praise

'[A]ll the details — including a not inconsiderable number of red herrings... Painstakingly analyses the evidence. The author's career... gives him just the right sort of experience and voice for the task... One of the most intriguing aspects of this book is the discussion of what the Turkish intelligence service MIT (and indeed, President Recep Tayyip Erdoğan) really knew and when.'
JONATHAN FRYER,
Lecturer in Comparative Sociology and the Politics of Africa
UNIVERSITY OF LONDON, SOAS

'A bombshell.'
DAILY MAIL

'Shocking evidence.'
DAILY EXPRESS

'Immensely readable...
an essential read on Middle Eastern politics.'
NEW WORKER

'A cracking read.'
Marco Giannangeli
Security and Diplomatic Editor
SUNDAY EXPRESS

THE KILLER PRINCE?

MBS AND THE CHILLING SPECIAL OPERATION
TO ASSASSINATE *WASHINGTON POST*
JOURNALIST JAMAL KHASHOGGI
BY SAUDI FORCES

Owen Wilson

This edition published for the first time by Gibson Square

UK Tel: +44 (0)20 7096 1100
US Tel: +1 646 216 9813

rights@gibsonsquare.com
www.gibsonsquare.com

ISBN 9781783342006

The moral right of Owen Wilson to be identified as the author of this work has been asserted in accordance with the Copyright, Designs and Patents Act 1988.

All rights reserved. No part of this publication may be reproduced, stored in a retrieval system, or transmitted, in any form or by any means, electronic, mechanical, photocopying, recording or otherwise without the prior consent of the publisher. A catalogue record for this book is available from the Library of Congress and the British Library. Owen Wilson, copyright.

Papers used by Gibson Square are natural, recyclable products made from wood grown in sustainable forests; inks used are vegetable based. Manufacturing conforms to ISO 14001, and is accredited to FSC and PEFC chain of custody schemes. Colour-printing is through a certified CarbonNeutral® company that offsets its CO2 emissions.

Contents

Time Line 7

Part 1: What is certain? 11

... Flying Home 12

1	Mysteries	14
2	A Blip	21
3	Saudi Secrets	23
4	The Insider	32
5	The Crown Prince	40
6	Tysons Corner, Virginia	32
7	Exodus	60
8	'Certain circles'	73
9	Plotting	81
10	Caught	83
11	The Attack	99
12	'Is he facing charges?'	109

Part 2: A movable feast 112

I	3 October	113
II	'Friends'	118
III	Five Eyes	121
IV	Who Benefits?	127
V	Thunderbolt	131
VI	Meticulous Planning	133
VII	Cat and Mouse	137
VIII	The Mood in Riyadh	140
IX	Pastor Brunson	145
X	Horse-Trading	151
XI	Dr Death	156

XII	'Regular tourists'	166
XIII	Apple Watch – iCloud	173
XIII	Crucial Hours	180
XIV	'Rogue operators'	188
XV	Last Words	194
XVI	Uncomfortable Truths	198
XVII	Bone Saw	203
XVIII	'Crap'	209
XIX	'Pre-meditated'	215
XX	Theatre	225
XXI	The Recording	235
XXII	High-five	242
XXIII	*Diplomatik Vahşet*	251
XXIV	Lies Ahead	263

Conclusion

Erdoğan and Khashoggi	263
The Killer Prince?	266

Time Line

Winter 2018 Saudi Arabia is paying advisors up to hundreds of millions to aggressively lobby the Trump administration for an export license for Westinghouse to build 16 nuclear reactors (an essential stepping stone to developing a nuclear bomb) at $80 billion in Saudi Arabia.

6 May 2018 Hatice Cengiz, a 36-year-old PhD student at Fatih Sultan Mehmet University in Istanbul, walks up to Jamal Khashoggi holding a talk at a conference in the city and requests an interview. She has good Arabic after attending a religious university in Cairo and field work in Oman and has been following Khashoggi's Twitter account for a few years. He doesn't respond but she waits outside the lecture room. It is the beginning of a relationship. Months later he proposes to her.

8 May 2018 Donald Trump rips up the 2015 Iran Nuclear Treaty to the dismay of Turkey and the delight of Saudi Arabia.

Summer 2018 US Intelligence agencies intercept secret Saudi plans to move against Jamal Khashoggi, a US resident and Washington Post blogger. The information is disseminated to US intelligence stations in security briefings. The Trump administration takes the decision not to act on Government Order ICD19-'Duty to Warn' to let Khashoggi know.

1 August 2018 Hedgefund Brookfield completes its $4.6 billion acquisition of bankrupt Westinghouse from IP3 consortium founder Toshiba

3 August 2018 Hedgefund Brookfield completes its $1.1 billion upfront-payment for a 99 year lease on 666 Fifth Avenue owned by Kushner Companies, saving the Kushner-family company from impending bankruptcy by defaulting on a $1.4 billion mortgage repayment with accrued interest due in January 2019

August/September 2018:
US and British intelligence intercept chatter about an impending plot against Khashoggi
10 September Jamal Khashoggi and his son Abdullah fly to Istanbul and meet Hatice Cengiz. He proposes to her which Abdullah passes on to his family in Saudi Arabia by telephone
The Saudi consul-general orders the installation of a tandoori oven that can reach 1000 degrees – the temperature commonly used for incinerating human remains – in the garden of his residence (al-Jazeerah reports in 2019).
Khashoggi visits the consulate on Friday 28 September at 11.50am in vain for the divorce papers and is told to come back on 2 October
Saturday 29 September, Khashoggi speaks at the Middle East Monitor conference in London and is interviewed on BBC World Service's NewsHour

1 October, Monday
4.30pm The first trio of elite Saudi soldiers arrive on a scheduled flight at Atatürk Airport and are captured on CC-TV: maj. Naif al-Arifi, 32, royal guard Muhammed al-Zahrani, 30, and brig. gen. Mansour Abahussein, 46. They check in at the Wyndham Grand and make a reconnaissance tour in consular Mercedeses to Belgrad Forest (at 6.28pm) and Yalova near Istanbul. The consulate's intelligence chief al-Muzaini arrives on the same flight
10.15pm Jamal Khashoggi flies from Heathrow to Istanbul on Turkish Airlines flight TK1984

2 October, Tuesday, Atatürk Airport
1.45am	Three Saudi operatives arrive on scheduled flights – lt Meshal al-Bostani, 31, royal guard Khaled al-Otaibi, 30, and Abdulaziz al-Hawsawi, 31 – and check in at the Wyndham Grand
3.29am	A Saudi-government Gulfstream jet with tail marking HZ-SK2 lands at Atatürk Airport from Riyadh carrying nine Saudis: prof. lt-col. Salah Tubaigy, 47, Turki al-Sehri, 36, sgt Maj. Waleed al-Sehri, 38, lt Thaar al-Harbi, 39, brig. gen. Maher Mutreb, 47, royal guard Fahad al-Balawi, 33, Col. Badr al-Otaibi, 45, Saif al-Qahtani, 45, and maj. gen. Mustafa al-Madani, 57
4am	Jamal Khashoggi arrives on Turkish Airlines flight TK1984 and is captured on later leaked CC-TV entering his Istanbul apartment at 4:58am with his fiancée Hatice Cengiz. He is captured on CC-TV leaving his flat at 12:17pm

Saudi consulate, Istanbul

9.55am	Brig. gen. Mutreb enters the consulate alone in a suit; other death squad members follow
11.05am	Saif al-Qahtani and Al-Madani, dressed in a check shirt, sneakers and jeans, enter the consulate together
Present at the consulate:	the 'negotiation-group' – Mutreb (group leader), Waleed al-Sehri, Turki al-Sehri, al-Balawi, al-Harbi, Badr al-Otaibi – and from the 'intelligence/logistics' groups: al-Zahrani, Tubaigi, al-Madani, al-Qahtani
Arrival at the	consul-general's residence at 11:04pm in Mercedes 34 CC 3071: from the 'intelligence/logistics' groups: Abahussein (operation leader), al-Arifi, al-Hawsawi, Khalid al-Otaibi, al-Bostani
11.50am	'Ekrem Sultan' calls Khashoggi to finalise the paper work. Khashoggi confirms he will be visiting the consulate after 1pm
12.50pm	Non-Saudi staff working at the consulate are told to leave the building or remain in their rooms
1.14pm	Jamal Khashoggi is captured on later leaked CC-TV entering the consulate, handing his phone over to Hatice Cengiz at the security gate
1.14pm	The second Saudi-government Gulfstream jet, with tail marking HZ-SK1, files its diplomatic flight plan and is airborne from Riyadh for Istanbul
1.30pm	While former London-embassy colleague brig. gen. Maher Mutreb yells 'traitor' and Jamal Khashoggi pleads 'I can't breathe', he is strangled and dismembered in pieces, possibly still alive, by prof. lt-col. Tubaigy with a bone saw (his body parts are disposed of and his fingers, head and a video of the operation may be prepared for sending on to Riyadh on Saudi-government Gulfstream HZ-SK1 landing at 5:15pm
around 2pm	Zeki Demir, a technician is called to the consul-general's residence to light the gas oven in the garden used for barbecues (evidence at a trial-in-absentia in July 2020 in Istanbul)
2.52pm	Impersonator al-Madani is captured leaving the consulate's back door with a false beard in Khashoggi's clothes but his own trainers on later leaked CC-TV footage; Hatice Cengiz doesn't see him as she is waiting at the front
around 3pm	Six vehicles, including two vans with blacked-out windows, leave the consulate and its occupants are captured on CC-TV. Occupants buy large suitcases around Istanbul as a decoy
3.09pm	Two of the cars, Mercedes Vito minivan 34 CC 1865 and Audi 34 CC 2464, arrive at the consulate-general's residence and plastic bags and suitcases are rolled into the residence
3.30pm	The consulate closes with no sign of Khashoggi
after 4pm	Hatice Cengiz speaks to the Turkish gatekeeper and calls the consulate. An Arab man comes down and tells her to go home
4:41pm	Hatice Cengiz calls Erdoğan's chief advisor Yasin Aktay in Ankara who calls Saudi ambassador Waleed Elkhereiji
4:53pm	Mutreb leaves the consul-general's residence
5.30pm	Khashoggi's fiancée Hatice Cengiz is seen on CC-TV outside the consulate
5.50pm	Turkish authorities open their formal investigation (says President Erdoğan)

Atatürk Airport

5.15pm	The second Saudi-government Gulfstream jet, with tail marking HZ-SK1, lands and waits
6.20pm	HZ-SK1 takes off with six of the Saudi squad re-filing as a diplomatic flight taking the shortest route out of Turkish airspace: Mutreb, Waleed al-Sehri, Turki al-Sehri, al-Balawi, al-Harbi, Badr al-Otaibi (the Saudi prosecutor will demand the death penalty against the first four); its first destination is Cairo, Egypt, before returning to Riyadh
10.54pm	Before take-off the first Gulfstream jet with tail marking HZ-SK2, is searched by police for the presence of Khashoggi. It is allowed to take-off for Dubai, before flying on to Riyadh with seven of the Saudi hit team: Abahussein, Tubaigy, al-Zahrani, Khalid al-Otaibi, al-Arifi, al-Bostani, al-Hawsawi (the Saudi prosecutor will only charge the first two – demanding the death penalty against Tubaigy)
00.10am	Khashoggi impersonator al-Madani and Saif al-Qahtani leave Turkey on a scheduled

flight

October 2, Tuesday Southaven, Mississippi (GMT -6), President Donald Trump speaking at a rally for Senator Cindy Hyde-Smith

'You have to pay.'
DONALD TRUMP: We protect Saudi Arabia. Would you say they're rich? And I love the king, King Salman. But I said 'King – we're protecting you – you might not be there for two weeks without us – you have to pay for your military. You have to pay'… They have got to reimburse us.

October 3, Wednesday Moscow (GMT +3), Russian Energy Week 2018, Vladimir Putin seated next to Saudi energy minister Khaled al-Falih

'A traitor.'
VLADIMIR PUTIN: Watching some media outlets, I see that some of your colleagues are pushing forward the theory that Mr Skripal is almost some kind of human rights defender. He is simply a spy, a traitor to his homeland. You get it? There is such a thing – a traitor to one's homeland. He is one of them. [Applause!] Imagine: You are a citizen of your own country, and all of a sudden you have a man who betrays his own country. How will you, or any representative of any country sitting here, look at him? He's simply a scumbag, that is all there is to it.
rferl.org/a/putin-slams-traitor-sergei-skripal-bastard/29523407.html

October 3 Wednesday evening Riyadh (GMT +3) MBS interviewed by 6 Bloomberg journalists

'I would know that.'
Bloomberg: So… U.S.-Saudi relations are just as good now as they were 24 hours ago before the President said 'You have to pay'?
MBS: Yes of course… I love working with him. I really like working with him and we have achieved a lot in the Middle East… We have good improvement in our trade – a lot of achievements, so this is really great.
[…]
Bloomberg: What's the Jamal Khashoggi story?
MBS: We hear the rumors about what happened. He's a Saudi citizen and we are very keen to know what happened to him. And we will continue our dialogue with the Turkish government to see what happened to Khashoggi there.
Bloomberg: He went into the Saudi consulate.
MBS: My understanding is he entered and he got out after a few minutes or one hour. I'm not sure. We are investigating this through the foreign ministry to see exactly what happened at that time.
Bloomberg: So he's not inside the consulate?
MBS: Yes, he's not inside.
Bloomberg: Turkish officials have said he's still inside.
MBS: We are ready to welcome the Turkish government to go and search our premises. The premises are sovereign territory, but we will allow them to enter and search and do whatever they want to do. If they ask for that, of course, we will allow them. We have nothing to hide.
Bloomberg: Is he facing any charges in Saudi Arabia?
MBS: Actually, we need to know where Khashoggi is first.
Bloomberg: So he might be facing charges in Saudi Arabia?
MBS: If he's in Saudi Arabia I would know that.
Bloomberg: So he's not the person mentioned by Saudi Press Agency?
MBS: No, definitely not.

October 18 Vladimir Putin at the Valdai Discussion Club in the Russian Blacksea resort Sochi

'I hope America will not go as far as Saudi Arabia did.'
RAGIDA DERGHAM: Thank you, my name is Ragida Dergham. I am Founder and Executive Chairman of Beirut Institute. It's a think tank for the Arab region with a global reach… On Saudi Arabia, of course, the world is preoccupied with the developments, and I'm wondering what consequences or… Do you see that there may be consequences, on your particular relationships, Russian-Saudi relations, given that you have been eager to have good relations and beyond.
VLADIMIR PUTIN: Now concerning Saudi Arabia. What is it that is bothering you? I can't understand. We have built really good relations with Saudi Arabia in recent years. Please, specify your

question about Saudi Arabia. What is it that is perplexing you in this regard? Why should our relations with Saudi Arabia break down?

RAGIDA DERGHAM: As you know, because of the developments in Istanbul, at the Saudi Consulate, there is a big interest worldwide in the investigation regarding the assassination or the killing of Jamal Khashoggi, the journalist who was our colleague and has been a participant in the Valdai Group. So this is what I am talking about. Right now, of course, there is pressure on President Trump that may reflect on the mid-term elections, and there are countries pulling out and countries being concerned, I mean, media and others are concerned about continuing to be present in Saudi Arabia given the alleged feeling that maybe someone in the government may be involved in this atrocity, of killing of Jamal Khashoggi. That is what I meant. Do you think it will impact your relations with Saudi Arabia at all?

VLADIMIR PUTIN: As far as I know, the journalist, who has disappeared and whom you have just mentioned, lived in the United States of America. He lived in the US, not in Russia. In this sense, the US, of course, bears certain responsibility for what has happened to him. This goes without saying.

He was the one to go to the United States for asylum. In this connection, I would like to say the following. First, we should wait for the results of the investigation to become available. How can we, Russia, start spoiling relations with Saudi Arabia while being unaware of what has really happened over there?

As far as I can judge, this man was to a certain extent a member of the Saudi elite. In some way or other, he was connected with certain ruling circles. It is hard to say, what is going on there.

But we can see that complicated processes are also taking place within the US elites. I hope America will not go as far as Saudi Arabia did. But we don't know what, in fact, has happened over there. So why should we take any steps directed at downgrading our relations, if we do not understand what is really happening?

If someone understands it and believes that a murder has been committed, then I hope that some evidence will be presented and we will adopt relevant decisions based on this evidence. This gives me a pretext to say something else.

From time to time, there are steps taken against Russia and even sanctions are imposed, as I have repeatedly said, on the basis of flimsy excuses and pretexts. They groundlessly claim that we have allegedly used chemical weapons, even though, incidentally, we have destroyed our chemical weapons, while the United States has failed to do so despite the obligation to that effect it assumed.

So, there is no proof against Russia but steps are being taken. According to claims, the murder was committed in Istanbul, but no steps are being taken.

Uniform approaches to problems of this kind should be sorted. To reiterate: Our policy towards Saudi Arabia has evolved over a long period of time, over many years. Of course, it is a misfortune that a man has disappeared, but we must understand what has really happened.

valdaiclub.com/events/posts/articles/vladimir-putin-meets-with-valdai-discussion-club/

12 February 2019 Tom Barrack, representative and beneficiary of The Iron Bridge said in Abu Dabhi of the Khashoggi assassination: 'For us to dictate what we think is the moral code there … I think is a mistake.' Echoing Vladimir Putin's words of 18 October, the Lebanese American also said, 'the atrocities in America are equal or worse than the atrocities in Saudi Arabia.'

7 September 2020 Saudi court commutes the death penalty of Maher Mutreb, Salah Tubaigy, Fahad al-Balawi, Turki al-Sehri and Waleed al-Sehri into 20 years in prison. Three other defendants (Mansour Abahussain, Mustafa al-Madani/Mohammed al-Zahrani, Saif al-Qahtani?) receive 17 years each and one a sentence of 10 years in prison.

11 February 2021 President Joe Biden declassifies the assessment by the Director of National Intelligence that MBS 'approved' the operation to 'capture or kill' Jamal Khashoggi.

20 July 2021 Tom Barrack arrested on secret foreign-agency charges related to the UAE.

AUTHOR'S NOTE: For reasons that will become clear, this book has no index and may at times repeat certain facts to establish a different point.

PART 1

What is Certain?

Flying Home

※

Having just spoken at a London conference, Jamal, a tall bearded man, says goodbye to a friend at the Queen's Terminal, Heathrow's steel-and-glass Terminal 2. It is early in the evening on the last Monday of September 2018. Dressed in a light-yellow shirt and rolling a suitcase, the tall and bespectacled man walks through airport security to his 10pm Turkish Airlines flight to Istanbul. Just before take-off he sends one last text to his fiancée at home – *'I'm on the plane right now, I'm coming home to you. In love, loving and passionate.'*

Landing at Atatürk Airport, he rolls his suitcase with his coat curled around the handle to the taxi stand and arrives for the first time at his new apartment in Istanbul around 4.30am. His fiancée joins him half an hour later at what is intended to be their future home, carrying groceries in a plastic bag. Later they go down to have breakfast in their apartment complex's branch of Dilek ('desire'), an Istanbuli chain serving pastries and pasta.

At a quarter to 1 in the afternoon, the tall man, now wearing a dark blazer, and the younger woman cross the busy streets of Istanbul. Hand-in-hand they hail a taxi.

Both are beaming and relaxed. He is about to collect the documents from his consulate that he needs to get married to her in Turkey. She is a Turkish citizen, but he is a Saudi. He had arranged it while having breakfast with a few calls.

On the Friday before, four days earlier, they had also gone to the consulate together. They arrived before noon, but the administrative staff had not been able to process the paperwork in time. He had to catch his afternoon flight out to London. He had waited for as long as he could and had barely made the flight out. The consulate staff had proposed he come back today.

After the consulate visit, the couple intend to look for the last items to buy for their stylish new-build apartment near Istanbul's oldest district. She has already organised most of the furniture and provisions. They are planning to have dinner at around 5 or 6pm and to set the date for their marriage later that week after which they will start living together. The ceremony will be a no-nonsense affair – just family and a few friends. He had been more interested in how they would celebrate it and what they would wear than she was. Given the hardship in the world, she doesn't like the idea of spending money on the wedding, or looking forever for dresses to wear.

The man takes precautions just before going through the security road-block in front of the Saudi consulate. Top palace officials in his home country take a lively interest in him and have for at least half a year been offering him high-level government positions back in Saudi Arabia. They had done as well the year before when he first moved to the United States. Actually, it was more accurate to say that he had escaped to the US. He doesn't trust courtiers bearing gifts.

Nor does he want to take any unnecessary chances. Before he enters the consulate's security zone to be patted down, he hands his mobile phones to his fiancée so that what is stored on them cannot cause trouble once he is inside.

'*See you shortly, darling, wait for me here*', he says to her.

A few moments later he greets the smiling, nodding, elderly, light-blue blazered usher of the consulate and is gone.

The woman has taken the day off and has decided to wait outside anyway. How long can it take to pick up a few documents? On Friday she had waited for an hour and a quarter.

By 4 pm, two and a half hours later, however, there is still no sign of him. She is getting anxious now. She calls her sister and discovers that the consulate closed at 3.30pm.

She goes up to the guard at the gate and then rings the consulate's number to see where her fiancé is.

She is told '*everyone is gone*'.

1
Mysteries

On Saturday 6 October Turkish officials leaked to Reuters a blunt message that a man had been murdered on Tuesday 2 October in the Saudi consulate in Istanbul. The news about a murderous assault behind diplomatic doors ran like a thunder bolt through the world media. It is highly unusual for one government to accuse another government of criminal behaviour. It is even rarer for such an accusation to be made so suddenly, if not a first for diplomatic offices to be used as a killing ground.

Immediately, the international media was spell-bound by this real-life whodunnit. Over the next months the story would blow up to a running-news murder mystery akin to the hunt for Saddam Hussein and Muammar Gaddafi. The affair's tentacles would wrap around Turkey, Saudi Arabia, the US, Russia, Great Britain, Israel, Iran and Egypt.

Astonishingly, the murder victim at the heart of the drama was a character close to retirement who had at best a role in the periphery of the kingdom. He was an affable conversationalist, but could keep his cards close to his chest without his friends realising it. This almost nineteenth-century character slipped effortlessly between roles: diplomat entrusted with explosive national secrets, war correspondent, newspaper editor, centrist pundit, PLO champion and secret donor to subversive opposition movements. Straddling these contradictory roles, he had along the way established friendships with kings, princes, presidents, thinkers, and even super-villains such as the founder of al-Qaeda, Osama bin Laden.

A kaleidoscope of contrasting opinions described him. One person who got to know him in 2018 thought that this nebulous character 'did not appear to be guided by any particular ideology' but was 'sharp, quick-witted... always on the lookout for a good debate'. A long-standing friend thought that 'he engaged people that disagreed with him' and could be wildly indiscreet. Another friend who had also known him for a long time called him the 'most intellectual person in Saudi Arabia'. A high-ranking prince said of him that he 'has always been honest'. Other words used to describe him were 'big and burly' and 'soft and humble' and also 'pushy but in a good way'. His sons said that their father was treated like a 'rock-'n' -roll star' when they were with him in Saudi Arabia.

Turkey's media bombshell created the first big riddle in the Khashoggi affair, and one of the reasons for this book. Why? What had prompted President Erdoğan of Turkey to go nuclear in such a short period of time? And what was so special about this shadowy figure called Jamal Khashoggi, a person few had ever heard of? What kind of egregious secret was he party to that led to his assassination in such a deceitful way on diplomatic soil?

Furthermore, wrapped inside the Turkish allegation was another great riddle – and another reason for this book. Unlike nations such as Russia and North Korea, the desert kingdom had never before hunted down someone on foreign soil to assassinate them. It had never before murdered any Saudi nationals abroad in general. At least, not openly. As a personal advisor to Erdoğan would say, 'It is an attack that destroys all traditions'. A UN report of 20 June 2019 would assess it as 'just unthinkable' before the killing of Khashoggi became known.

Who was the main suspect in the murder mystery?

Saudi Arabia's *de-facto* ruler, Crown Prince Mohammed bin Salman, minister of defence, deputy prime minister, CEO of its single oil company, president of both its economic and security council, or more popularly 'MBS', looked like the man with his hand on the trigger. He was a relatively new entry on the world stage and had popped on the global-news radar only a few times since his appointment on 21 June 2017. Unusual for a leading Saudi royal, he exuded youthful vigour and was only thirty three years of age. He came across as a colourful, feisty, unorthodox character who didn't hesitate to pick on people his own size. Notably he had imprisoned senior royal relatives, officials and businessmen in a Riyadh five-star hotel for a shake-down of almost a trillion dollars to fill the royal coffers. Another time, he had kidnapped the Lebanese prime minister Saad al-Hariri on his visit to Riyadh, making him announce his resignation on Saudi television (as well as having him roughed up, it was rumoured). What could possibly be MBS's interest in Jamal Khashoggi – a butterfly to a falcon? Khashoggi was 59 and hadn't been privy to Saudi court secrets for years.

MBS, appointed as crown prince on the 21st June 2017, was known to be cracking the whip inside Saudi Arabia to establish his new authority. He had set up a hit team known to US intelligence as the Saudi Rapid Intervention Group or *Firqat el-Nemr*, the 'Tiger Team'. It was deployed to subdue dissidents inside and outside the kingdom. The group was involved in Saudi Arabia's routine campaigns of forcibly repatriating and detaining nationals – including activist women – in royal palaces inside the kingdom. There were rumours of physical abuse and sometimes even torture. It wasn't pretty, and sadly nothing out of the ordinary for the authoritarian kingdom. But the group wasn't known to have a license to kill and murder those critical of the Saudi regime.

Why the dramatic break with the past on this occasion? What reason could be grave enough for Saudi Arabia's royal palace to disrupt longstanding tradition – if not Saudi religious laws – and assassinate a relative nobody in a Jason-Bournestyle plot? Why would the crown prince wager his own and his country's reputation on a minion?

Saudi palace intrigue was traditionally consensus-based, staid and non-violent compared to the desert-kingdom's neighbours. Indeed, Turkey's President Erdoğan's government had barely survived a precipitous coup on 16 July 2016 – from which Erdoğan had only been saved by a fluke tweet. Saudi royal succession was placid rather than violent, venomous and internecine, despite the unimaginable wealth involved. King Faisal had been killed in 1975, but his death was tragic and not political in nature. Yet here suddenly was one of Saudi Arabia's thirty-three million subjects slain outside the kingdom in one of its consulates.

The overture to these mysteries began far away from the remote corridors of power MBS and the other state leaders inhabited. On Tuesday 2 October, Jamal Khashoggi had flown into Istanbul from London. With a short greying beard, suffering from a terrible cold but with an open, ready and inviting smile, the fifty-nine-year-old Saudi *bon vivant* had moved the previous year from Saudi Arabia's second city to a sleepy suburb of Washington DC where he was officially a US resident.

The weekend before his death, Khashoggi had spoken at a wonkish 25th-anniversary conference in London on the PLO Oslo Accords commemorating the beginning of the Middle-East peace process. He had stayed at the Ambassadors Bloomsbury hotel, a short walk away from the conference venue. Although not an official diplomat, Khashoggi had in the past taken meetings with the PLO and Hamas on behalf of Saudi Arabia as a supernumerary emissary. Despite his severe cold, he had met up with friends from Saturday through Monday. On Tuesday he had arrived back in Istanbul and went to the Saudi-Arabian consulate in the Levent business district to obtain papers needed for a marriage license in Turkey. His failure to re-emerge from the building would have taken quite some time to percolate through to the world media.

Except for one thing. Since December 2017, Jamal Khashoggi had his own page on the website of the *Washington Post* in a new online section called Global Opinions. The *Post* published pieces of his in Arabic – in which language his pages 'spiked in traffic' – and English. One had appeared in the print edition of the paper.

It was this media connection that had led to the first reports about his mysterious disappearance on 2 October on the *Post*'s website, four days before the Turkish government's bombshell. Jamal Khashoggi's fiancée Hatice Cengiz had alerted *Washington Post* Istanbul-bureau chief Kareem Fahim that Khashoggi had failed to re-emerge four hours after visiting the Saudi consulate in Istanbul.

Fahim duly posted the item on his own *Post* blog that day. The internet in the Middle East soon buzzed with rumours. The news that a one-time Saudi secret-service liaison to al-Qaeda had disappeared also instantly circulated among secret services around the world. Clearly, the CIA, MI6 – not to mention Russia's FSB and GRU, Mossad, France's Deuxième Bureau, Germany's BND, China's Ministry of State Security, and the intelligence services of other countries that sold arms to Saudi Arabia, the world's largest arms purchaser as a result of its war in Yemen – took an interest in order to assess what the implications were for their country's leaders. Some of these agencies – the ones that had found out in advance of Saudi plans to strike against Jamal Khashoggi at the Istanbul consulate – were already secretly covering events for their paymasters.

It was at this point that the news machine gained a momentum of its own. There was little chance that the *Washington Post* or other press journalists find out any more on their own, however. In Britain, journalists had been able to do their own investigative work during the excruciating deaths of former KGB spy Alexander Litvinenko from nuclear isotope Polonium 210 poisoning in London (2006), or Dawn Sturgess's after the poisoning of former GRU spy Sergei Skripal and his daughter with top-secret Soviet *novichok* nerve agent in Salisbury (2018) in the UK. Turkey and Saudi Arabia are sealed when it comes to journalists or researchers trying to dig into sensitive subjects. The idea of a Freedom of Information request would be laughable. Both countries – like Russia, China, North Korea, or, for that matter, the world's other authoritarian regimes – had draconic ways of deterring what they considered meddling in their affairs. Even foreign intelligence agencies risked severe prison sentences, or worse in Saudi Arabia.

In the months that followed it would seem as if the Turkish media had done its own investigative work on the Khashoggi affair. But any 'discovery' of new information depended on the Turkish or Saudi Arabian governments' leaking of data – not on journalists hunting down independent sources. Releases were initially handed to a small number of leading global outlets, such as Reuters, the *Washington Post*, and the *New York Times*. But once the fire was lit, most were handled by *Sabah* ('morning') newspaper in Turkey.

Sabah was a good showcase of how Turkey's regime operated. A one-time independent paper, *Sabah* had been seized on a technicality in 2007 by Erdoğan's government and sold to media conglomerate Çalik Holding for a knock-down price with a government loan. Çalik's then CEO was President Erdoğan's son-in-law, who had since moved on to become his minister of finance (he would resign as minister in 2020 and take the blame for Turkey's economic malaise, relieving the pressure on his father-in-law). Occasionally a few other Turkish media sources with similarly corrupt official ties and kickbacks received leaked information. The modest number of leaks by other governments went to their home media, but not always as we will see.

When trying to establish the facts of the Khashoggi affair, the team of UN special rapporteur Agnes Callamard noted this absence of free media scrutiny.

She announced an international human-rights inquiry into his killing on 25 January 2019 and was assisted by lawyer Helena Kennedy QC, and by other international experts, including the New York law firm Walden Macht & Haran. Her report of 20 June 2019 addressed the issue of leaks and noted that 'there is rarely space for scrutiny from anyone outside the intelligence system. Outsiders may be readily manipulated'. As a result, the report set aside 'leaks reported by journalists' and only used them 'to corroborate information gathered independently by the inquiry'.

The first part of this book tells the story based on the facts as we know them through the UN's independent verification (the text will refer to the relevant paragraph of the UN report where particularly helpful). But its next part deals with the third riddle this book aims to delve into: the media stories that emerged. Its aim is the opposite of the pin-point of the UN inquiry which sought to nail down facts and apportion blame. Instead of ignoring media leaks on principle, as the UN inquiry team did, their time line is reconstructed here because they shaped the unfolding narrative of the Khashoggi affair. The power of these leaks created an evolving reality that had real consequences, rippling like a stone dropped in water. The UN report called this 'a worrying tendency to value Intelligence information and leaks of it, over facts and evidence.' It may have been worrying, but it is what always happens, particularly when authoritarian regimes are involved as they keep a tight lock on what stories may be verified – usually none.

Unlike in the Skripal case, these leaks were freely deployed by the leakers to manipulate real consequences as there was no media counterweight to them in either Turkey or in Saudi Arabia, the places with facts on the ground. The press geographically located elsewhere had no access either. In fact, it only had leaks of its own. Instead of only scrutinising the facts (as the UN investigation did), in the second part of the book it is this nebula of news stories and their consequences that will be scanned. Through these 'real' consequences the puzzle of government leaders' shifts in behaviour become intelligible.

By going back to the very first instance of a statement or release – rather than media repeats elsewhere – as they were fed into a news-cycle that sought to answer the questions 'who did it?' and 'will the culprits be punished?' – a pattern emerged. This pattern emerged even clearer when considering additionally what impact such a press leak sought to achieve and whether its release contained hard facts or merely suggestive facts. Normally this isn't necessary, but it is when the suppliers are authoritarians or intelligence services. They have a dog in the fight that is not necessarily the truth.

From this not only a new story emerged in which Jamal Khashoggi's background takes centre stage, but also one in which Ankara's role is as murky as Riyadh's. And that theirs was not the only tenebrous one. Though the affair was mainly about hurt national pride inside Turkey, it is ironic that outside the country, due to his opposition to Saudi Arabia as the villain of the piece, the authoritarian President Erdoğan came to be seen as a defender of honourable government.

Although on the face of the Khashoggi affair was a stand-off between governments, its tentacles would also touch some of the world's most visible billionaires. They included then-president of the US Donald Trump, his friend Tom Barrack, Vladimir Putin, owner of Amazon Jeff Bezos, King Salman of Saudi Arabia, his son Crown Prince Mohammed, while in the background hovered the world's richest man Sheikh Mohammed bin Zayed, the ruler of the UAE and bidder for Newcastle United Football Club. In addition there were aspiring billionaires such as Jared Kushner, Donald Trump's son-in-law, and President Recep Erdoğan. In 2015, President Erdoğan had moved into the *Ak Saray* (white palace) in Ankara built at close to $1bn with taxpayers' money. Erdoğan's government had stopped publishing the palace's costs once they overran the budgeted $615 million. The fate of clubbable insider Jamal Khashoggi was not just about geopolitics but also very personal for this rarified class of the world's richest people.

None of the governments involved in the affair come off as hugely principled. The temptation to tell tales is great because they can, they reckon the gravity of the situation demands it, and often perhaps because it is easier that way for all the officials, their promotions, and the institutions involved. But there is a crucial difference in countries with a free press. While they may put up roadblocks, Western officials know that they do not have sole control over the facts. Journalists, elected officials, and members of the public, can check them if they wish, decide whether what they are being told makes sense or not, and say so without fear of life and limb.

If there is one moral of the Khashoggi affair, it is that this individual freedom to establish the facts is still as potent as when it was accidentally reborn in the sixteenth-century Netherlands. If that freedom didn't (still) exist strongly in the leading super in the world, the US, Jamal Khashoggi's rendition would be just another tool for the small groups in power to lord increasingly as wizards of Oz over others. Minute-maid facts – here today, contradicted tomorrow – would be another. It is hard to see how the story in this book could be published in, say, Saudi Arabia, or even Turkey. By laying out all the media facts, the self-serving agendas and distortions created by all the governments involved reveal themselves.

As a media phenomenon, the Khashoggi affair is also significant because it shows what happens when official facts are always fudged, and echo-chambers are created. The media starts to look like a giant, national Truman Show.

The UN report of Agnes Callamard's team will feature in greater detail at the end of the book. But even this report didn't escape the manipulation problem.

While having a determination to fight 'confirmation bias', more time, skills, money, better access than any 'outsider' to secret material in possession of the Turkish and other governments, the team was not given Saudi Arabia's raw data and Turkey provided highly screened access – as meticulously catalogued by the report.

The Khashoggi affair exposes what daily life is like in a country like Turkey and Saudi Arabia: facts are enslaved to officials' stories – 'true' until the government decides to change the story and introduce different facts that fit with the new version. The facts are as subject to government manipulation as the discussion of them, which officials carefully guide to disguise their media monopoly. Often, paradoxically, dictatorial governments are far more skilled in manipulating the media than their peers who have to deal with a free press. There will be a whole ministry devoted to programming the population – such as the Saudi ministry of information, the Russian ministry of communication, or the Chinese ministry of information technology – that would be still-born in a country where there is freedom of speech. Turkey's road to repression started under Erdoğan, who from 2003 reversed eighty years of democracy building. There continue to be outlets that are critical of the government. However, they are contained and no more than isolated exceptions that prove the rule. The fact that Turkey called out Saudi Arabia on its Khashoggi plot had little to do with free speech and far more with a sword fight between two totalitarian regimes.

Years after the assassination of Jamal Khashoggi, we still don't know exactly what happened. The Turkish government has not even disclosed all the evidence in its possession to Turkish courts investigating the crime.

The opening scene of this book we know for certain is true. Jamal Khashoggi went missing after entering a Saudi consulate. Even though his body was never found, we also know for certain that he was assassinated and we know the names of the people who executed him in the consulate. But as to what exactly took place, and how and why, readers will still have to make up their own minds and weigh up what is true and what is fabrication.

The only way is to sift through the evidence like a latter-day Sherlock Holmes, looking at it from different angles. At the end of the book, I suspect, the foremost question will remain, why a risky assassination in a foreign country? There are several answers, though they are not equally plausible. Nor are the motives of the main characters transparent. Even over the most likeable ones a question mark hovers, Khashoggi himself included. But, as with all famous assassination plots, the events surrounding Khashoggi's death certainly cast a brief light into the murky world of espionage and high-stakes international intrigue.

2
A Blip

On Tuesday 2 October, Jamal Khashoggi's enigmatic disappearance remained a small blip on the radar. If after the *Washington Post*'s blog and other coverage no further news broke his disappearance would have to be filed away as a loose end. All that could then be said was that Jamal Khashoggi might or might not have been arrested and repatriated to Saudi Arabia – fate unknown, as with other Saudis before him. Ambiguous? Yes. Tragic? Without a doubt. A major global-news story chipping away at the most demonic conspiracy of the century? Less so in a world where people simply vanish with regularity in authoritarian regions.

Yet four days after Khashoggi's unexplained disappearance, the story, instead of disappearing into the din of the daily news, was saved from oblivion by precisely the country that had no time for its own independent journalists – Turkey.

After initially seeming as uninformed as anyone else, it was the Turkish government that lit the blue touch paper when two of its officials stated to Reuters that 'Mr Khashoggi has been killed at the consulate.' And, just to twist the knife further, the anonymous officials added 'We believe that the murder was premeditated and the body was subsequently moved out of the consulate.'

The officials leaked this information anonymously to the paper because they supposedly were not authorised to speak. It set the tone for the future and a variety of reasons would be given for this approach: protection of sources – intercepted communication or human informers – ongoing investigations, hampering of future prosecution, etc. It all also added to the fevered speculation and sense of mystery.

Yet no government makes such an accusation unless they have copper-bottomed evidence. They 'wouldn't announce this kind of thing, if they didn't have some other information which is leading them in that direction', a British pundit on al-Jazeera observed. That was the key.

Particularly, if it was the Turkish government accusing the one in Saudi Arabia. With a tanking economy and over 100,000 of its citizens detained following a 2016 putsch – plotted by only a fraction of that number – Erdoğan's standing was fraying abroad and brittle at home.

Saudi Arabia, however, with its economy floating on oil and Mecca and Medina, the holiest places of Islam within its borders, could lay claim to Turkey's traditional leadership from Ottoman days over Sunni-Muslims in the Arab world – particularly under their new *de-facto* ruler, young and photogenic MBS.

Turkey's breath-taking accusation of premeditated murder immediately bracketed Jamal Khashoggi and the crown prince together before the world. This was because the day after the alleged killing, none other than MBS himself had officially and vocally protested Saudi innocence of Khashoggi's disappearance and current whereabouts.

'We have nothing to hide', he himself had said unequivocally and on the record about Khashoggi in a Bloomberg-website interview that covered a broad range of other topics and by chance was scheduled on Wednesday evening 3 October (published two days later on Friday).

From 6 October, when the Turkish government engaged the global news machine, its authorities began to leak a steady and grisly stream of detailed information about the murderous events in the Saudi consulate, destroying MBS's reputation in the process with a thousand cuts.

A new reputation would emerge. Gone was the image of young and dynamic new broom, carefully cultivated with the help of global advisors such as McKinsey, Booz Allen, lobbyists and top PR agencies, over the course of fifteen months – organisations which had been paid many hundreds of millions of dollars. He was now cast as a ghoulish potentate in the mould of Vladimir Putin, Saddam Hussain, and the Assads.

Fanning the flames further, President Erdoğan, MBS's fellow-authoritarian, signalled in a number of personal statements that he would not stop until he had achieved his objective – whatever that was exactly. Despite his own gloves-off vendetta against Turkish journalists, Erdoğan would be given two op-eds in billionaire Jeff Bezos's *Washington Post*. He called the murder 'savage' and 'planned' and would give many press conferences.

Holding the line set by the crown prince in his Bloomberg interview, the kingdom pretended it had no idea what the fuss was about. But the drip-feed from Turkish 'sources' would prove irresistible and keep MBS and the assassination in the world's media-spotlight. How much these Turkish 'sources' manipulated the news story becomes clear in the second part of the book and in contrast with the facts as we know they occurred and pieced together in this first part of the book.

That is not to say that the second part is just about media smoke. In a nutshell, the forensic question at stake in the second part is whether or not Khashoggi died around 1.25pm on 2 October, or much later. If the latter, he will have been tortured and died a far more gruesome death than we have been led to believe by the countries involved in the Affair. It is the clues to this question that are packaged in the stories that were planted in the media. Aided by these, the reader will have to decide what really happened.

3
Saudi Secrets

∽

The son of a merchant, Jamal Khashoggi was born in Medina, the second holiest city in Saudi Arabia, on 13 October 1958 to a well-connected family. Medina in the sixties, when he was a young boy, had many more historic religious buildings not yet bulldozered as a consequence of Wahhabism's (the Saudi denomination of Islam) contempt of idolatry. His family roots were Turkish and his grandfather Mohammed Khashoggi had moved from the city of Kayseri, in Anatolia, to the Hejaz region (now in Saudi Arabia) of the Arabian Peninsula when both were still under Ottoman rule. Khashoggi, or *kaşıkçı,* is in fact the Turkish word for spoonbill, a bird with the spoon-shaped beak related to the ibis.

Jamal Khashoggi with his sons Abdullah (left) and Salah (middle) and their wives and two grand children. His third wife Dr Alaa Nasief is seated bottom right.

Mohammed became personal physician to founder-King ibn Saud, a status that allowed the Khashoggi family to achieve prominence in court circles. Mohammed was the father of late billionaire arms dealer Adnan Khashoggi, the middleman in Ronald Reagan's Iran-Contra scandal in the 1980s. Adnan was also once a neighbour of Donald Trump's and sold him a $200-million yacht. By coincidence, one of Khashoggi's royal patrons, Prince Alwaleed bin Talal, later bought the yacht from Trump and rented it out to the makers of James Bond movie Never Say Never Again as the villain's lair. Khashoggi's aunt Samira was the first wife of Mohamed al-Fayed, the Egyptian former owner of the famous London store Harrod's who had been refused a UK passport on account of not being 'a fit and proper person'. (To his friend Turan Kişlakçi Khashoggi disowned his family's connection to Adnan, however.)

After receiving his primary and secondary education in Medina, Jamal Khashoggi went to the US to study business administration at Indiana State University, graduating with a bachelor's degree in 1982. His first wife was Rawia al-Tunisi. They had two sons, Salah and Abdullah, and two daughters, Noha and Razan. They were all educated in America and three of them took US citizenship, while Salah, the eldest son, became an investment banker in Saudi Arabia.

Following his graduation, Khashoggi returned home to Saudi Arabia, where his first job was managing a group of bookshops. By the mid-1980s, however, he was writing for English-language newspapers such as the *Saudi Gazette* and *Arab News*. From 1991 to 1999, he worked as a foreign correspondent in such countries as Afghanistan, Algeria, Kuwait, Sudan, and in the Middle East, reporting on the First Gulf War.

To the world outside Saudi Arabia he became at this time well-known for his interviews with Osama bin Laden. Even though a Saudi, bin Laden was then a prominent member of the Afghani *mujahideen* resistance against Soviet-Russia's push into Afghanistan. Bin Laden was funded by both the Saudis and Americans – spear-headed by the Bush family – who were seeking to stem the spread of Communism by proxy. It was only after the Russian withdrawal from Afghanistan in February 1989 that bin Laden gradually turned on his American backers through forming al-Qaeda, a new resistance movement aimed at routing the influence of his US supporters after the successful ousting of the Soviets.

It was as foreign correspondent that Khashoggi had become the go-to asset for the Saudi and US intelligence services and impressed powerful Saudi royals such as longstanding intelligence chief Prince Turki bin Faisal. Khashoggi was a foreign correspondent in Afghanistan, Algeria, Kuwait, Sudan, and other Middle Eastern countries, presumably doubling as journalist and Saudi intelligence asset. During his time in Afghanistan, Jamal Khashoggi visited Osama bin Laden, first at his hideout in the Tora Bora mountains, later while bin Laden was in hiding in the Sudan. Khashoggi was one of the few links (if not the only one) to bin Laden that the Saudi and US intelligence services had.

This link was Khashoggi's big career break. According to a report by *Washington Post* columnist David Ignatius, 'Khashoggi couldn't have travelled with the *mujahideen* that way without tacit support from Saudi intelligence, which was co-ordinating aid to the fighters as part of its co-operation with the CIA against the Soviet Union in Afghanistan.' He was not the only secret agent. His uncle Adnan Khashoggi sold guns to the Afghans – paid for by the Saudis and Americans – and would get caught up in Reagan's Contra Scandal. At the time, Khashoggi was privately critical of (then) Prince Salman, MBS's father, head of the Saudi committee for support to the Afghan *mujahideen*. Salman was funding Wahhabi extremist groups that were undermining the efforts of the other guerrillas, Khashoggi thought.

Even before his meetings in Soviet times with bin Laden, Khashoggi had had a personal interest in political Islam. After the Iranian revolution in 1979 that ended the reign of the shah of Persia and led to the rise to power of Ayatollah Khomeini, he began attending Islamic conferences and meetings in Indiana, USA, and became very religious for a while. Khashoggi admitted that as a young man he had joined the Muslim Brotherhood, the reformist movement begun in Egypt in the 1920s. At the time, however, the brotherhood was still supported by Saudi Arabia and membership was not seen as an act of rebellion.

Khashoggi had since renounced the movement. He would not have been able to work for Saudi royal government otherwise. To his friend Turan Kışlakçi he said that 'in the 1990s, I left because I thought there was no room for intellectuals in the religious community'.

He fully accepted Saudi Arabia's strict adherence to Wahhabism, however, and did not criticise its links to the Saudi royal family. His fiancée Hatice Cengiz, said he nonetheless sketched to her his move over thirty years from 'Islamist', to 'intellectual', to 'sympathiser' of Mohamed Bouazizi, the Tunisian street-vendor. Bouazizi's death by self-immolation catalysed the Arabian Spring and the Muslim Brotherhood's attempts to carry over religious populism into democratic votes in the Middle East.

Jamal Khashoggi had known bin Laden for a long time. They had first met in Jeddah in the early 1980s. Khashoggi was one year younger and they were both at the time in their mid-twenties.

'Osama was just like many of us who became part of the [Muslim] Brotherhood movement in Saudi Arabia,' Khashoggi said. 'The only difference that set him apart from others, and me, he was more religious. More religious, more literal, more fundamentalist. For example, he would not listen to music. He would not shake hands with a woman. He would not smoke. He would not watch television, unless it was news. He wouldn't play cards. He would not put a picture on his wall. But more than that, there was also a harsh or radical side in his life. I'm sure you have some people like that in your culture. For example, even though he comes from a rich family, he lives in a very simple house.'

While they were both in Afghanistan Khashoggi got to know bin Laden better. This time, he was impressed by his enthusiasm and devotion. In 1987, this gave him Khashoggi his first scoop.

'I interviewed Osama – a gentle, enthusiastic young man of few words who didn't raise his voice while talking,' he said. They discussed the condition of the *mujahideen* and what bin Laden was doing to help them. 'I did not know him thoroughly enough to judge him or expect any other thing from him. His behaviour at that time left no impression that he would become what he has become.'

Al-Qaeda, the Sunni-Islamist terror organisation, was first founded in 1988 as the Soviets were withdrawing from Afghanistan. Bin Laden talked of its purpose, spreading *jihad* through central Asia and not just Afghanistan.

Arab News (1988): Jamal Khashoggi (centre) on the left and Osama bin Laden (centre) right.

Jamal Khashoggi wrote a large two-page piece on al-Qaeda and the *mujahedeen* for *Arab News*, headed on the left page with a beaming bearded Khashoggi posing with a rocket-propelled grenade launcher (not a 'rifle' as a *Washington Post* article had it) and on the right page with bin Laden smiling – for a change – and looking down, while both were surrounded by pan-Arab youths. It contained no talk of attacking the United States or Europe, merely the Soviets. When Khashoggi first met his friend Barnett Rubin, later a senior fellow at NYU, at the US consulate in Jeddah a year after the Russian withdrawal he gave Rubin a copy of the article.

Bin Laden and Khashoggi met for the last time in the Sudan. This was in 1995, the year its president Omar al-Bashir reinstated Sharia law and was in the sixth year of his three-decades-long dictatorship.

'Osama was almost about to change his mind and reconcile and come back to Saudi Arabia,' Khashoggi said. 'It was a lost opportunity.' A year later, in early 1996, President al-Bashir started secret negotiations with the CIA to either expel or extradite bin Laden in return for lifting US sanctions against Sudan.

New Yorker writer Lawrence Wright, who wrote *The Looming Tower* and knew Khashoggi for well over a decade and a half, said that Khashoggi had warned bin Laden when the latter stated he wanted to drive the US from the Arabian Peninsula: 'Osama, this is very dangerous. It is as if you are declaring war. You will give the right to the Americans to hunt for you'.

Although Khashoggi had been asked to try to persuade bin Laden to renounce violence and failed, he retained the ear of powerful members of the ruling house. He was surprised when bin Laden announced he was declaring war on America in 1997 and shocked by the attacks on 9/11. He gave up the idea of creating an Islamic state in Saudi Arabia. 'I think we must find a way where we can accommodate secularism and Islam, something like what they have in Turkey,' he said later.

When bin Laden was killed in 2011, Khashoggi wrote on Twitter: 'I collapsed crying a while ago, heartbroken for you Abu Abdullah [bin Laden's nickname]. You were beautiful and brave in those beautiful days in Afghanistan, before you surrendered to hatred and passion.'

The rewards for loyalty to the Saudi royal family during the turbulence in Afghanistan were great. In 1991, Khashoggi had become editor of *al-Madina*, one of Jeddah's oldest newspapers, and in 1999 Khashoggi rose further to become the deputy editor-in-chief on *Arab News*, the biggest English language daily in the kingdom, and a key interlocutor for western journalists with the Saudi royal family, whose formal apparatus was often incomprehensible to outsiders. He also became a go-to source for foreign journalists trying to understand the rise of Islamism and Islamist terrorism.

Four years later he became the editor-in-chief of the leading Saudi daily *al-Watan*, a paper on the liberal spectrum in the kingdom and one of Saudi Arabia's three main papers. But here he fell foul of Saudi Arabia's deeply-conservative religious sectarianism. After less than two months, he was dismissed by the Saudi Arabian ministry of information because one of his *al-Watan* journalist had dared to ask the then crown prince whether the *mutaween*, Saudi's oppressive religious police, was going to be reformed.

MBS was to loosen the *mutaween*'s power over Saudi Arabia fifteen years later, but in 2003 religious conservatives still had the upper hand. They blamed him for allowing the question. Their knives were out for Khashoggi and he had to flee into quasi exile in London. This was not a moment too soon. Maggie Salem Mitchell, director of the Qatar Foundation International, who befriended Khashoggi around this time, recalled that in order 'to save his life, [the Faisal clan of princes who owned *al-Watan*] got him out of the kingdom'. If that was literally the case, it meant that his assassination in Istanbul was not the first time a corner of the Saudi establishment had considered his death.

As fate would have it, London turned out to be Khashoggi's second major career boost. In Afghanistan he had been an intelligence asset, but London heralded his entry into the inner circle of Saudi intelligence. Khashoggi became diplomatic adviser to ambassador Prince Turki bin Faisal, the urbane grandson of Saudi Arabia's founder ibn Saud and son of King Faisal. Prince Turki was Saudi-Arabia's top intelligence chief for more than two decades and knew every secret in the kingdom. He abruptly resigned from his powerful post 10 days before 9/11, the precision attacks on the US with three planes manned mainly by Saudis.

It was unheard of. Only months earlier his twenty-two years in service had been extended with another four years. Luckily for Khashoggi, Prince Turki had been allowed to return from the cold as ambassador a year and a half after 9/11 as Saudi Arabia was desperate to manage its fall-out.

Khashoggi's grand office when stationed at the Saudi Embassy in Washington, DC.

Two weeks after the 7/7 attacks in London, Prince Turki was again promoted to Washington. The bibulous, cigar-smoking then ambassador to the US, Prince Bandar bin Sultan, suddenly left as he was implicated in the scandal of mysterious planes exfiltrating Saudi royals to Riyadh. The scandal related to the US-wide flying ban after 9/11 that grounded all airplanes, except mysteriously those of Saudi royals. Prince Turki and the US-educated Khashoggi sparred closely to direct popular fury in the United States away from the kingdom and cover over the Saudi tracks of 9/11.

During his four years abroad Jamal Khashoggi mingled freely with American, British and Saudi intelligence officers. Arab-specialist John R. Bradley wrote in the *Spectator*, that the Pentagon thought highly of Khashoggi. They even included him and two other Saudis in top-secret talks about regime change under which the US would govern Saudi Arabia (and its oil reserves) via an appointed council of distinguished Saudis.

Turki and Khashoggi's hard work paid off. President George W. Bush in the end angled this retaliatory 9/11 invasion at Sadam Hussein in Iraq, who had no involvement in 9/11 but did sit on considerable oil reserves and had previously fought with Bush's father, president George Bush Sr. King Abdullah must have thought as highly of Khashoggi's discretion and loyalty as the Pentagon to allow talks to proceed that put his own dethronement in the hands of a commoner.

As a reward for adroitly bouncing off the regime-change for which the Bush neocons were baying, Riyadh permitted Khashoggi to return to lead *al-Watan* as editor again in 2007 despite the opposition of hardline clerics against him. But he was dismissed a second time three years later, this time for himself criticising the kingdom's harsh Islamic rules that MBS was to relax decades later. It was to mark the last time he had hands-on power over developments in Saudi Arabia.

He deeply regretted this. 'The clergy. They didn't like me,' Khashoggi said about the distrust of his most vociferous opponents in Saudi Arabia. 'They didn't like the way I ran the paper. Totally lobbied against me and they got me out. I miss journalism and I think it's a very interesting time in my country. I see change, and I would like to be part of that change.'

While Khashoggi called himself a journalist, and he did indeed chronicle current events, his job was a lot more restricted than that. The Saudi media are semi-governmental institutions. Unlike Khashoggi's equivalents in the US or UK, his primary job was not to publish news awkward to the regime or, indeed, holding them to account. In addition in the hermetically-sealed kingdom, a key task was to sequester any intelligence that the palace did not wish to see dispersed to Saudi subjects. Although the newspapers in Saudi Arabia are privately owned by different branches of the royal family, they are effectively semi-government institutions. They are guided by the palace in Riyadh which can fire top leadership.

Jamal, said Hatice Cengiz, told her that he was initially forbidden to write about the Arab Spring (2010-2012) as Riyadh was fearful the US government was about to foment an uprising in Saudi Arabia – the Obama version of regime change in the Peninsula. Khashoggi did as he was instructed. He was also not allowed to write about the Saudi financed el-Sisi coup in Egypt in 2013. He deplored the Saudi aid to el-Sisi, but again he did what the palace wanted. When the bans were relaxed once the Arab Spring had lost its sting, Khashoggi wrote a book on it (2016), his third. The other two were on Saudi's dependence on foreign labour (2013) and its US relations (2002).

'There could be some criticism with red lines for the media', in the words of London-based Saudi exile, Yahya Assiri, a former Saudi air force officer, graduate of London's Kingston University, and media commentator. In Saudi Arabia, this meant mainly criticism of the position of the Saudi's orthodox Whahabbist clerics in the kingdom. The clerics were the only power who could stand up to the royal family and so it was in the interest of the palace to permit as much discussion as possible to keep the kingdom's ultra-conservatives in check.

Even after his editorships and service abroad, Khashoggi remained privy to secret intelligence through his exceptional contacts and the close friendships he had struck within the rarefied stratosphere of Saudi Arabia's most influential princes. Khashoggi knew the opaque inner workings, processes and political alignments of the influential yet impenetrable top of the Saudi royal family inside out. According to some reports, Khashoggi even continued to have the rank of 'advisor to the royal court' of King Abdullah after the king had removed him for the second time as editor of *al-Watan*. Khashoggi himself told his friend Turan Kişlakçi he 'had worked four or five years for the government'.

When King Abdullah died on 23 January 2015 and his brother Salman became king, Khashoggi contributed widely to the Arab media and foreign broadcasters as a political commentator for MBC, BBC, al-Jazeera, and Dubai TV. Between June 2012 and 18 November 2016, his opinion columns in London-based (but Saudi royal family owned) newspaper Arab-language *al-Hayat* ('life'), aimed at the Saudi and Arab diaspora, were regularly shared on the website of Saudi-royal-family owned news channel al-Arabiya. He also wrote for two other London-based Saudi-sponsored papers, online *majalla.com* ('magazine.com') and *Asharq al-Awsat* ('the middle east').

MBS (left) and Jamal Khashoggi in 2015/2016.

Khashoggi's Istanbul friend, Turan Kişlakçi recalled that, despite the change of guards in Riyadh, Khashoggi retained the backing of the new king as well as MBS as the latter wielded more and more power in the kingdom. Both father and son liked it when Khashoggi whole-heartedly approved of their military coalition against the Shiite Houthis in Yemen. He deftly theorised about it and called it the 'Salman Doctrine', a strategy whereby Saudi Arabia would 'lead and take initiative'– strikingly flattering praise for MBS's hawkishness – while the US 'provides logistical and intelligence support when needed.'

Nor did Khashoggi cross the new court's red lines as to Qatar, the growing thorn in MBS's side. On 17 January 2016, Khashoggi wrote in Qatar's English-language newspaper *The Peninsula*, 'Today I criticise ... the liberals.' He chastised them for attacks on 'religiously committed persons' and chided the liberals for using 'the same tactics' as their ultra-conservative opponents. Pouring oil on troubled water, he said both sides would call each other names without evidence, 'of being conspirators, or of being in the Muslim Brotherhood, or part of the alleged conspiracy of the American-Qatari-Turkish alliance.' As an advocate of Palestine – the subject of the London conference speech before his death – he also included 'those who care about the Gaza strip'.

It even looked as if Khashoggi might once again regain influence as an editor. In 2015 he agreed to become editor-in-chief of al-Arab, a new news channel based in Bahrain – a relatively poor nation on the Arabian Peninsula with friendly Saudi relations. Al-Arab was backed by Khashoggi's sponsor Prince Alwaleed bin Talal, one of Saudi's richest royals, who partnered with US financial news channel Bloomberg Television, which also co-owned Haberturk TV in Turkey. Bloomberg's co-owner also owned *Haberturk* ('Turkish news') newspaper and independently-minded *Sabah* before the Turkish government seized it on a technicality and sold it at a knock down price to Erdoğan's friend at the Demirören group with a state loan after which it became an AKP mouthpiece.

Al-Arab was meant to become a rival to Qatar's al-Jazeera TV and Saudi's al-Arabiya. However, it was closed down by the Bahraini government on its first day. Misjudging the local red lines, Khashoggi had allowed the new channel to air an interview with a member of Bahrain's Shiite opposition to the nation's Sunni rulers. Khashoggi's friend Maggie Salem Mitchell recalled saying to him, 'Dude, what did you think was going to happen?'

To foreign reporters Khashoggi remained a godsend, an unofficial spokesperson for the Saudi royal family and a Kremlin-watcher who could read power shifts and divine subtle meanings from the robed courtly pageantry that swirled around marble buildings, ormulu ornaments and Louis XV chairs, and passed for Saudi politics. This was the man Kareem Fahim, the Istanbul Bureau Chief of the *Washington Post*, knew as Jamal Khashoggi. 'The only time I ever spoke to him was when I was calling to get some sort of government comment. So he had this dual role of journalist and consummate insider and occasional spokesperson for the Saudi government', Fahim said.

4
The Insider

Those who knew Khashoggi on the international pundit circuit agreed that he did not fit the profile of a rebel at all. He was deeply attached to his country and was at best a lukewarm critic of the kingdom. Joyce Karam, the Washington Bureau Chief of London-based Saudi paper *al-Hayat* and a long-time friend, judged, 'He is not exactly Saudi opposition'. 'He always walked a fine line, you know, sometimes agreeing with Saudi policies and sometimes disagreeing with it.' In fact, because of his tendency to circle the centre, some Saudi critics living outside Saudi Arabia feared that Khashoggi had never really given up his intelligence work for the palace at all and was a Saudi spy.

Barbara Slavin, Iran expert at the Atlantic Council, a sixty-year-old DC think tank, said Khashoggi was 'very intelligent, pleasant, thoughtful' and 'was telling [MBS] that if you keep putting people in prison for even modest criticism you will defeat the whole purpose of [your] reforms'. Mike Franc, director of DC programmes at the Stanford University Hoover Institution told the *Atlantic*, 'I don't recall he ever said anything mean about a person – even MBS. He never uttered a nasty word about him'.

Nonetheless – in a repeat of what happened during the Arab Spring in 2010 – in 2016 the palace once again forbade Khashoggi to publish his thoughts.

Remarkably, this time the ban had little to do with any (implied) criticism he might have had of the Saudi government, its policies, the royal family, or indeed MBS himself or Wahhabi religion. It, in fact, had nothing to do at all with any critique of Saudi Arabia itself, the royal family, or MBS himself, or the Saudi government's foreign policies.

Rather, the ban was imposed because of Khashoggi's criticism of the new president-elect Donald Trump. Khashoggi had called him 'contradictory' at a rarified energy conference held by think tank The Washington Institute. The conference had taken place in the US capital two days after Trump had won the 8 November 2016 election. Billed as a 'commentator' by the organisers, Khashoggi said Saudi Arabia should form 'a bulwark against' Trump. The reason for the 'bulwark' was that he doubted whether Trump, who wanted the US to be closer to Russia, really understood that 'supporting Putin means supporting the Iranian agenda'. His deep concern was that 'Iranian hegemony' should be countered and this was entirely within MBS's red lines.

It was all quite interesting, yet hardly likely to keep Donald Trump or his periphery awake at night. They were celebrating their unexpected victory after the FBI had revived the investigation of Hillary Clinton, days before the election, in relation to her use of a private email address and server as Foreign Secretary (something Ivanka was to do as well in her official capacity while her father was president). Moreover, the Institute was a distinguished but wonkish think tank of the kind that rarely creates waves or headlines. The furthest Khashoggi's words got to were two lines in the middle of someone's blog post – a long way from Fox News where the president-elect might have even noticed them, if he had any idea who Khashoggi was.

Instead, however, Riyadh took Khashoggi's opinion as if the nation's future was on the line. Stung by Khashoggi's words, the Saudi government issued an official press release to distance itself from him and declaim the role of unofficial spokesperson he had performed over the past decade. 'Jamal Khashoggi does not represent the government of Saudi Arabia or its positions at any level', the press release said to remove any doubt. Riyadh seemed to be making a giant mountain out of a tiny if not invisible Trump molehill. It was baffling.

Saud al-Qahtani, the director of Saudi Arabia's Media Center, was the conduit through which the palace relayed its ban to Khashoggi. It seems, however, as if Khashoggi was puzzled by MBS's new red line on Trump that contradicted MBS's hatred of Iran. Two weeks later, on 21 November 2016, Khashoggi took part in a panel discussion between 5 to 6pm on 'Fighting Terrorism' at the World Police Conference (WPC). It was held at Doha's top hotel, the space-ship-on-the-sea Sheraton Grand, in Qatar and opened by Qatar's Prime Minister and Frane's Foreign Minister. There was a glittering cast of global influencers: CEOs, former prime ministers, and former functionaries such as Jean-Claude Trichet, former President of the European Central Bank, and Lord Kerr, Britain's highest career diplomat. WPC had billed Khashoggi as CEO of the defunct al-Arab channel in Bahrain. As panel member, Khashoggi again criticised Trump and repeated on Twitter the same anti-Trump warning he had given at the DC think tank days after Trump's surprise win.

Riyhad's reaction was electric. It was now full-out war between Khashoggi and the Media Center. Al-Qahtani called him in a fury to say he was 'not allowed to tweet, not allowed to write, not allowed to talk'.

'You can't do anything anymore – you're done', al-Qahtani had shouted angrily at Khashoggi over the phone.

From that day, Khashoggi's seven-year-long weekly column stopped appearing in *al-Hayat*, the London-based Arab paper owned by MBS's nephew Prince Khalid bin Sultan, a grandchild of founder King ibn Saud's and former deputy under MBS's father when he was still minister of defence. Khashoggi later also received a letter confirming his media ban in writing, which hurt his pride deeply.

But Khashoggi did as he was told. His torrent of tweets ended abruptly from 21 November, and so did his media appearances and conference attendances.

The vehement reaction of the palace made little sense. Except for one detail. The Saudi government's relations with the Obama government had been frosty. But MBS saw the vain and volatile billionaire and soon-to-be president as his mark to improve US-Saudi relations. It was a few weeks before MBS's scout, energy minister Khalid al-Falih, headed to New York to meet Trump's transition team led by Jared Kushner and to flash Riyadh's hundreds of billions.

One thing, in particular was on MBS's wish list: the kingdom's nuclear capability. Or rather, the lack thereof. As opposed to its rivals for influence in the Middle East, Saudi Arabia merely had plans. Shiite Iran had an operational nuclear reactor since 2011 and 'Muslim Brotherhood' Turkey had advanced plans to build one in 2018, like many other Middle-Eastern states. It wasn't really the energy he was interested in. A nuclear reactor was the key stepping stone to nuclear weapons. Israel had bombed Iraqi and Syrian reactors to rubble for that reason in, respectively, 1981 and 2007.

Without realising it, Khashoggi was jeopardising Riyadh's nuclear policy – or so the palace thought. It was now or never for Saudi Arabia.

Iran's nuclear programme was the one that had got away. The Shia-fundamentalist country was now so close to developing its own atomic bomb that the Obama administration had desperately tried to force Iran to abandon its nuclear-weapon strategy. It did so through severe sanctions that made Iran agree to a 2015 nuclear carrot-and-stick treaty, the Iran Nuclear Deal. Under the deal, Iran agreed to use nuclear power only for civilian ends and permitted stringent independent verification and monitoring by the International Atomic Energy Agency. Not forever, but for a period of time at any rate.

It was Iran's nuclear potential that Saudi Arabia feared most of its sworn enemy. For almost a decade, nuclear capability had become the most-desired military asset the Saudi government did not yet possess in its ample arsenal. This was true for Khashoggi's sponsor King Abdullah as much as King Salman and MBS.

Although MBS is at times portrayed as a green and impetuous leader, in wanting nuclear arms he was no outlier in the kingdom.

Quite the opposite. Iran's growing closeness to a nuclear bomb caused great anxiety in Riyadh, even before MBS and his father ruled the palace. In 2008, King Abdullah and the US had still signed an accord in which the kingdom voluntarily agreed not to enrich uranium itself if it ever built nuclear reactors. In effect, King Abdullah had bound Saudi Arabia to not building a nuclear weapon since home-grown enrichment of uranium is the *sine qua non* for any country wanting to join the club of nuclear powers.

Ever since Iran's nuclear reactor started generating energy in 2011, Riyadh had made clear that it had changed its mind about the 2008 accord with the US. Obama's Nuclear Deal that was being thrashed out in Geneva around Iran's nuclear program was meant to hamstring the country and convince its Gulf neigbours that Iran wouldn't be able to put together the bomb despite having a nuclear facility. Regardless, if Shiite Iran could potentially make nuclear arms, Saudi Arabia wanted to be treated the same way by its US ally.

Khashoggi had no problem with MBS's stance. At the time of the negotiations, Khashoggi was still deeply wired into King Abdullah's court. Riyadh and Khashoggi hated Obama's July 2015 deal in equal measure. A major bone of contention was that the deal did authorise Iran to enrich its own uranium. Admittedly, this was only for the lower grade of enrichment for civilian use, but that didn't take away from the fact that the US had allowed Iran, Saudi's mortal foe, to do something it had denied its loyal (if one set aside the cloud cast by the 15 Saudis who took part in the 9/11 precision bombing) ally. It spat in the face of Riyadh.

When King Salman, and the new minister of defence MBS, took over the reins on 23 January 2015 they naturally also took charge of Saudi Arabia's strategy to thwart any deal in Geneva, except on the strictest terms. But in this respect the new king and his son failed. On 15 July 2015, the day of Obama's Iran deal's announcement, Khashoggi would politely tweet from Riyadh 'reality forces us to be against'. His polite tweet was positively hectoring compared to the silence that was Riyadh's official response.

However, behind the scenes there had been horse trading between the Obama administration and the new King Salman and his new defence minister MBS. Obama had something that the new Saudi regime wanted. When the new king and MBS let Obama's Iran deal pass in July 2015, the US gave the young, ambitious new Saudi minister something very important in return – Obama's seal of approval and logistical support to the Saudi-led airforce bombardments of Iran-backed Houthi rebels in Yemen. What MBS had lost on the deal, he won in getting the US's backing for his invasion and being seen as the man who could knock heads together on the Arabian Peninsula within months of being appointed. This feat Khashoggi had enthusiastically endorsed as the 'Salman Doctrine'.

Enter retired US general Michael Flynn, the man who was Donald Trump's first pick for national security adviser. Unbeknownst to Khashoggi and the US media – but not presumably the US intelligence services – Michael Flynn was warming up the Trump transition team led by Jared Kushner to the idea of selling nuclear technology to the Saudi royal family under the header of a scheme called 'The Iron Bridge'. Dating back in its origins to 2015, this idea was first hatched by retired US generals and six US nuclear power companies in a consortium called IP3. The ostensible goal of the consortium was to build some 40 civil nuclear installations in Saudi Arabia.

In November, Khashoggi was blind-sided as to this impending change of US direction under Trump. Like everyone else, he saw a president-elect who lacked the US's traditional mistrust of Russia's Putin. As Russia traditionally sided with Iran, for him that meant a weaker position of Saudi Arabia in the Middle East if Putin gained greater influence.

Flynn's subsequent official appointment lasted all of twenty four days, as he turned out to be a liar and confessed as charged to the felony of perjuring himself under oath to the FBI. Flynn would also concede that he had been on the payroll of IP3 and had made sponsored trips to Saudi Arabia as early as 2015. He had failed to disclose the latter detail on his White House security clearance. Had they been disclosed, his financial ties would have tainted his advocacy of IP3's 'Iron Bridge'.

Yet by the time of Flynn's mayfly decline and fall, his lies no longer mattered. The 'Iron Bridge' scheme had been inserted through the warp threads of Trump's White House. As a sign of his gratitude for Flynn's work, Donald Trump issued on 1 December 2020 a broad pardon to Flynn of 'any and all possible offenses' as one of the last acts of his presidency.

The scheme suited the transition-team-Trump outlook on many levels. Trump liked it, too. Resuscitating moribund traditional US industries had been one of the core planks of the Trump campaign and those around him. It played well with his elder hamburger-and-fries voters, not least septuagenarians like himself whose ideas had formed in the seventies.

Coal was one of the dead-end industries Trump championed, even if it didn't stand much of a long-term chance against the price drops in renewable energy, or the plentiful cheap oil from fracking that had made the US once again the world's top oil exporter. Even coal-gobbling behemoth India started to switch away from it. In 2017, the price of solar power would precipitously halve to $40/mwhr in India and would drop further, whereas coal cost at least $60 and would only go up in the future as a result of inflation of the cost of mining and transporting it alone. Trump's campaign promises to save the mineral did wonders for the local US coal industry. Peabody Inc., the world's largest private-sector coalminer, emerged from its 2016 bankruptcy buoyed by Trump's election promises.

Nuclear energy was like coal, another industry on its last legs in the US. In the case of nuclear-power, Trump's passion for this out-dated industry teetering on the brink of bankruptcy worked out slightly differently. It appealed to his love of cutting deals and photo opportunities with outsized cheques and bragging about what a great and shrewd businessman he was.

Not that the deal was any good on paper. With sunshine available in abundance for solar power in the Middle East, selling expensive, capital-intensive

1970s nuclear technology to Saudi Arabia made no obvious sense even if Saudi Arabia possessed up to 7% of the world's uranium deposits. Compared to the rapidly decreasing cost of 'mining' solar power, the financials of nuclear energy looked border-line suicidal. Moreover, for liability reasons no one had dared to test new technology since the Three Mile Island (1979) and Chernobyl (1986) disasters (the Chernobyl disaster had even shattered the USSR and the Iron Curtain). Indeed, MBS and his energy-minister al-Falih were already placing a $200bn bet on solar power with Japan's Softbank.

But the key thing the 'Iron Bridge' had going for it was that it was the first hurdle to owning a nuclear arsenal. What Flynn and his fellow generals at IP3, in effect, were trying to cash in on before the sun set on the US nuclear-energy industry was selling the dream of an atom bomb to Saudi Arabia before the industry had bankrupted itself. And Trump was good at selling dreams.

The 'deal makers' newly in charge in of the White House levers saw an eager, rich client who could afford to buy US technology at eye-popping headline-making amounts. Tom Barrack, a Lebanese American, Trump's closest friend, confidante, fellow septuagenarian, fellow billionaire with close ties to the Middle East, and a fellow deal maker, got actively involved in the 'The Iron Bridge'. On behalf of the Trump administration, he wrote the white paper on it of 21 March 2017. In this document he also proposed that he would be given ambassadorial or special envoy status to see it through.

It wasn't until 19 February 2019, half a year after Khashoggi's assassination, that House of Congress Democrats would publish a report exposing the whole fishy IP3 scheme with the help of whistle-blowers. The report cast a shrill light on the back-stage manoeuvring and its hairy skirting of US criminal federal law.

The congressional report laid out for the first time what had been going on. The year 2015 was not only the year of Obama's Iran Nuclear Deal and when King Salman ascended to the throne with MBS in tow, but also when Flynn made his first IP3-sponsored trips to Saudi Arabia. The retired generals who founded the IP3 consortium had clearly sensed a major opportunity in Riyadh with a new king in charge. In particular, they noted that Saudi procurement was now in the hands of the new minister of defence, MBS. Here was a thirty-year old with a hunger for big-ticket successes.

All this preparatory work got caught up in a vortex of swirling expectations with the surprise election of Donald Trump in November 2016. MBS saw in him a very pliable partner from whom to finally acquire the basic technology that opened the door to the world's most devastating weapon. When Saudi energy minister Khaled al-Falih, MBS's right-hand man, met Trump's son-in-law Jared Kushner in November 2016 his secret mission was thus about far more than cultivating goodwill after the frosty relations with the Obama administration. The ultimate prize was leap-frogging the other countries in the Middle East and gaining the lead position on nuclear power. No wonder MBS didn't want any Saudi to mouth-off Trump – Jamal Khashoggi included – while the palace was trying to woo him into a close friendship with high stakes and a top-secret goal.

While progress snowballed in secret, Khashoggi was furious about being muzzled. He lived in Jeddah and was no longer an insider at the new court and didn't understand why he was being silenced by Riyadh without being given a reason why.

The report revealed that, on Trump's Inauguration Day, Michael Flynn texted, 'we are good to go' and instructed IP3 'to put things in place'. By an unforeseen lucky break, Angela Merkel cancelled her visit to DC on 14 March due to a snowstorm when MBS was also in town on a visit as Saudi Arabia's Minister of Defence. Jared Kushner, who had hit it off with both al-Falih and MBS, swiftly manoeuvred MBS into the slot that had freed up. His father-in-law received MBS in the Oval Office. In their discussions the three of them covered 'The Iron Bridge' as part of a package of $200 billion 'investments' over 4 years by Saudi Arabia.

The snowy-winter air in Washington DC was thick with billions of dollars. Three days later the IP3 generals proposed in a private letter to MBS that Saudi Arabia buy Westinghouse, the leading but bankrupt US nuclear power company, with IP3. Toshiba, the IP3 member that owned the company outright, would sell it to this new Saudi-IP3 consortium. Nor did MBS make any bones about what was foremost on his agenda during his visit to the US capital. A day after the letter, MBS said on CBS's 60 Minutes, 'if Iran developed a nuclear bomb, we will follow suit as soon as possible.' Even so, lacking inside knowledge of 'The Iron Bridge', this comment would not have given Khashoggi much of a clue as to Riyadh's nuclear game plan. King Abdullah's government had said exactly the same thing whenever Iran's reactor came up.

Next came Donald Trump's first official visit to Saudi Arabia, which MBS and Kushner had teed up together. On 20-22 May 2017, Riyadh pulled out all the stops and the new US president was received like a king in Riyadh on his first presidential visit abroad. Donald Trump was decorated by King Salman with a gold necklace of the highest Saudi order, appeared to curtsy, opened an anti-terrorism centre with King Salman and Egypt's president el-Sisi who had flown in, and shook a cutlass at enthusiastic royals and princes during a traditional Saudi sword-dance.

And here was the photo opportunity Trump had been aiming for. With great ceremony, he also signed an immediate $110bn Saudi spending deal rising to $350bn over several years, as if he had just sold the first condo in a new building. Hailing the triumph of his first 5 months in office, he held up a large cardboard cheque in front of the camera while MBS appeared a little embarrassed, unused as yet to brassy sales patter at mutual press conferences.

In secret, the Trump administration was subsequently to issue seven authorisations to US companies to share nuclear intelligence – two of them weeks after the assassination of Jamal Khashoggi. Al-Falih and MBS's new best friend Jared Kushner, and Donald Trump's senior advisor in charge of the White House 'Office of American Innovation', oiled the wheels. Things were going so well that MBS boasted in 2017 that Jared Kushner 'was in his pocket.'

MBS and IP3 were not the only ones to benefit while these dealings were taking place beyond the media and Khashoggi's eye line. Jared Kushner's family's imperilled fortunes were rescued from being wiped out on 3 August 2018 by Brookfield Asset Management. Two days earlier, on 1 August, Brookfield had purchased bankrupt nuclear-power plant builder Westinghouse for $4.6 billion from IP3 member Toshiba. Like Toshiba, the Kushners' company's survival was severely compromised. Toshiba had filed for bankruptcy of Westinghouse on 31 March 2017, as a result of Westinghouse's mounting losses that were risking Toshiba's future. The Kushners' company was approaching bankruptcy through default on a $1.4 billion mortgage repayment plus accrued interest on 666 Fifth Avenue in New York that was due in January 2019. Brookfield, however, paid $1.1bn on 3 August for a 99-year lease on the property, which allowed the Kushners to redeem their loan, because, unusually, Brookfield paid upfront in cash.

What MBS wanted throughout this period was a warm bath of applause for Trump coming from Saudi Arabia, having been told how acutely sensitive the new president was to criticism of any kind. MBS didn't have to rely on second-hand reports as he had friends who had known Trump intimately for a long time.

Billionaire Jeffrey Epstein was one such friend. He knew Trump well from the 1990s and early 2000 and boasted to a *New York Times* reporter as early as 2013 that he was friendly with MBS and that they spoke frequently. Two days before the election, after the reopening of the FBI investigation of Hillary Clinton had thrown the race wide open again, Jeffrey Epstein flew to Riyadh on 7 November 2016. MBS was also in Riyadh at that time and had a well-publicised meeting with fellow billionaire Amazon's Jeff Bezos about investing in Saudi Arabia. Epstein's Gulfstream GV-SP – later dubbed the Lolita express for ferrying underage girls around for his sexual gratification – landed at 6:35pm from Paris and flew back two days later on Election Day at 3.17pm.

Jamal Khashoggi, once the consummate insider, had no idea. Meanwhile MBS's power grew rapidly as he deftly secured Trump as Saudi's biddable ally. In Riyadh, he leveraged this success to push his superior, Crown Prince bin Nayef, out of the way and become the first in line in Saudi's royal succession.

5
The Crown Prince

Who was the mastermind of the Khashoggi Plot?

Certainly, at the time of the assassination, the *de facto* head of Saudi Arabia was Crown Prince Mohammed bin Salman, or MBS as he is commonly referred to. Strictly speaking, MBS's eighty-two-year-old father King Salman ruled the kingdom. But Salman had suffered a stroke before he ascended the throne and he had not yet fully recovered. He was also afflicted by Alzheimer's. Though when the *Guardian* newspaper reported this in 2015, Riyadh immediately issued a strong-worded official rebuke, saying the new king was 'Most certainly not suffering from dementia or any other kind of mental impairment, nor has he suffered a stroke'.

Even so, in the day-to-day-running, MBS was in charge of the kingdom. What, then, was on MBS's mind in the lead-up to the assassination of one-time Saudi courtier Jamal Khashoggi?

In 2018, MBS was the darling of the West where he was seen by pundits and governments alike as a desperately-needed reformer in a country stuck in the dark ages and run in increasingly geriatric succession by the sons of King ibn Saud – a man who had died in 1953 at the age of 78. Shortly after becoming crown prince, MBS had opened cinemas and restricted the powers of the religious police. Women were allowed to drive and visit sports stadiums. On 19 March 2018, he had even relaxed the rule that Saudi women wear a black *abaya* covering their face, promulgating that it was not a matter of sharia law. The first public concert featuring a female singer had been held. His late 2017 shakedown of the starchy generation of older princes was unorthodox but understandable, it was argued, as the kingdom was suffering from the low oil prices and needed cash.

Dynamic MBS planned to diversify the economy, moving Saudi Arabia away from its slavish dependence on oil. He even set up a $200bn investment plan in solar energy with Japanese Softbank, the subject of Jamal Khashoggi's last-ever tweet. He also spent an awful lot of money buying Western arms. Tantalisingly, he iconoclastically toyed with the idea of privatising the state oil company Saudi Aramco, the world's most profitable company, in order to plug the gaping hole in the royal coffers of the desert kingdom. Although it would only float 5 per cent of the company, the West had been excluded from owning part of the company ever since nationalisation in the seventies (from then owners, the US oil companies Texaco, Exxon and Mobil, three of the Seven Sisters). Global investors salivated at the prospect of owning shares in this unbeatable company and there was a chorus of international applause for MBS.

But by traditional Saudi royal-succession rules, MBS should not have been even close to a position of royal power in the first place. Saudi Arabia was founded in 1932 under King ibn Saud. After he died in 1953, he was supposed to be succeeded in turn by all his surviving sons. He had forty-five sons, thirty six of whom survived him. Six of them had indeed subsequently become king and almost a dozen were still alive in 2017.

Among the still surviving sons there was, for example, the relatively spruce seventy-six-year-old Prince Ahmed, with whom King Salman shared the same mother, ibn Saud's favourite wife Sudairi. Ahmed was one of the youngest children of ibn Saud and his thirty-first son. And when King Salman ascended the throne in 2015 as the sixth ibn Saud son to become king, he had picked as his crown prince another son of ibn Saud's as Saudi tradition demanded. He chose his youngest living half-brother, the septuagenarian Prince Muqrin, and also made him first deputy prime minister. After King Salman's death Muqrin, ibn Saud's thirty-fifth son, would become King Muqrin – and the seventh son of ibn Saud to ascend the throne.

Or so it seemed for a brief while. After just three months, King Salman replaced Muqrin with his nephew Prince Mohammed bin Nayef. Bin Nayef ('bin' means son of) was the first crown prince in his fifties since 1982. Connoisseurs of Saudi palace intrigue noted that he was also the son of Prince Nayef (who was crown prince before Salman, but died in 2012), Prince Salman and Prince Ahmed's brother and the fourth son of Hassa al-Sudairi.

Salman's choice of Nayef's son meant that the new king shattered the sixty year tradition of passing the Saudi crown to a son of ibn Saud. Not only that, he strengthened the Sudairi succession line. There was, furthermore, some historical validity to this palace coup. Salman and Nayef were 'Sudairi sons' and their mother was their father's favourite of his twenty-four wives.

However, it was really a matter of power. Ibn Saud's tenth wife Sudairi had no fewer than seven sons, whom together had formed a block amongst ibn Saud's thirty-six surviving sons. In 1964, the al-Saud clan forced ibn Saud's chosen successor King Saud, his oldest living son, to abdicate. The new king, Faisal, had given the kingdom's five key positions of power to senior half-brothers from different mothers who had supported him in the coup against Saud. The only exception were the Sudairis. They received two of these positions.

In practice, the real Saudi line of succession was made up of the brothers holding the great offices of state. When Abdullah, son of ibn Saud's fourteenth wife Fahda al-Shammari and head of the national guard since 1964, became king, he had appointed his Sudairi half-brother Sultan (minister of defence since 1964).

Upon Sultan's death, he appointed the then minister of the interior, his Sudairi half-brother Nayef, as his heir. When he died within a year, he appointed his Sudairi half-brother Salman, who had received the governorship of Riyadh from Faisal in 1964.

Abdullah himself had become regent in 1995 when King Fahd, Sudairi's oldest son, suffered a debilitating stroke. From that moment, he constantly plotted against the Sudairi succession. Though unsuccessful, Abdullah did ammass an enormous fortune over this period. When he died in 2015 he had become the world's richest head of state after the Sultan of Brunei and the King of Thailand.

Jamal Khashoggi knew this time very well indeed. He had made his career under Abdullah and knew the intrigue inside out as he held the rank of a royal advisor to the king when Abdullah died.

In June 2017, in a further game of palace chess, King Salman removed this new-generation crown prince, too, by royal decree and replaced him with Mohammed bin Salman, his own son. He had slyly laid the groundwork for this promotion by appointing MBS as deputy crown prince under Crown Prince bin Nayef. It was Abdullah who had originally created this deputy tier in 2014 for his half-brother Muqrin in an attempt to wrench power away from the Sudairis through the backdoor. Ironically, it became the way through which Salman segued his son into position.

It was not just that one had to go back to the reign of ibn Saud (1932-1953), Salman's father, for a crown prince as young as MBS. He was different in other ways, too. Born in 1985, MBS was the eldest child of King Salman's third wife Princess Fahda bint Falah. Several of King Salman's other sons, who studied overseas to perfect foreign languages and earn advanced degrees, had spent time outside the royal cocoon and built impressive résumés. One became the first Arab astronaut, another a deputy oil minister, yet another the governor of Medina Province. MBS, however, was exclusively educated in Saudi Arabia and did not speak English as fluently as they did, although he understood it well.

Rachid Sekkai, who taught him English and later worked for the BBC, said he toyed with a walkie-talkie in class and was more interested in playing in the garden and cracking jokes with his brothers and the guards. When the chance came to visit America, he refused to go to the US embassy for a visa to be finger-printed 'like some criminal', according to a State Department cable. But two thirds of Saudi Arabia's population was under 35 and he was a popular choice with them as they could identify with him and his passion for computer games. He was rumoured to have spent $70,000 on Battle Pass and five hours playing Resident Evil. They saw him as one of their own. Unlike older royals, he was comfortable shaking hands with women outside the kingdom.

While his father was still governor of Riyadh Province (and highly feared),

MBS was brought up in a palace that was built like a fortress. After a private Saudi education, he studied law at King Saud University in Riyadh, graduating fourth in his class. Another prince of the same generation said he got to know him during high school when one of their uncles held regular dinners for the younger princes at his palace. He recalled MBS being one of the crowd, saying he liked to play bridge and admired Margaret Thatcher.

Salman had as many as twelve sons (and one daughter) with three wives. But he picked MBS, his seventh son, as his favourite and heir. At the age of twenty four, MBS was appointed as his father's personal advisor. When his father moved on from the governorship of Riyadh and became second deputy prime minister and defence minister, MBS stayed on as private advisor. Clearly Salman was very impressed with his young son. Other appointments followed when Prince Salman unexpectedly became crown prince in 2012, then king in January 2015.

As king, one of Salman's first appointments was to elevate MBS as his minister of defence. This introduced MBS to world leaders and gave him a lot of sway in the West given Saudi's massive arms procurements.

It was in his new capacity as minister of defence that MBS also first began to wield Saudi executive power, though with at best equivocal success. In neighbouring Yemen, the rebel Houthi militia of the Shiite Zaidi sect and forces loyal to the former president Ali Abdullah Saleh (ousted in 2012), took the capital city Sanaa on 21 March 2015 and proclaimed themselves the official government of Yemen. Saleh's successor Abdrabbuh Hadi was a Sunni muslim and retained his control over the principal port of Aden, however, while al-Qaeda and Isis (Daesh) were able to occupy other parts of Yemen. The Houthi then marched on Aden and president Hadi fled on the 25th of March to Saudi Arabia.

Hadi was understood to be languishing in Riyadh under house arrest, but in retaliation of his defeat, MBS as Saudi defence minister organised a Sunni coalition of Gulf states – including the impressive emirati forces of his neighbour and friend Prince Mohammed bin Zayed – and the coalition began air strikes on Houthi positions and a naval blockade. What really united the Sunni Gulf states behind Saudi Arabia was that their arch-enemy Iran was gaining a Shiite bridgehead on the Southern Arabian Peninsula by supporting the Houthi rebels. Interestingly, MBS did not inform the head of his National Guard, Prince Mutaib bin Abdullah, the son of the previous king, when the first air strikes were launched and half a year later Mutaib was also ousted from all offices in MBS's 2017 Ritz Carlton purge.

Having total command of Yemeni airspace, MBS expected a quick victory over the Houthi and, consequently, the restoration of the Sunni Hadi regime which he then could take credit for. At the start of the war, he was often photographed visiting troops and meeting with military leaders. But as a military leader, MBS took frequent holidays, putting himself out of contact for days on end. Soon the campaign reached stalemate and turned into a war of attrition, and his appearances with coalition forces grew rare as the fight began to be called Saudi's Vietnam War.

Instead of a quick victory, civilian casualties mounted, and MBS drew growing criticism from human rights groups, while diplomats pointed out that the death toll for Saudi troops was higher than the government acknowledged publicly. The prolonged war and the Saudi-led blockade also led to a famine in Yemen. Half of the war-torn country's population – fourteen million people – were on the brink of starvation and it was estimated in 2018 that 85,000 children died from malnutrition.

In order to counter these negative headlines and keep tighter control over the narrative inside and outside the kingdom, MBS had established the Centre for Studies and Media Affairs under his right-hand man Saud al-Qahtani to propagate a positive spin on the Yemen war in Washington, DC. At vast annual expense, the Center hired numerous Washington and London-based lobbying and public relations firms to assist in the PR campaign. When the *Economist* dubbed him the 'architect of the war in Yemen', MBS's smooth response was that, instead, he was waging war on 'Islamic terrorism'.

As oil prices were dropping, MBS paid for the costly war by slashing the state budget and freezing government contracts in the name of austerity. He cancelled the bonuses that made up one third of the salaries of government employees, having to reinstate them seven months later in the face of public anger.

For himself, however, he could not resist buying a 440-foot yacht, the Serene, from a Russian vodka billionaire for $500 million. Fearing assassination, he was said to sleep on board. He also bought Château Louis XIV near Versailles, France, the world's most expensive home with a $300 million price tag. This modern palace was built by Saudi property developer Emad Khashoggi, a cousin of Jamal Khashoggi's. The Leonardo da Vinci painting 'Salvador del Mundo' cost him $450 million in the most expensive art sale in history – it was rumoured to be berthed on the Serene.

None of this affected MBS's popularity among young Saudis. On the one hand, they were unlikely to hear about it. The country's controlled news media lent a helping hand by building up MBS's image as a hardworking, business-like leader, less concerned with the trappings of royalty than his predecessors – his profligacy was one of the secrets blanked in the Saudi media on palace orders from the Center for Studies and Media Affairs. And on the other hand, MBS gave them what they wanted: relaxation of Saudi's stifling religious oppression.

King Salman had indeed made a shrewd choice. Given Saudi Arabia's increasingly geriatric echelons of power and a crown cascading down aging and infirm brothers, Salman himself being one of them, many young Saudis admired MBS as a dynamic representative of their generation who addressed some of the kingdom's problems in a forthright manner rather than in the traditional crab-like way: two steps side-ways, one step forward. To them he was the swashbuckling prince defending their point view.

MBS had an eye for what really engaged young Saudis. It wasn't religion, as it had been when Jamal Khashoggi and Osama bin Laden were students. During the months before Jamal Khashoggi's assassination, MBS was planning a £4 billion takeover bid for Manchester United – despite the fact that its owners the Glazer family said they had no immediate intention of selling the club. Soccer was the most popular sport on the Arabian peninsula. Saudi Arabia's neighbour Qatar, the richest country in the world, had snagged the 2022 FIFA world soccer championship and its announcement in 2017 had swelled Qatar's national pride and started a sports one-upmanship with its neighbours. MBS was making sure that he delivered what his twenty million young Saudi fans expected from him.

But there was far more to King Salman's faith in MBS than merely his son's appeal to Saudi Arabia's youth. King Salman rewrote history when he dropped the ibn Saud succession rule. It also meant that he trusted his son to be his wingman and a ruthless and effective operator in the royal palace to deal with the the power of the other senior branches of the royal family. There was also Salman's younger Sudairi brother Ahmed who remained a heavyweight even though he had lost his government positions when Salman became king Abdullah's heir in 2012. MBS had his work cut out for him.

Even before King Salman installed him as crown prince in 2017, it was clear that MBS was on a mission to move aside his predecessor, Crown Prince bin Nayef. Bin Nayef seemed unassailable as a competent long-time hard-line counterterrorism expert who had good connections in Washington and the support of many of Saudi's leading royals. But the White House saw an early sign of the ambition of the young prince in late 2015, when – breaking protocol – MBS delivered an obloquy on the failures of American foreign policy during a meeting between his father King Salman and President Obama.

Early in 2016, bin Nayef suddenly retired to his villa in Algeria. Previously he had taken hunting holidays there, but this time it was different. He stayed away for weeks and was often incommunicado. Even CIA Director John Brennan, who had known him for decades, had trouble reaching him. A diabetic, it was said, bin Nayef was suffering from the prolonged effects of injuries from an assassination attempt where an al-Qaeda suicide bomber detonated a bomb surgically implanted in his rectum. Crown Prince bin Nayef was, in actual fact, avoiding the predations of MBS, (then) his deputy crown prince.

King Salman did not sit on the side lines either. He had already united his own court with that of his son's when he ascended the throne, thus handing MBS control over access to the king. In April 2015, King Salman had also made MBS head of the lucrative Saudi Aramco oil company, the chief engine of the economy. MBS replaced Khalid al-Falih, who became energy minister and one of MBS's close associates.

In December of the same year, MBS announced as minister of defence the formation of a military alliance of (Sunni) Islamic countries to fight Islamic terrorism. Counter-terrorism had long been the province of bin Nayef, but the new alliance gave no role to him or his interior ministry. When MBS listed the countries of the alliance, a number of them said they knew nothing about it, or were waiting for information before deciding to join. By not intervening, the king made it clear that MBS had his tacit approval here, too.

In April 2016, MBS also launched his economic bid for royal succession. To show the breadth of his thinking, the deputy crown prince unfolded an ambitious plan for the future of the kingdom's finance. Called Vision 2030, it was every bit as bold and aggressive as King Salman's change of the royal succession rules in Saudi's plush corridors of power. The plan sought to increase the country's employment numbers and improve education, healthcare and other government services, and move the economy away from its sole reliance on oil. A National Transformation Plan, laying out targets for improving government ministries, came shortly after. It also called for transparency and accountability, indirectly admitting that they had been missing before and that these were important values. Khashoggi, then still living in Saudi, was a supporter of the plan, Cengiz said in her book, and had even lobbied to become an advisor.

A luxury beach resort was planned for the Red Sea coast between al-Wajh and Umluj where women would be allowed to wear bikinis in the pool and beach areas. Twenty two islands would see hotels with Donald Trump style bling spring up, adding a projected $6 billion to Saudi GDP. Over $2 billion was invested in an entertainment authority that MBS established. This government branch staged live music concerts, comedy shows, wrestling matches and monster truck rallies. A large sports, culture and entertainment complex was to be built, along with a theme park.

Any criticism of the relentless rise of MBS was silenced by calls to Saudi journalists telling them they had been barred from publishing, and sometimes from travelling abroad. One Saudi journalist published an article about MBS on his website, the *Riyadh Post*, where he said that the prince's popularity was based on a 'sweeping desire for great change' and the hope that he would 'turn their dreams into reality'. But he also qualified his praise: 'If you fail, this love withers quickly, as if it never existed, and is replaced by a deep feeling of frustration and hatred.' The website was blocked the next day. It was not a mistake Jamal Khashoggi made when discussing MBS sensitive matters. Even though he was a prominent Saudi journalist, his writings never attracted the cross hairs of MBS's sniper al-Qahtani.

While still deputy crown prince to bin Nayef, MBS also made well-publicised foreign trips to Europe, the Middle East and Washington, where he stayed at the Georgetown home of Secretary of State John Kerry. In September 2015, dinner at Mr Kerry's house ended with MBS playing Beethoven's Moonlight Sonata on the piano for his host and other guests. He attended the G20 summit in November 2015, leading the German secret service to predict bluntly in a leaked report that Crown Prince bin Nayef would not become king. Then in May 2016, Secretary of State Kerry was a guest on MBS's yacht, the Serene, and in June 2016, the two men shared an *iftar* dinner, breaking the Ramadan fast.

MBS's influence in Washington was channelled through Sheikh Mohammed bin Zayed, the crown prince of Abu Dhabi, or MBZ, deputy supreme commander of the United Arab Emirates Armed Forces, and one of the richest men in the world with $1.3 trillion at his fingertips and a personal fortune of $15 billion. A favourite of the Obama administration, he was a respected voice in the Sunni world. Both princes shared an innate hostility to Shia Iran and the Muslim Brotherhood, whose Islamic populism they considered direct threats to their hereditary form of government after the Arab Spring (2010-2012). It helped that MBZ had a personal antipathy towards Crown Prince bin Nayef.

From the moment his father became king in 2015, MBS had no time to lose to consolidate his power base. His father was seventy-nine years old. Apart from Abdullah, who had reached the venerable age of ninety, the rule of each of the preceding kings had ended by that age. The old guard among the royal family continued to see MBS as a power-hungry inexperienced upstart and the knives were out for him.

The groundwork for bin Nayef's *coup de grace* was laid on 17 June 2017 when King Salman issued a decree restructuring Saudi Arabia's system for prosecutions. It stripped bin Nayef of his long-standing power base of overseeing criminal investigations. He was, in addition, placed under house arrest, while those loyal to him were purged.

Still bin Nayef refused to give up his claim to the throne. But during an end-of-Ramadan celebration at the palace the crown prince was led to a separate room to 'meet the king'. Instead, court officials – including MBS's henchman al-Qahtani – took his phones and talked in on him. They wore him down deep into the night as he grew tired, suffering from diabetes and the after-effects of the terrorist attack on his life. Finally, King Salman met alone with the exhausted bin Nayef to discuss his position. Still he would not yield. It was prince Khalid al-Faisal, governor of Mecca, who persuaded him finally by pointing out that his claim to the throne as son of King Faisal was greater than bin-Nayef's. And yet he had not complained when Salman passed him over. 'In this family, we obey the king.'

To the other royal princes it was meanwhile broadcast by rumour that bin Nayef had abdicated because of his addiction to painkilling drugs. Relieved of all his functions by Salman, he was removed from royal succession. In a final humiliation the former crown prince was forced to pledge public loyalty to his successor when MBS became crown prince on 21 June 2017. The bitter pill was gilded by MBS, who moments before, kneeled and kissed bin Nayef's hand, promising to always ask for his counsel.

Donald Trump was one of the first foreign leaders who phoned to congratulate MBS. The two had quickly formed a special bond. A month after Trump's election in 2016 a high-level Saudi delegation close to MBS had met with Trump's transition team, and Saudi Arabia, via the soon-to-be crown prince MBS, was one of the first to issue an invitation for a full-blown state visit to Riyadh – which happened with much pomp and circumstance on 20-21 May 2017 at vast expense.

The 2016 Saudi delegation, led by MBS's associate energy minister Khalid al Falih, had shrewdly concluded about the Trump transition team that 'The inner circle is predominantly deal makers who lack familiarity with political customs and deep institutions, and they support Jared Kushner'. Trump's transition team equated international relations with deal flow, seeing the state department as a giant sales agency. Saudi relations with the Obama White House had been frosty, but Trump's team offered an opportunity to burnish the Riyadh-DC relationship with a golden glow. Al-Falih met with Kushner and talked about spending hundreds and hundreds of billions on deals and more deals. They also offered their clout to help resolve the Israel-Palestine crisis, a set of negotiations dear to Jared Kushner's inexperienced heart. The outcome of these efforts were trailed as the 'deal of the century' by Trump but remained ineffectual.

On 4 November 2017, MBS made his public move against his aged royal adversaries and their flunkies who had grown rich and powerful under King Abdullah. He ordered hundreds (estimates ran up to 500 but the figure was around 300, 11 of them princes) of senior princes and wealthy businessmen, politicians, clerics and government officials to be detained at Riyadh's palatial 492-room Ritz-Carlton hotel. Within the hotel they were free to move around, watch national geographic on TV, and enjoy its men-only spa with two extravagant staircases winged in grand curves leading to a domed pool area, all framed overhead with an explosion of azure and aquamarine framed in gold and white. They were prevented from leaving by guards loyal to MBS only.

If ever there was a test of Salman's faith in his seventh son, this was it. The secrecy surrounding the move had to be hermetic. The palace was rife with courtiers who owed allegiance and favours to the Abdullah branch. Even one word of royal gossip in the wrong ear and Saudi Arabia's power brokers would have found a plausible excuse not to attend to escape being held hostage by the new crown prince. MBS passed with flying colours. And where did Khashoggi rank in this high-stakes power play? He had, like many, made his career during Abdullah's twenty year long regency and reign. But he was no more than a foot soldier compared to the grand men gathered at the Ritz-Carlton. He commanded no great power, fortune of his own, or state office in the kingdom.

Imprisoned at the hotel, the detainees were relieved of their functions and only released after they gave up billions of dollars to a new anti-corruption committee set up by the new crown prince. It was run by Saudi prosecutor general Sheikh Saud al-Mojeb who said the guests received 'the same rights and treatment as any other Saudi citizen' (he might have added that they were even presented with the bill of their stay after their release from the hotel). Bank accounts were frozen and the hotel's internet and telephone lines were disconnected while they remained under house arrest. MBS's aide Saud al-Qahtani was a key part of the corruption negotiation team inside the Ritz Carlton.

MBS ripped out the spine of the former Abdullah regime. Two brothers of the powerful Bin Laden family, directly related to Osama, and part owners of the privately-held Binladin construction group, were given a room in the Ritz Carlton. The group built everything for the Saudi government and was now engaged with MBS's vision 2030. The brothers were left watching TV and agreed to hand over their 36.2 per cent share on 26 April 2018. Purged of bin Ladens, the group would change its name.

Another owner, Bakr, Osama bin Laden's half-brother, transferred his 23.58 per cent on the same date, too. But he was moved to custody in a different place rather than released. MBS had a personal score to settle. As CEO of the firm Bakr had haughtily rebuffed an approach by MBS in 2015 to become a board member. Riyadh would only release Bakr from detention in January 2019 to alleviate international pressure building up as a result of the Khashoggi affair.

MBS also took care of rivals within his own branch. Prince Ahmed, MBS's uncle and the king's remaining Sudairi brother, had been tipped off hours before MBS's Ritz Carlton plot began. He escaped just in time and went to live in self-imposed exile in London in a £50 million home. Although Prince Ahmed had been removed from succession in 2012, he remained highly influential as a heavyweight candidate for the throne among ibn Saud's remaining children. His Sudairi-ibn Saud claim to the throne was like gold to silver compared to MBS's and it was wise to run before the hotel scythe landed.

Senior royals bitterly complained that MBS used his power as chief of his father's royal court to block their access to King Salman during the Ritz Carlton months. With some further tacit encouragement from his father, MBS then set about restructuring the intelligence agencies, another Saudi power base staffed by royal branches sceptical of him.

Outside the kingdom, MBS began to throw his weight around in the first month of his appointment as crown prince. In June 2017, he led a blockade of Qatar, the base of al-Jazeera, the more successful pan-Arab rival to Saudi broadcaster al-Arabiya. Qatar's neutral attitude to Shiite Iran despite being Sunni traditionally irked Saudi Arabia. For Qatar it was a necessity. Its main oil and gas field, the source of the minute state's vast wealth, reached far underneath the Persian Gulf and crossed over into Iran's territorial waters. MBS didn't care and was poised to do the same as in Yemen and invade the country with his emirati ally MBZ.

MBS alleged that the Gulf state was supporting Shia terrorism from Iran. Qatar was 90 per cent Sunni and denied this, though the tiny gas-rich state admitted that it had provided assistance to some Sunni Islamist groups such as the Muslim Brotherhood. Yet it said it did not support Sunni militant groups linked to Isis (ISL or Daesh) or bin-Laden's al-Qaeda.

It was a subtle point to make, as far as MBS was concerned there was no daylight between the Muslim Brotherhood and Isis or al-Qaeda. Riyadh deeply mistrusted the Muslim Brotherhood and how it had surfed the populist Islamic wave that had gripped the Middle East.

MBS saw the brotherhood as the main threat to Saudi royal rule in the kingdom and was determined to stamp it out where he could. The general appeal of religious extremism was waning, but in its stead the brotherhood was capturing minds and hearts in the Arab world. After the Arab Spring, the brotherhood had hijacked Egypt's first-ever elections following President Hosni Mubarak's unseating by popular revolt. The Muslim Brotherhood's President Morsi had soon set about to restore dictatorial powers for himself in the image of Iran. Morsi had done so in such a calamitous fashion that he was soon generally disliked as much as Mubarak. He had been deposed in a 2013 coup led by Abdel el-Sisi with the Egyptian army and Saudi support while Salman was Saudi minister of defence and MBS his adviser.

One person MBS was able to convince that the brotherhood was as evil as al-Qaeda was Donald Trump, half a year into his presidency. On 9 June 2017, he told reporters in front of the White House, that action was necessary as the 'nation of Qatar unfortunately has historically been a funder of terrorism at a very high level'. He had not yet told his White House staff, however, that he was going to side with MBS and MBZ.

If he had, they would have pointed out an important kink in his argument. As it was, it took them some time to convince the president that the US's most important airbase in the Middle East was based in Qatar, hosted by the US's long-standing and loyal ally the emir who he had just been accused of being a terrorist. Trump didn't know this and MBS and MBZ were subsequently told to stand down from invading Qatar in no uncertain terms. Just in time.

Like the war against Shia-governed Yemen, the Saudi blockade of Qatar continued to drag on, however. It was effectively nullified by imports from Iran and airlifts organised by Qatar's fellow Sunni, the president of Turkey, Erdoğan whose gradual rise to power was closely aligned with the Muslim Brotherhood.

Turkey's support for both Qatar and the Muslim Brotherhood annoyed MBS immensely.

Although 70 per cent Sunni, Turkey had fought Saudi's orthodox Wahhabism – which had spread in opposition to the sultan – for centuries and tended to ignore the Shia-Sunni divide of Muslims in its foreign policy, striking a pragmatic rather than dogmatic course. President Erdoğan had just survived his own army putsch and populist Islam was his power base rather than the army. Iran and Qatar were Erdoğan's natural allies whereas el-Sisi's army-backed dictatorship in Egypt was a natural fit with the Saudi and UAE camp.

It was all these problems and the gathering weight of international headlines against him, that had made MBS decide to brush up on his overseas image with a lavish world tour projecting his brand of youthful Saudi Arabia.

In the UK, he met Prime Minister Theresa May, Queen Elizabeth and Prince William. Then he flew on to the US where he visited Washington, Hollywood and Silicon Valley, meeting President Trump, Bill and Hillary Clinton, Henry Kissinger, Michael Bloomberg, George W. Bush, George H.W. Bush, Bill Gates, Jeff Bezos, Oprah Winfrey, Rupert Murdoch, Richard Branson, Mayor Eric Garcetti of Los Angeles, Michael Douglas, Morgan Freeman and Dwayne Johnson. He also met with prominent Jewish groups and garnered almost universal praise.

It begged a certain question. Given the world stage MBS bestrode with such keenness, what was so special about Jamal Khashoggi that he merited the interest of Saudi Arabia's top leader in September 2018 when the first preparations for the Khashoggi Plot were hatched?

6
Tysons Corner

Grounded in Jeddah Jamal Khashoggi remained deeply aggrieved by his continuing media ban. He later said in a TV interview, 'all that I write, I write as an honest advisor'. It was grating to Khashoggi that the beginning of Trump's presidency was treated with the same media black-out as the Arab Spring and the el-Sisi coup in Egypt. The new Riyadh courtiers merely gave orders and no explanations. It nurtured his resentment.

He travelled to London in April 2017 to stay for three weeks with Dr Nawaf Obaid, who had studied at Kings College, London, and received his PhD from MIT. He was also, like Khashoggi, a former advisor to Prince Turki when Turki was ambassador in London and Washington DC and dealing with the crisis caused by 9/11. Khashoggi mooted a plan to move to the US to his friend. But al-Qahtani called Khashoggi during this London sabbatical and told Khashoggi that all would be forgiven once he returned home to Jeddah. Obaid, who later told the *Washington Post*, said it was all part of al-Qahtani's 'hot-cold approach' to keep Khashoggi in check.

Khashoggi listened once again to al-Qahtani's siren song and did return to Jeddah. But he didn't stay for long. The climate for anyone belonging to the Abdullah clan was not safe and Khashoggi was warned to leave, said his Turkish friend Turan Kışlakçi. He escaped with two suitcases during Ramadan – 27 May to 25 June in Riyadh, 2017 – and left for his $400,000 condo in Lillian Court, 1625 International Drive, Tysons Corner in Fairfax County, Virginia, USA. Tysons Corner was fifteen kilometres from Washington, DC, half an hour by DC's Metro, and Khashoggi still owned the place from his US embassy time.

It was well-timed, as one would expect from someone with top-level intelligence contacts and who had in 2003 also been helped to escape narrowly to safety in London. In the middle of June, King Salman and MBS would stage their palace coup against sitting Crown Prince bin Nayef.

As his cover Khashoggi had submitted an application for a fellowship at the prestigious Woodrow Wilson Center in DC. His application described a book project 'to explain American life to the Saudi reader and Arabs in general', which would be an 'eye-opener' on 'schooling, educational reform [and] control of public funds' as well as mortgages (housing being the problem that affected most ordinary Saudis as royals owned most of the land in Saudi Arabia). He proposed travelling to US rural towns and describing how town meetings worked and the elections of mayors and governing boards.

Lillian Court, Tysons Corner.

He was still torn on the 4th of July, 2017, whether to return to Saudi Arabia or not. On that day Maggie Salem Mitchell, director of the Qatar International Foundation and his friend since 2001, hosted a dinner at Clos Maggiore in Covent Garden, London. At the party in the wood-panelled restaurant with ivy on the walls, branches with flowers in the courtyard, as well as a magnificent wine list including rare vintages of Château Pétrus, he discussed his options: 'To keep quiet, to sit in his house in Jeddah and smoke cigars... or to go to Istanbul or the US.'

Once he had settled on the US, though, Khashoggi faithfully maintained al-Qahtani's media ban, even if he applied for political asylum. In August, nonetheless, he posted his first tweet since his 18 November 2016 ban. Saudi information minister Awwad al-Awwad had called him in Virginia on 13 August to say Riyadh's objections to his views had been lifted. 'I return to writing and tweeting. Grateful to his highness the minister of information for his kind efforts, gratitude and loyalty to the crown prince. No free pen is broken and no tweeter is silenced under his reign', Khashoggi wrote agreeably in Arabic and not very truthfully given his own nine months' media exile.

What was happening behind the scenes in August would be pieced together by the *Washington Post* on 22 December 2018 in an in-depth investigation into Khashoggi's text messages and papers, including a 200-page trove they had been given access to.

During this call, Awwad al-Awwad asked Khashoggi would he be interested in setting up a pro-Saudi think tank? Khashoggi had duly submitted a proposal for a 'Saudi Research Council' based in the US with a funding of $1-2 million, something akin to the Qatar Foundation International run by his friend Maggie Salem Mitchell. To show his allegiance to MBS and al-Qahtani he publically tweeted on 23 August: 'I am not "in exile" please don't use that painful description'. Instead, he called himself an 'expatriate'. His stay in the US was just temporary and 'I will return to my country'.

In effect, Khashoggi's 'research council' would act like an advance post of al-Qahtani's cyber-war department, the Centre for Studies and Media Affairs. 'Irresponsible media' connect the kingdom to terrorism, and the idea, Khashoggi wrote in his proposal, was to monitor 'potential negative news... that might explode against the kingdom', 'notify the ministry' and allow the country to 'regain its positive role and image'. The think tank would be an amalgam of his previous semi-government roles in Saudi intelligence, and as newspaper editor, advisor, spy and diplomat, and the statutes would provide the agreed red lines.

There was one sticking point. Al-Awwad wanted Khashoggi to return to Saudi Arabia to discuss the proposal directly with MBS. He declined and the project ended up in the long grass.

It is a sign that the palace lifted Khashoggi's media ban before securing his willingness to cooperate with the MBS regime in one financial guise or another. Even if he started criticising Saudi Arabia publicly from the US, it hardly mattered. None of the Saudi media would touch him and the Trump Administration would simply ignore him as he clearly no longer had anything to do with the palace. Though irritating at worst, he would get lost in the cacophony of pundit voices on the many American media. Besides, his children and wife still lived in the kingdom and they were al-Qahtani's Media Center leverage to pressure Khashoggi to turn down the volume as and when necessary.

And so when Khashoggi was approached by Karen Attiah of the *Washington Post* to write a piece for its new online section called 'Global Opinions' accepting the commission was no longer against the palace's direct orders. Someone had given Attiah Khashoggi's WhatsApp and she made the first approach.

As could be expected by anyone who knew him, Khashoggi pushed the envelope. He published this first piece for the *Washington Post* on 18 September – 'Saudi Arabia Wasn't always This Repressive. Now It Is Unbearable'. He wrote plaintively, 'I have left my home, my family and my job, and I am raising my voice. To do otherwise would betray those who languish in prison. I can speak when so many cannot. I want you to know that Saudi Arabia has not always been as it is now. We Saudis deserve better.' In one of the first emails he wrote to Karen Attiah, he said he never imagined his Saudi Arabia would be filled 'with intimidation, lies, and hate' like el-Sisi's Egypt.

Attiah was thrilled. She told her colleagues she had no idea Khashoggi was based in the US and it would be his 'coming out' declaration. Not that it had been an easy piece to edit. She realised 'that he was thinking in Arabic, and writing what he could in English, and I would try to fill in the spaces of what he meant. It took a bit of work'.

The online traffic generated by Khashoggi's first blog 'spiked' in its simultaneous Arab translation and superseded the *Post*'s expectations. Even so, the impact was modest. Unlike MBS's surprise announcement on 27 September that he had lifted the 1957 driving ban for women in Saudi Arabia – the last country in the world to have one – the US and international media paid little attention. MBS, however, was globally lauded for modernising Saudi Arabia and relaxing its strict religious rules along the lines that had previously landed Khashoggi in trouble.

Even after Khashoggi's public 'coming out', palace officials continued to make contact with Khashoggi to discuss job opportunities in Saudi Arabia. One offer even saw Khashoggi running one of Saudi Arabia's most important media networks upon his return. They told him that, despite everything, MBS's trust in him remained unshakeable and that palace doors remained open to him. Al-Qahtani himself called in September to persuade Khashoggi to return and in a follow-up call in October he continued to pass on friendly messages from MBS. It was also on 26 October 2017 that Khashoggi also had his last text exchange with the Saudi US ambassador, MBS's brother KBS.

But despite the amiable tone, the palace knew they had lost the battle and that Khashoggi was continuing with his application for political asylum. In his October call, al-Qahtani urged Khashoggi to keep 'writing and boasting' about Saudi Arabia. It was a shot across the bow, given Khashoggi's online piece for the *Washington Post* in which he accused Saudi Arabia of oppression and publicly announced his life as a political exile. In December, Khashoggi was granted political asylum in the US – a speedy result as it usually takes around six months.

Back in Saudi Arabia, Khashoggi's family bore the brunt of his departure as al-Qahtani tightened the thumbscrews. The abuse levelled at his third wife, Dr Alaa Nasief – who practised as a holistic business and life-coach and was trained in Myers Briggs testing, hypnotherapy, and other mediation techniques, and ran a company in Jeddah – caused her to divorce Khashoggi after seven years of marriage. His sons Salah (b1983) and Abdullah (b1985, the same year as MBS) from his first marriage were given travel bans and could not leave the kingdom for their work. In their calls to him, they urged him to settle his differences with MBS to stop their harassment. Salah, a Jeddah investment banker, cut off contact for months as a result of his father's continued association with the *Washington Post*.

Even so, Khashoggi still thought he could fix things with the crown prince. Secretly bypassing palace officials, he made a direct appeal to MBS and once again offered his allegiance and assistance to the crown. Both MBS and he, after all, shared a reformer's mindset. A leading businessman told *Washington Post* writers anonymously that Khashoggi asked him in the Autumn of 2017 to give the crown prince a personal message, that MBS needed an honest advisor like him. In her book, Cengiz said he connected this offer to Vision 2030, MBS's masterplan for Saudi Arabia.

What Khashoggi still couldn't imagine was that as far as MBS was concerned the self-exiled courtier was evidently toxic rather than honest. His pension continued to be paid and his visit to the Saudi US embassy had ended with an amiable chat with MBS's brother KBS. But that was a front to throw Khashoggi off the scent. The palace's ideological framework had radically changed from what it was like under King Abdullah.

MBS told the businessman in confidence that an advisorship would never happen given Khashoggi's ties with Qatar and the Muslim Brotherhood. A CIA intercept around this time also caught MBS telling his close associate Turki Aldakhil – the CEO of al-Arabiya network and later his ambassador to his friend MBZ, the ruler of the emirates – that he wanted to go after Khashoggi 'with a bullet'. As far as MBS was concerned, there was little daylight between Khashoggi and a Shiite terrorist. (The leak of this explosive intercept happened in February 2019, but the CIA must have had it in its possession in 2018. So the question was as much why the US leak was handed to the media at that point in time as whether the intercept established MBS's premeditation regarding the aim of his Tiger Team. In other words, there was a US goal being achieved behind the scenes that was separate from establishing the truth about the events of 2 October).

On 6 November 2017, MBS began the Ritz Carlton purge of what was left of the Abdullah clan in positions of power. In the same month, MBS opened the international bidding process to build two nuclear reactors (though MBS said he was planning a total of sixteen). The former ensnared one of Khashoggi's richest royal patrons – the colourful, talkative entrepreneur, vegetarian, fitness-fanatic and lover of stylish sunglasses Prince Alwaleed bin Talal. Alwaleed was one of King Salman's half-nephews through founder-king ibn Saud's sixteenth wife Munaiyir. He owned at various times part of Murdoch's News Corporation, Disneyland, Lyft, Citibank and also luxury hotels such as the Mövenpick chain at which Khashoggi's assassins would stay in Istanbul. In a Bloomberg interview after his release on 28 February 2018 Alwaleed joked uneasily that he had used his time as market research for the Four Seasons hotel chain in which he also owned a substantial share. Until the payment MBS extracted from him during his Ritz Carlton stay, Prince Alwaleed was one of the world's richest men.

Khashoggi accepted Karen Attiah's proposal to write more online pieces for the *Post* after the success of his first piece among Arab readers, and did so in a crescendo of five quick blasts – almost a quarter of the number of pieces he would write for her Global Opinions section: 'Saudi Arabia's Crown Prince Wants to Crush Extremists. But He's Punishing the Wrong People', 31 October, 'Saudi Arabia's Crown Prince Is Acting Like Putin', 6 November, 'Saudi Arabia Is Creating a Total Mess in Lebanon', 13 November, 'Saudi Arabia Has Devastated Yemen – But a Lesson from 1965 Can Help Fix the Mess', 22 November, 'Saudi Arabia Is Paying the Price for Betraying the Arab Spring', 5 December.

Like these five think pieces, his *Post* blogs were written in an even-handed tone when critical of the kingdom's new policies, and indeed were occasionally laudatory. Despite everything, Khashoggi continued to think of himself as an 'independent writer' and did not see himself as a writer for the 'opposition'. Deep in his heart, he saw himself as a monarchist who fought for the same corner of modernisers as MBS within the palace. They differed on the method and he was appalled by the Ritz Carlton coup that had revealed the real MBS. On 13 November 2017, Khashoggi told the BBC World's Hard Talk that he was 'worried for my country, my children and grandchildren – one-man rule is always bad, in any country'.

Khashoggi had to file his *Post* copy in English, though Attiah told the *New York Times* that his 'English wasn't great'. When he 'got settled in a little bit more, he found assistants or translators who helped him', she said. The *Washington Post* would then translate his English copy back into Arabic and publish both alongside online.

Khashoggi's five pieces published were such a success in Arabic that the *Post* made him an online commentator in December. He wasn't a staff member, but they did give him a masthead on its Global Opinions website. It was a great moment for him, and he was very proud of his new title.

'When is the press release? When is the press release?', he kept pushing his *Washington Post* editor Attiah for the announcement.

Khashoggi was equally excited to visit the *Post* news room with Attiah.

'His eyes lit up' Attiah recalled, 'I wish we could build this in the Middle East' he said.

Jamal Khashoggi on his first visit to the Washington Post news room.

In fact, the *Washington Post* Global Opinions could be the 2.0 version of al-Arab, his TV station in Bahrein that closed down on its first day. Already in September, he mooted to Attiah that the *Post* would create an Arabic Section of

Global Opinions, a Middle Eastern *International Herald Tribune* – the onetime Europe-only paper which the *Washington Post* used to co-own with the *New York Times*.

Khashoggi bombarded her with WhatsApps and emails, using many thumbs-up emojis. In his last messages to her he repeated his dream of creating a broader platform [of] honest news and commentary in Arabic with the *Post*. 'He was pushy – not in a bad way, but very', Attiah said. He asked 'When are we meeting about this?'

Personally, however, it was a tough time. Khashoggi was lonely and suffered from deep mood swings during this time as a result of severing his ties with the palace and his family. He WhatsApped his *Post* editor Attiah, 'I'm really sad and depressed. They put travel bans on my family. They're trying to get to me. It's making me sad.'

His condo in Lillian Court was pleasant enough. It was one of a cluster of three low-slung apartment buildings around a New England style shared club house with a pool and recently renovated gym. When Khashoggi had bought it, Tysons Corner was still a sleepy place. But since then it had become a commuter satellite-town with its own metro stop on Washington DC's Silver Line and the corporate base for Freddie Mac, Hilton, Booz Allen and *USA Today*. But it didn't compare to the comfortable family life he had had in Jeddah.

Nor was he making any money in case his Saudi pension was stopped. The *Washington Post* paid him $500 per blog. Yet it didn't pay him for help with his English or with research. He wrote one or two pieces a month and was to receive a total of $11,000 for 22 articles over a year, if one included the posthumous piece his translator sent to Attiah on 3 October 2018. Setting to one side the prestige of having an online masthead and his love of punditry, there was no more than pocket money in the association with the *Post*. On the other hand, invitations from American universities to give guest lectures on the Middle East started to arrive and no doubt the association with the *Post* helped spread the word of his deep expertise.

With time on his hands until he found something new, Khashoggi embraced Twitter with a vengeance. He had opened his account in January 2016, ending the year with the last tweet in November that year on Trump before the ban. Writing in Arabic, Khashoggi now reached 1.72 million followers across the Arabic-speaking world after the ban ended in August 2017. In a year and a few months he would tweet over 54,100 times and followed 753 people, including KBS and MBS's top media aide Saud al-Qahtani (though not MBS himself).

He also threw himself with enthusiasm into meeting new people in DC. Khashoggi gave guest lectures and met people on DC's foreign-policy circuit and even met regularly with Saudis who unreservedly towed MBS's line, debating issues with them without acrimony.

In his quest for a new circle of friends, Khashoggi was anything but high-handed. Sigurd Neubauer, a researcher, got to know him during this period and met the Tysons Corner Pain Quotidien. 'Everybody who was interested in Saudi Arabia or in the region, he would make himself available to', Neubauer said. Another new friend was Turkish PhD student Selim Sazak of Brown University whom he met half a dozen times in DC. Sazak told the *Independent* news site he thought Khashoggi was 'sharp, quick-witted' and a 'contrarian' who was not 'guided by any particular ideology'.

With his US residency secure in December, Khashoggi could finally look forward with his life. He sought funding for a variety of projects while travelling to dozens of conferences. Unbeknownst to his close friends and family, Khashoggi also reconnected in early 2018 with Hanan Atr a female acquaintance from the past, a strikingly attractive fifty-year-old Egyptian living in the UAE. They had first met at the 2008 Arab Media Forum held in Dubai, UAE, and she regularly visited DC on business. In early 2018 they first met again with friends. Alone in Tysons Corner, Khashoggi eagerly developed their relationship in a romantic direction. He enjoyed spending time together with her and buying her beautifully wrapped gifts and after a few weeks he presented her with a diamond engagement ring much to her surprise and delight.

7
Exodus

༈

As Khashoggi was finally putting his life in exile back in order in Tysons Corner, the palace stopped contacting him with job offers. Though he remained a person of interest to al-Qahtani's Center, he was in a place where he could do relatively little harm as MBS ploughed on with his ambitious agenda for Saudi Arabia. Having purged key positions in the kingdom of opponents, he focused once again on his nuclear aspirations and negotiating with the Trump adminstration to give IP3's Westinghouse 'much praised' AP1000 design the $10bn tender for its first two reactors.

The UAE, ruled by his friend MBZ, had signed the US's gold standard on '123' agreements controlling weapons and civilian grade uranium in 2009, the year after King Abdullah, and its first reactor would open in 2019. MBS, however, had no intention of signing an 123 agreement which he considered close to insulting to the kingdom. The reason given publically was the presence of natural uranium deposits in Saudi Arabia. Al-Falih told Reuters that if Trump didn't agree with MBS's demands he wouldn't have a 'seat at the table'. Apart from staunch opposition in Congress, the US problem was compounded by the fact that MBZ's UAE would be released from its 123 obligations if Saudi received US nuclear technology without them. Trump needed to throw a bone to MBS to keep Westinghouse on track.

After successfully convincing Donald Trump in 2017 that the Muslim Brotherhood was a terrorist organisation like al-Qaeda rather than a pan-Arabic political movement, in 2018 MBS wanted Trump to undo Obama's Nuclear Deal. He and King Salman had let it pass at the time in exchange for US support in Yemen, but they still deeply resented the preferential green-light it gave Iran's enrichment of uranium to a non-weapons grade. Unravelling the deal would revive sanctions on Iran and keep its economy in the doldrums and clip its regional power.

In a *Washington Post* blog of 3 January, Khashoggi again addressed what he thought of the palace's handling of the 2015 negotiations, but in a more forth-right manner. In a blunt throw-away line he said that the palace had not performed its duty 'to short-circuit the Iran nuclear deal'.

Khashoggi wrote too soon. Four months later, on 8 May 2018, Donald Trump landed MBS a mammoth home victory when he officially nullified the treaty. In doing so the White House's objective was not political (block enrichment of uranium by Iran, stop nuclear proliferation, and, hence, ease Saudi Arabia's concerns about an Iranian nuclear bomb and Iran's growing power in the region). Instead it was transactional. The White House was paving the way for completing its $350bn-plus deal with Saudi Arabia. Trump and Kushner were pushing IP3's 'Iron Bridge' scheme with Saudi Arabia while Russia, China and France were also circling MBS's tender to build two reactors. Removing the Iran roadblock was the open sesame that MBS demanded. Playing the long game, MBS had deftly swatted three flies with Saudi's very large cheque book. It was also very impressive.

The next stop for MBS was to convince public opinion in the West that he was a safe pair of hands and that he was turning Saudi Arabia into a forward-looking twenty-first-century country as a trustworthy, progressive and modern leader. This was the objective of his world tour – unprecedented for a Saudi ruler – that started in the US with visits to Donald Trump and Oprah and anyone well-known in between, including Queen Elizabeth II in Buckingham Palace. Often gone were the traditional exotic flowing robes in favour of a suit – jeans when visiting Mark Zuckerberg at Facebook – and a vast PR machine swung into action to craft his international image as a reliable Westerner in charge of an otherwise backward country. This reality make-over would be a *sine qua non* for success. Without it Trump would lose against the battle-hardened opposition in Congress to selling nuclear technology to Saudi Arabia.

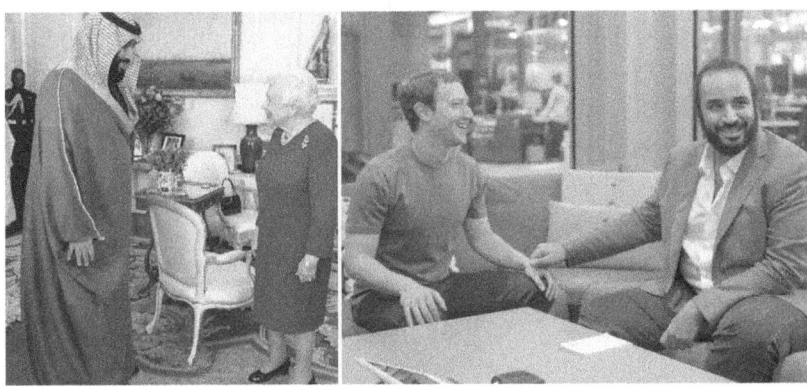

Stops on MBS's world tour, from Queen Elizabeth II to Mark Zuckerberg.

As this took place on the world stage, Hatice Cengiz and Jamal Khashoggi met for the first time in Turkey. The date was 6 May 2018, two days before Trump officially cancelled the Iran deal after signalling his intentions for a couple of months.

Khashoggi was a speaker at the five-star Istanbul Marriott on new security arrangements in the MENA (Middle East and North Africa) region at the al-Sharq Forum, a think tank set up by Waddah Khanfar, the energetic former director general of Qatar's al-Jazeera. In Turan Kışlakçı's recollection, he himself first introduced thirty-six-year-old Hatice Cengiz to Khashoggi. But Cengiz told the *Financial Times* in August 2019 that she walked up to Khashoggi 'during a coffee break and introduced myself; I said to him that I wanted to interview him for a political website'. She flatteringly told the fifty-nine-year-old Khashoggi she had been following him closely on Twitter as a PhD-student for his insights and wanted to interview him. In her 2019 memoir, Cengiz added that she was chaperoned by a friend.

Khashoggi did not immediately agree to the interview but after his lecture she waited outside the lecture hall where he joined her for half an hour to do the interview with her in Arabic.

Despite the fact that only 0.5 per cent of the population speak Arabic in Turkey, quite exceptionally, Cengiz spoke the language fluently. She came from Bursa – the automotive and silk capital of Turkey, two hours to the south of Istanbul – from a conservative family which settled originally from Armenia. She was the second child and had an older and a younger brother and attended a local religious secondary school called *imam hatip* just when Erdoğan came to power in 2003 as leader of the AKP. At the time, this type of school was rated poorly except by religious families.

These schools had a singular position in Turkish culture. In most of the Muslim world, children are educated in religious schools called *madrasas*. But Turkey's founder Kemal Atatürk had closed all of them in his country and replaced them with secular state-run schools. It triggered a constant battle in Turkey to reintroduce religious schooling and the *imam hatip* – Turkey's version of a *madrasa* – educated an ever-fluctuating percentage of school children, enrolling both genders from 1976. The school taught Arabic to read the Koran and its commentaries in the original language and men, but not women, could go on to become imams.

Under Erdoğan they were once again in the ascendant. From a few per cent of pupils in 2002, they educated over ten per cent in 2017. From 2003, Erdoğan had quadrupled the budget of the *diyanet* ('directorate of religious affairs') in order to promote the Hanafi denomination of Sunni Islam. The *diyanet* was the employer of Turkey's official state preachers of this denomination and a third were women, of whom a sizeable number ranked higher than imams. Even so, religion remained segregated and under Erdoğan the public presence of women was once again disappearing, literally, behind a veil.

After attending *imam hatip*, Hatice went on to study for three years at Sunni-Islam's most prestigious university in the Middle East, the al-Azhar University in Cairo, Egypt, where the four Sunni denominations are taught. She spent a lot of her spare time reading widely. Her heroine was Gertrude Bell, whose travels through and writings on the Middle East she discovered in Cairo. Later, in 2015, she saw Queen of the Desert, the Werner Herzog bio picture of Bell, with Nicole Kidman opposite James Franco in the role of the nine-year older Henry Cadogan, whom Bell had wanted to marry. While panned by the critics, Hatice loved the movie. She felt a great affinity with the pan-Arab motivation that drove Bell, and her courage. And maybe, yes, Gertrude Bell was a 'serious spy', Hatice told Kemalist magazine *Sözcü* ('spokesperson') in February 2019 when they interviewed her on the publication of her memoir *Cemal Kaşıkçı* (Jamal Khashoggi).

In her memoir she added that she lost interest in her Cairo studies and returned to Turkey in 2006 to various jobs as a tourism guide. This may appear an odd choice, but it is considered an important office by the Turkish government in shaping its official image among foreign visitors.

Having won a place at Istanbul University's Theology Department in 2010, she followed her religious studies up with a Masters at Sabahattin Zaim University and lived in Oman from 2016-2017 for research into its unique 'inter-sectarian' model – Oman's half-Sunni half-Shia population co-exists peacefully unlike anywhere else in the Middle East. At the time of meeting Khashoggi, the thirty-six-year old was doing her PhD in history at the Fatih Sultan Mehmet University.

Istanbul University ranked fourth in Turkey, and has an extraordinarily demanding entrance exam, but the latter two institutions dangled at the bottom of the Turkish university league table, well past the 100 mark. Why did she pursue her graduate degrees at these unprepossessing universities with their close links to the AKP government? That was not her only professional connection to the regime. Cengiz wrote her first published essay for the official magazine of Turkey's Foreign Policy Institute, a prestigious think tank headed by a man dubbed at its 40th anniversary 'our diplomacy guru' by Mevlüt Çavuşoğlu, Erdoğan's foreign minister. She dreamt of being an academic and an investigative journalist she said ambitiously.

These were not the only peculiar aspects of her background. Her father was a baker and her two brothers worked in the bakery, she wrote in her memoir. But when two more children were born (her two sisters) her father had to work harder. Yet the fifteen-year length of her university education and, indeed, studying for a first degree in Egypt are exceptional among ordinary Turkish families, not least a baker's one. Cengiz also wrote that she considered studying law at a US university (even though a JD is a graduate degree in the US) a far greater expense than Cairo's al-Shazar's university – whose tuition and living costs were $10,000 per year, already an astronomic figure in Turkey. She couldn't pursue this US dream because of 9/11, she wrote. Studying in Cairo was first put forward by the mother of a school friend at her religious *imam hatip*. As we will see later, in an interview with the *New York Times*, she gave a different explanation of how her studies had been financed.

There wasn't much time for the interview during the al-Sharq conference and Khashoggi and Cengiz had but a short meeting at the Marriott. She emailed him later in the US that she regretted she hadn't been able to get the interview published, as his public profile as an Arab journalist was modest in Turkey. But she emailed the piece to him and he 'liked it very much' and wrote 'that it was valuable that she cared'.

'Hatice, it doesn't matter. I appreciate your efforts, I appreciate it. When I next come to Turkey we can talk longer.' Khashoggi had playfully added, 'Our meeting is a start'.

Cengiz eagerly responded, asking whether he might be able to expand the interview and 'to talk in more detail'.

By return, he suggested that they should meet again when he was back in Istanbul. From this second meeting, she continued conducting formal interviews with him. Alongside their relationship as friends blossomed quickly.

In his personal life, Khashoggi told her, he 'felt great solitude' and longing for Saudi Arabia. He was 'so isolated' from everything in the US and didn't know what was happening to his friends in the Saudi government. Cengiz sensed a 'great political and emotional loneliness'. He also confessed to her he didn't want to tell his family in Saudi Arabia how depressed he was.

A recent picture of Jamal Khashoggi, Yasin Aktay, Prince Alaweed bin Talal, and President Recep Erdoğan.

'Night after night I am in the US, on my own, and I watch the developments in my country. Being single causes me real pain and I cry. But I don't want to tell this to my children', he said to her.

Hatice Cengiz (far left), Jamal Khashoggi and Turan Kışlakçı' (far right) at a a Turkish-Arab Journalists' Association Friday meeting, Summer 2018.

Candidly he said that, after his last marriage had broken up for political reasons due to his self-exile, he had decided he 'wanted to get married again'.

'Suddenly, I saw a completely different human being, and then a special, direct dialogue began', Cengiz recalled. They started to include the future in the things they discussed. Whenever Khashoggi was feeling down, Cengiz would cheer him up and remind him of the future.

Their wide-ranging conversations intensified, Cengiz said. Cengiz was connected to senior policy circles in Turkey, and so was Jamal. He had longstanding friendships with leading people in the Turkish media but also knew senior politicians close to President Erdoğan, and had many Turkish friends apart from Turan. Indeed, he also knew Erdoğan with whom she said he had 'a friendship', and whom he met at least once during their months of growing closer together.

Jamal Khashoggi did indeed plan to get married again. As in his professional life, he was exploring two choices. And so, on 2 June he married his Egyptian friend, Hanan Atr. It was a religious ceremony conducted under Sharia law by Anwar Hajjaj, an imam and professor at the American Open University in Virginia, USA as well as witnesses Khaled Saffouri and Ragheed Aqla. A long-term friend of Khashoggi's also attended the ceremony and took pictures of the smiling couple dressed in white and blue.

Jamal Khashoggi and Hanan Atr married at his home in Tysons Corner, Virginia, in June 2018.

Khashoggi next visited Istanbul in July where he and Cengiz met again at a musical event held at Turan Kışlakçı's Turkish-Arab Journalists' Association. They now called each other regularly.

He told her about his lonely time in his apartment in Washington, DC, where he was cut off from his family and friends and often cried. Though he did not tell her about his marriage to Hanan Atr, he did tell Cengiz that he was a a much happier man after meeting her.

In August Khashoggi was back in Istanbul, and they chatted every Friday at Turan's Association and their affectionate relationship blossomed in earnest. She found him 'wise', 'mature' and a 'beautiful person'. He was gregarious, energetic and in love with life, and they shared a deep intellectual interest in the politics, religion, history and culture of the Middle East. He enjoyed how she thought about the

Sunni-Shia divide and how to bridge its violent antagonism.

'No kebabs' for him, observed Cengiz in turn. Istanbul as the former heart of the Ottoman empire had a long and refined gastronomic tradition, and Khashoggi enjoyed eating fish and always 'tasted the best things in restaurants'. 'He was upset if he didn't eat well.'

Hatice Cengiz and Jamal Khashoggi in Istanbul, Summer 2018.

After returning to the US in August, Khashoggi texted with exhilaration, 'I came home safe and sound. I want us to be together as one'. He was in love and wrote to her, she said, that 'no one has loved me like you do.'

In September Khashoggi had again made up his mind. He met his new Egyptian wife for the last time. Their passion to get married legally, they both agreed, had dissipated despite the religious ceremony in June.

He then took Turkish Airline flight TK8 at 11:30pm on Friday 9 September and arrived in Istanbul at 5pm a day later on Saturday 10 September. His son Abdullah also arrived in Istanbul on the same day and together they met with Hatice at Turan's Association where Khashoggi proposed officially to Hatice.

He now told her that he had four children from his first wife, who lived in Dubai. He said he had been divorced three times and again told her that his most recent marriage had ended less than a year ago for political reasons. Evidently, Abdullah had no idea of his father's marriage to Atr and did not contradict the facts as Khashoggi laid them out before Cengiz.

'It didn't matter to me', Cengiz said about the multiple marriages. They went to buy their engagement rings that day, and Abdullah announced to his three siblings in Saudi that their father had a new fiancée and was finding a new home in Turkey.

Cengiz had meanwhile told her conservative Turkish family of her impending marriage plans. She had also gone to the nearby marriage office of the Fatih district (captured on CC-TV) to find out what marriage formalities applied to Khashoggi as a Saudi citizen. She was told about the two forms he needed and that they could only be certified in Turkey at a diplomatic mission or in Saudi Arabia itself.

After Jamal's proposal to Hatice in the presence of his son, his friend Turan went to Hatice's father to ask for her hand on his behalf. 'I want you to go and talk to him and find out what their requests are', Khashoggi – who didn't speak Turkish – had asked him.

Hatice's father was not immediately enthusiastic. He had reservations about the twenty-four-year age difference and about Jamal's poor health. He came round and would give his blessing, however, as long as they observed all the correct civil-marriage formalities under Turkish law, and did not merely follow the rites of an Islamic religious marriage (as Hanan Atr had on 2 June). He was wary of Saudi men as they were used to having several wives.

Later, standing in front of the consulate on his vigil, Turan would express his irritation about this. But for Hatice's father's insistence, Khashoggi would still be alive. But her father's caution was prescient in view of the fact that Khashoggi had never mentioned to his Turkish circle of friends his fourth marriage in June. Cengiz, too, appeared prescient in having urged Khashoggi to use his high-powered Turkish contacts instead of the Saudi consulate to get their marriage paperwork.

The formalities Hatice's father had in mind also included the traditional Muslim *mehr* (dowry, *mehir* or *başlik parasi* in Turkish) for the bride – an apartment in her name, or at any rate one they would co-own as well as a certain sum of money in view of her 'economical situation'. It was meant 'to safeguard his daughter' he told Turan. But when all his conditions were accepted by Turan, he gave his consent to the marriage after all and agreed to meet his future son-in-law.

Hatice's father then spoke to her and asked her to think carefully about the age difference. Khashoggi left a voicemail for his fiancée with his thoughts on the matter, 'You are intelligent and strong, and you have a quality that will make you one of the best writers in Turkey among the writers who know the Arab world. I love you because you are Hatice, but I am attracted to you as a true intellectual and journalist. I love you very much. I'll see you very soon. *Bye bye.*'

Within twenty days of proposing, Khashoggi had 'met my parents and bought an apartment for us. He was practical', Cengiz told the *Financial Times* approvingly in July 2019.

They first looked for the place where they would live and would, then, get married. Still there was not much time left in September to get the marriage ceremony organised as well, as Khashoggi had at least three speaking commitments.

Khashoggi had been far more excited about the nuptials than she was and asked what they should wear on their wedding day. But she had responded, 'let's take care of practical matters first.' Cengiz preferred simple convenience over elaborate and costly celebrations, particularly when there was so much suffering in the world, she said – it was perhaps a difference from Saudi custom, and one of the things Khashoggi liked about her, she later told *Sabah*.

Khashoggi 'loved people, the crowds, the noise' and wanted to live in Fatih ('the conqueror'), the historic district of Istanbul and heart of the former Ottoman-Byzantine-Eastern Roman empire. But Cengiz was less keen on life in cramped, winding streets with crumbling ancient architecture.

Two weeks later, on 25 September, Khashoggi exchanged on their apartment in 'Castle 2' Topkapi Europe Residences (avrupakonutlarikale2.com) in the Zeytinburnu ('cape olive') district, just outside the ancient Roman walls of Constantinople built by emperor Theodosius. Located in this bustling but dishevelled working-class district, the new residences were nonetheless an oasis of calm.

Avrupa Konutlarikale Kale-2 (Europe Residences) built in 2016, the main gate on the right.

In her own book, Cengiz made it seem a modest home. In fact, it looked very much like an updated and opulent version of Khashoggi's Lillian Court condo in Tysons Corner. It was an elegant luxury regeneration development completed in 2016 with large, floor-to-ceiling brown-metal windows, pink-cream marble internal corridors, wide balconies, landscaped gardens, CC-TV, gated security, tennis courts, indoor pools, a fitness centre, a sauna and even its own mosque with minaret in its landscaped gardens with pergolas providing shade from the punishing summer sun. As often in Istanbul, the development's historical references rioted – it was built on almost the exact location where Mehmet Fatih had breached the St Romanus gate with a giant cannon called 'Basilic'. This state-of-the-art piece weapon helped terminate what was left of ancient Rome in Asia and the gate became known as cannon gate, or 'Topkapi'. At the apartment complex the two disparate terms were amicably joined to create 'Topkapi European Residences' for marketing purposes.

No 16, an 1800-square-foot second-floor apartment with three bedrooms, ensuite bathroom, balconies, and a large sitting room and galley kitchen was utterly modern yet within easy reach of all government buildings, and it had distant views of the ancient sights such as the Hagia Sophia, mosques, and, well in the distance, Topkapi Palace, the famous seraglio of the sultans and the former heart of the Ottoman empire. Mehmet Fatih had chosen the place when he put up his encampment on a bluff, yet the nineteenth-century Ottomans renamed it Topkapi Palace as an honorific, regardless of the fact that the bluff overlooked the Bosphorus and was far removed from 'Topkapi' itself.

More practically, perhaps, the building was a 100 yards from the metro and near the new seventh Istanbul campus of Cengiz's latest alma mater, Fatih Sultan Mehmet University, as well as 15 minutes from CNN Turk, Fox TV and media offices such as those of *Yeni Şafak* – where Khashoggi's friend Yasin Aktay was a leading columnist.

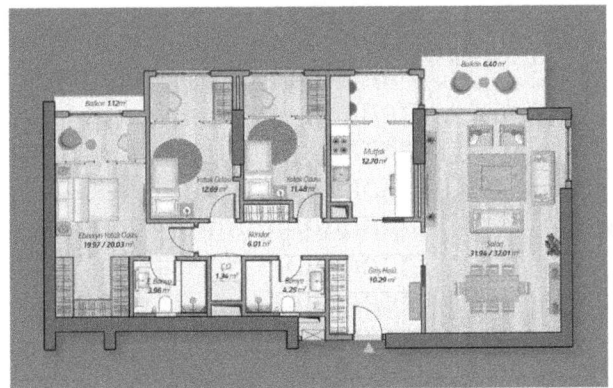

Apartment 16 on the second floor of Castle 2 Topkapi Europa Residences Block D

'Open the blinds', Khashoggi had excitedly said to Cengiz. From the windows, you could see the Fatih Mosque, another Sultan Mehmet landmark.

'I'll go and pray there when we are married and have tea in your father's bakery.' He was enamoured with the prospect of breakfasts in Fatih, whose many minarets reminded him of the buildings of his youth in the holy city of Medina. He spoke often nostalgically about missing Eid, the end of Ramadan, in his home town.

Although their new apartment was built to an exceptional standard, its price was relatively modest for Washington, DC, standards at just over $250,000, particularly after the pounding the Turkish lira had taken at the hands of President Donald Trump who disliked Erdoğan and whose administration crossed Turkey. No ordinary Istanbuli would ever be able to afford living there.

It is not clear how well-off Khashoggi was. But, in addition to his palace salaries over the years, he had earned incidental income along the way. On 2 December 2009, for example, a businessman who called Khashoggi 'Uncle J' transferred $100,000 into his account for an interview by Khashoggi of Malaysian President Najib Razak, published on 14 December in *al-Watan*. The interview was designed to help create an elaborate smokescreen of gold-plated Saudi wealth around Razak's slush fund and piggy bank of well over $10bn. Called Malaysia's sovereign-wealth fund '1MDB', it paid for Razak's wife's lavish purchases of jewellery, houses and handbags and massive electoral bribes, and evidently also media interviews to maintain an aura of respectability. One of the eleven princes detained at the Ritz Carlton for corruption was Prince Turki, son of King Abdullah. His firm PetroSaudi was enmeshed in the 1MDB fraud.

Khashoggi's al-Watan interview with Malaysian President Najib Razak, part of the 1MDB slush fund scandal for which Khashoggi, al-Watan's editor, was paid $100,000 in 2009.

Khashoggi himself may not have been aware that he was part of the 1MDB fraud (though he did take the money to set up the interview without appearing to ask whence the exorbitant fee in exchange for an interview with the most senior statesman in Malaysia). But on 9 May 2018, the scandal shattered Malaysia's ruling party's uninterrupted rule since independence in 1957 and he must have read about it then. It was to ensnare Goldman Sachs with a $3.9bn settlement to avoid criminal investigation, and caused a 30 per cent drop in its share price.

Subject: Statement of Support for KSA by PM Malaysia
From: nawafobaid@aol.com <nawafobaid@aol.com>
Date: 20/11/2009 12:15
To: jamal@khashoggi.com; Tarek.Obaid@Petrosaudi.com

Uncle J :-

Please, publish this somewhere important in the paper!

Many thanks,

Nawaf

Jamal Khashoggi
Alwatan
Editor in Chief
+966 (2) 652-2020 Work
966 7 227 3333 Work
+966 (50) 531 6922 Mobile
+966 (2) 653 1646 Home
jamal@khashoggi.com
Editor@alwatan.com.sa
khashoggi@mobily.blackberry....

Email to Jamal Khashoggi to place the interview 'somewhere important in the paper.'

In between waiting for the deeds to the apartment to arrive and Khashoggi's hectic cosmopolitan schedule, Cengiz had started to order furniture to make the apartment habitable for the moment when they would live together as husband and wife.

By Friday 28 September, two days after the deeds came through and the day Khashoggi would leave for London, he decided to make things official. At 9.53am Khashoggi and Cengiz stepped into the Fatih Marriage Office together and the marriage official explained to Khashoggi the documents he needed to produce to

The office was no more than 10 minutes or so from the apartment. Khashoggi, suffering from his cold, chewing gum, seemed a little distracted. He was wearing a yellow jumper and red baseball cap and carried a brown coat with him. Cengiz wore her usual scarf and a long coat with bold checks and her satchel hung around her shoulders. They sat down at a desk with an official and Cengiz got up again to busy herself with a number of forms from a stand. She gave some to Khashoggi and kept some herself, which they all discussed. It was all captured on later leaked official CC-TV, and discussed in-depth on Turkish TV. get married in Turkey.

Subject: My brother
From: "Tarek Obaid" <Tarek.Obaid@Petrosaudi.com>
Date: 02/12/2009 11:23
To: Abdulazzziz Issa

Azzzzzzzzzziz,

I need to transfer to my friend $100,000 USD pls:-

SABB
SA7845000000028049930001
Account No 028-049-930-001
Jamal Khashoggi

Transfer from Prince Turki's PetroSaudi: $100,000 into Jamal Khashoggi's account.

An hour and a half after the Fatih Marriage Office consultation, Khashoggi and Cengiz would also make the 30 minute journey to the consulate with the papers for the unannounced visit. They had deliberated whether to go as Khashoggi told Cengiz he was worried 'something might happen'. In the end, he said 'Let's go'.

CC-TV still inside the Fatih Marriage Office at 10am on Friday 28 September.

As we know for the second consular visit after his early morning return from London on Tuesday, Khashoggi, who had been so reluctant to return to Saudi soil no longer felt worried. In the taxi drive to the Saudi consulate their mood was high-spirited and they talked about light-hearted matters. Khashoggi wanted a US-style two-door fridge but Cengiz had already ordered a standard one. She called the company from the car to change the model without success. Khashoggi had joked about it and they both laughed. They were also going to buy a washing machine and stove that afternoon so that she could move in after the marriage in a few days. So far their apartment was still empty, except for a double bed, a reclining La-z-Boy TV for Khashoggi with its price tag still attached, crockery, his clothes and his rolling suitcase. (She would only revisit the apartment accompanied by Turkish officials and a film crew making a documentary after the court cases in absentia against the perpetrators had reached a verdict. The apartment was still covered in black dust used by forensic teams to uncover finger prints.)

CC-TV still outside the Saudi consulate, around 11am on 28 September.

To Hatice and Jamal, their marriage was only a few rubber stamps away. Papers in hand, they might go from the consulate back to the Fatih Marriage Office to apply for the marriage license.

Jamal Khashoggi in the La-z-Boy he had just bought, price tag still visible.

In the evening, they would tell friends and family and pick the date for the civil wedding ceremony before Khashoggi had to leave again for the US on 10 October.

Cengiz planned to wear white – like Hanan Atr, Khashoggi's fourth wife in June. Khashoggi had asked her the week before, 'do you want children?' As he already had two sons and two daughters and two grandchildren, she wasn't sure what he wanted himself, and she had simply replied, 'if Allah doesn't want me to, I don't need to have children'.

8
'Certain circles'

From May, when Cengiz approached Khashoggi in Istanbul and became close to him, Saudi Arabia suddenly resumed its campaign against Khashoggi. The regular friendly calls from the palace with job offers started up again. At the same time, the social-media trolling of Khashoggi resumed as well. Ostensibly these were Saudi citizens disagreeing with him, but they were really officials ('flies') working under cover for al-Qahtani's Media Center. 'During May and July 2018 many activists noticed that there was an organised attempt to attack them online. Jamal Khashoggi was heavily affected by this attack', recalled Omar Abdulaziz, a Saudi social media expert of MBS's age and in exile in Canada because of his criticism of the palace.

The twenty-seven-year-old Abdulaziz got in touch with Khashoggi. 'I did a small study that was aimed at stopping them. I pitched the idea to Mr Khashoggi and he welcomed the idea. With other people like Tariq al-Mutairi [a young Kuwaiti online activist 'socially conservative and politically liberal'], we decided that we should set up a team to face this attack.' Safe in the US the new attacks irked him. So Khashoggi decided to support us. He decided to fund the project with five thousand dollars from his own pocket.' The project had code-name *Geish al-Nahla* ('bee army'), offering cyber protection to Saudi activists needing a safe platform from Lord of the Flies al-Qahtani.

Abdulaziz also said that he and Khashoggi had plans to post documents detailing human rights abuses carried out by Saudi Arabia and to spread the information via the tweets of young Saudi dissidents (reported by CNN). Khashoggi had pledged $30,000 towards the plan, which included sending untraceable foreign Sim cards to activists inside the country. (The former initiative but not the latter would be included in the October 2019 documentary by Anas Essam and Omer Ibrahim with which Abdulaziz cooperated.)

One of his own secret initiatives was to seek financial backing for a new organisation, Democracy for the Arab World Now (DAWN), which would rank countries, and he asked Nihad Awad, the founder of the Council on American-Islamic Relations (CAIR) for support. They had known each other since the founding of CAIR twenty five years ago and met at a DC Panera for breakfast, 'And we were just working on details' said Awad. It had been Khashoggi's job at the palace to keep tabs of all opinions and persuasions but now he was formulating his own brief. On its website CAIR defended its independence from accusations of being linked to the Muslim Brotherhood and Hamas, though even a staff-writer of the staid news agency AP News, opined in 2019 that CAIR were on the 'islamist' spectrum of Islam. The 'bombshell' of Khashoggi's secret cooperation was dropped by Kurdish media network Rudaw in Iraq on 17 October 2018.

Khashoggi and Abdulaziz had a lively WhatsApp conversation exchange of over four hundred texts, pictures and videos. In these, Khashoggi called MBS 'Pac-Man' and a 'beast' after the Ritz Carlton powergrab. To Abdulaziz he quietly pledged over $30,000 of his own money to further plans of spreading information to young activists in Saudi Arabia in secret. Abdulaziz was not the only one to whom he talked critically about MBS. 'MBS is now becoming the supreme leader', he told the *New Yorker*'s Robin Wright, as he compared MBS's position in the kingdom negatively to the veto power of Iran's ayatollah.

Publically, however, he remained the Khashoggi with a deep unconditional love for the palace. Dr Kristian Coates Ulrichsen, a young academic at Rice University knew the official Khashoggi. 'My impression was that Khashoggi remained a Saudi patriot to the end, and that any sense of freedom he felt at living in Washington and being able to express himself was tempered by a sense of concern at the path that he saw Saudi Arabia's new leadership going down.' 'Khashoggi spoke out about his country out of a sense of civic and patriotic duty and not because he wanted to see the crown prince fail; rather, he felt the crown prince and those around him were making mistakes, and was hoping that they would be able to learn from them', he said.

But there was also a public shift in his articles towards Qatar, the country MBS accused of funding the Muslim Brotherhood. In fact, he was to have been a guest speaker at the Gulf International Form's inaugural conference at the National Press Club in Washington, DC, on 16 October 2018, an event funded by the Qataris.

The treasure trove of Khashoggi's personal papers that the *Washington Post* was given, revealed that Khashoggi's topics for his pieces for the paper were closely discussed with his friend Maggie Salem Mitchell, the director of Qatar Foundation International. Between themselves, Salem Mitchell and Khashoggi agreed to keep this long-standing cooperation 'discreet'.

She would propose topics, draft material ('So do you have time to write it?', he contacted her early in August 2018), and urge Khashoggi to take a harder line against the Saudi government. She also gave him help with translations and assistants so that he could file his copy in English with the *Post*. As the director of the institute she controlled a lobby budget and had access to support staff. Khashoggi fudged the rules of independent journalism, but then what did the *Post* expect? Prestige doesn't pay a translation bill, and nor does $500.

Salem Mitchell, when asked to respond to the revelations, defended herself by saying she did it to help her friend succeed in the US as his English was rusty. She tried to make him feel welcome as he had left his wife and family behind and was lonely.

In his first months in Tysons Corner she went clothes shopping with him ahead of a talk at a Brookings Institution's forum in New York (16-18 September), during the first months of his self-exile. 'We're in Men's Wearhouse, and I was like, "Jamal, maybe you should get two jackets … one casual, one formal." He said, "Maggie, I'm a minimalist. I don't want to have a lot of things".'

They both drove to New York together with a Qatar acquaintance of hers and her partner Mike Franc, a director at Stanford's Hoover Institution, and helped Khashoggi prepare for a BBC interview at the forum along the way. His Saudi accent prevented him from saying the word 'Orwellian', which he specifically wanted to use. 'We had this stupid belly laugh, all of us trying to get him to say Orwellian', Franc recalled in the *Atlantic*.

In August 2018, Salem Mitchell prodded Khashoggi to write about Saudi alliances from the US to the European far right. When he sent her the draft, he had turned it into an article about Canada, and she castigated him severely: 'you veered off topic... IT'S HIGHLY PROBLEMATIC'. When he finally submitted the piece for his *Post* blog on 6 August it contained some lines in which the monarchist sounded like a democrat and he WhatsApped his friend the Qatari lobbyist, 'They're going to hang me when it comes out'.

In London on the Saturday before his death, Khashoggi said on BBC-24's Newshour about the conference he had just attended, 'An event like that would be difficult to hold today in the Arab world because we are retreating from freedom in most of the Arab countries. Most of the Arab world is currently collapsing, for example in Libya, Syria and Yemen and has no interest in discussing Palestine because they have miseries of their own. Then in countries like Saudi Arabia, my country, or in Egypt, they have no interest in those kinds of issues that motivate and rally the people because they want to subdue them instead.'

An anonymous source said that he had met Khashoggi at the end of September to discuss the war in Yemen. Like other high-level Saudis who had previously held the reins of power, he had become critical after it dragged on with huge loss of life. He disclosed to him with great reluctance that, 'he was getting proof that Saudi Arabia had used chemical weapons. He said he hoped he would be getting documentary evidence.' Reportedly the source was an academic.

While Khashoggi's *Washington Post* blogs were no doubt followed with gritted teeth at al-Qahtani's Media Center, it was nonetheless what the palace had signed up for when they lifted Khashoggi's media ban in the US. In truth, many of the things he now said could only be voiced by Arabs based in the US and would be as unwelcome anywhere on the Arabian Peninsula as Khashoggi's al-Arab in Bahrain – Qatar included. It wasn't a reason for assassinating someone, not least because one would be killing a US resident and journalist to boot in cold blood. That was an operation that would need a big idea to justify the extraordinary risk.

***

The Spring of 2018 was not only a milestone for Saudi Arabia. On 3 April 2018, Turkey had begun the construction of its first nuclear reactor by Russia's Rosatom. Regardless of the stringent international inspections it had agreed to, sixty-four-year-old Erdoğan had stolen a march on his rival for power in the Middle East, MBS. Like Iran, Turkey was one step closer to the bomb.

After the Arab Spring, Erdoğan had fostered alliances with regimes along two geographical lines that embraced populist Islam or the Muslim Brotherhood: Tunisia, Libya, Egypt, Sudan along one line and Syria, Iraq, Iran along the other. In between this sandwich lay Turkey's foe Saudi Arabia where the royal family perceived any religious populism as an existential threat, whether Sunni or Shia.

The 1979 fall of the shah as absolute monarch (and single owner of its vast oil revenues) in Shia Iran was seen in Riyadh as merely a precursor of the 2010 Arab Spring, which ended the non-religious regimes in Sunni Egypt, Libya and Tunisia, and half-Sunni Yemen. Whereas Erdoğan's closeness to the Muslim Brotherhood bolstered Turkey's lines of regional power, as recently as 2014 Saudi Arabia had classified the movement as a 'terrorist organisation'. King Abdullah had decreed a twenty-year prison sentence for anyone belonging to a 'terrorist group'. Long before MBS, Riyadh had stopped seeing eye to eye with the country from the moment Erdoğan rose to power in 2003.

Before Erdoğan, Turkey used be a sleeping giant, its religious extremism checked by coups by its generals in the tradition of Atatürk. But as president Erdoğan had become adept at projecting Turkish power well beyond its borders despite a modest annual military budget of $18bn that was dwarfed by Saudi's $64bn. Apart from challenging MBS's 2017 blockade of Qatar, Turkey had opened military bases in Qatar and Somalia and had been in talks for one with Sudan's brotherhood-linked dictator Omar al-Bashir of three decades, before the Sudanese army removed him in May 2019 following popular protests.

Routing Saudi power in the region and spreading the political message of the Muslim Brotherhood were the two prongs of Erdoğan's foreign policy. No wonder that Trump's kyboshing of the Nuclear Deal with its ally Iran was badly received in Ankara. On May 22, at a fast-breaking *iftar* meal with ambassadors, Erdoğan told them, 'We do not accept re-igniting issues, including the Iran nuclear deal... The main threats against our country and region are nuclear weapons.'

Whoever ruled the Saudi palace would be deeply concerned about Khashoggi's unfolding love for Cengiz and Turkey that transported him into Erdoğan's orbit. He might as well have publicly joined the Muslim Brotherhood.

Khashoggi's insights could be invaluable to Erdoğan in giving teeth to what Turkey does 'not accept'. Khashoggi knew like no other where the palace was divided. He had also been involved in Saudi intelligence, entrusted with vital secrets of the royal family, been authorised to develop close relationships in the US and Europe, and penetrated deep into Riyadh's secretive palace culture. Even after his time in the US and UK embassies with Prince Turki had ended, he took diplomatic meetings on behalf of King Abdullah's government. Azzam Tamimi of London's Finsbury Mosque recalled that Khashoggi had attended an international top with Hamas in Beirut on behalf of the foreign minister.

Khashoggi was aware of the problem. Asked by *Haberturk* about his Saudi friend and the 'many secrets he knew of the absolute monarchy' in Saudi Arabia, Turan Kişlakçi replied to that aciculate question that he had challenged Khashoggi on this closeness to the palace as advisor, and to Prince Turki (who is considered to have an air of intellectual superiority by his royal relatives, and as a result not very popular). Turan pointed out to Khashoggi, 'that is secret service and you are a journalist'. Khashoggi, however, had responded unapologetically about this blurring of lines in his life.

'There is part of the palace that at times would like to exclude the religious and the conservatives. I am part of it, and I am glad I am part of it. I have used it to make a difference, particularly to the PLO.'

But what if Khashoggi knew a secret so devastating that it could scupper Saudi Arabia's nuclear aspirations for a generation if known in the US? That would be an asset the palace could never allow Erdoğan to come close to. The only topic of that magnitude was 9/11 when Khashoggi had helped Prince Turki – the top royal who had abruptly withdrawn from the office 10 days before the attacks – save the Saudi monarchy from being toppled by Bush's neocons baying for action.

Even in exile, knowing that he was being watched, Khashoggi continued communicating with the palace on 9/11 developments. It was a clear signal to the paymasters of his pension that his public criticism of MBS had no bearing on his undying patriotism as a Saudi national. When, for example, he was approached by a former FBI agent working for the victims of 9/11, he promptly contacted KBS, the Saudi ambassador in the US, expressed his loyalty to the kingdom, and expressed he would claim 'the innocence of my country and its leadership'.

Apart from marriage, one of the other things Cengiz and Khashoggi discussed was his Saudi Arabian citizenship. As a result of Turkey's economic malaise, Erdoğan's government had dropped the requirements for Turkish citizenship by three quarters to a quarter of a million dollars, and Khashoggi could technically apply for Turkish citizenship at the same time as he purchased their Zeytinburnu apartment for that amount. But, he told Cengiz, Riyadh already called him 'the Turk' and he feared they would come after him more if he applied for Turkish nationality. He worried, in particular, that something bad might happen to his eldest son Salah, the banker in Jeddah.

Instead they agreed that Khashoggi would apply for US citizenship. It was a safer option. They would live between Tysons Corner and Istanbul, he would be safer as a US citizen than as a Turkish citizen and he would be flying around the world attending conferences anyway. Around September while still in the US he had applied for his US citizenship and was waiting for the paperwork to go through. It was a huge emotional step away from his homeland and Saudi family. But was also one that could have immediate practical consequences. Saudi Arabia doesn't grant multiple nationalities without express permission from the king. Under Saudi law his nationality could be cancelled with the stroke of a keyboard once he naturalised elsewhere.

Could Khashoggi have stuck a sharper needle into the eye of MBS while Riyadh's nuclear catch-up was entering another make-or-break phase? Six months earlier, on 7 March 2018, MBS had publicly said that Turkey was part of the 'triangle of evil', together with Iran and extremist religious groups such as the Muslim Brotherhood. The Saudi embassy in Ankara paddled back on MBS's words the next day and blamed the messenger for getting it wrong. But the words summarised the position in Saudi Arabia's palace quite well.

Khashoggi's calculation that breaking with the Kingdom risked no more than the cancellation of his Saudi passport or payments was as mistaken as Khashoggi's illusion that he was seen as an 'honest advisor' by MBS. It was fury at Khashoggi's treasonous move to Turkey and not his dissidence from the US that was the reason for his killing.

The Saudis confirmed it themselves on 15 November 2018. In a rare glimpse into the secretive and opaque Saudi justice system, prosecutor general Sheikh al-Mojeb made public his findings into the instructions that the Tiger Team had received to organise the extraordinary rendition of Khashoggi from the Istanbul consulate. His deputy al-Shalaan set out the details in a press conference.

Al-Shalaan said deputy-head of intelligence Al-Asiri had given the leader of the 15 operatives 'an order to bring back the victim by means of persuasion, and if persuasion fails, to do so by force'. MBS's top-aide and Khashoggi's nemesis Saud al-Qahtani had subsequently briefed members of the team that, further to his Center's intel, Jamal Khashoggi had been 'co-opted by organisations and states hostile to the kingdom'. Brigadier-general Maher Mutreb, Khashoggi's former London-embassy colleague, attended the al-Qahtani meeting as a key member of the team. Mutreb was 'to head the negotiation group in the team because of his previous relationship with the victim'. The two other groups within the team – 'intelligence' and 'logistics' (detail 169) – were also in attendance.

In his address, al-Qahtani furthermore made clear that it wasn't merely that Khashoggi was co-opted by foreign nations as an agent that was the problem. The real problem was far more serious than that. It was 'that the victim's presence outside of Saudi Arabia represents a threat to national security'.

When brigadier-general Mutreb yelled 'Traitor! This is what you deserve!' while Khashoggi was grabbed by the operatives under his command, he repeated what was really behind his cold-blooded assassination of his former intelligence colleague and former friend in London.

Jamal Khashoggi's significance was not lost either on Vladimir Putin, another world leader who viciously hunted down former Russian spies like FSB colonel Alexander Litvinenko and GRU colonel Sergei Skripal and had them killed outside Russia's borders.

President Putin offered his personal view on the Khashoggi affair on 18 October at a conference in Sochi – the Valdai Discussion Club, Russia's state of the union for his top officials and oligarchs.

Disregarding the fact that the world media considered Khashoggi's journalism the cause of his assassination – plain and simple – the very well-informed Putin observed instead, 'It is hard to say, what is going on there.' Leaking what was in Russia's intelligence files, he pointedly said about Khashoggi's *curriculum vitae*, 'As far as I can judge this man is to a certain extent part of the Saudi elite. In some way or other he was connected to certain circles in power'. While world leaders did not want to be photographed close to MBS at the G20 two months after the assassination, Putin publicly high-fived him to MBS's delight.

Putin had himself brought up the subject of 'traitors' on 3 October – the day after the murder of Jamal Khashoggi, and the same day on which MBS was to protest publicly and in person his innocence of Khashoggi's fate to Bloomberg in the evening.

On that day Vladimir Putin was taking part in a midday Q&A session at the Russian Energy Week conference in Moscow. But he had all of a sudden veered off topic and launched into a vitriolic broadside. It seemed so random at the time that his outburst made headlines around the world. Seated next to Vladimir Putin at the Q&A session and looking serene was Khalid al-Falih, MBS's trusted energy minister.

'Imagine' Putin fumed, pulling a disgusted face, 'suddenly someone goes and betrays your country. What do you think about him?… He's just a scumbag, and that's it.'

The word Putin spat out at the conference attended by oil-and-gas state ministers and CEOs of oil companies was '*poldonok*', a boorish Russian swear word.

The aim of his sudden outburst was on the face of it the former-GRU spy Sergei Skripal even though by October 2018 this affair had drifted to the backburner of the news cycle.

Putin had also commented that some 'are pushing forward the theory that Mr Skripal is almost some kind of human rights defender.'

It was an odd theory to bring up eight months after the fact. Sergei Skripal was a retired mid-ranking former Russian spy living in very modest circumstances in sleepy Salisbury. He had never gone on the record for anything, let alone human rights. At best, he had become in 2018 a mute symbol for human rights.

Jamal Khashoggi was also a long-standing member of the Saudi intelligence community. But the *Washington Post* blogger with his 1.7 million Twitter followers, could definitely be 'pushed forward' as a human rights defender because that is exactly how the Middle-East rumour-mill labelled him in the first 24 hours of his disappearance.

Jamal Khashoggi may not have been well-known enough in the Anglophone or Turkish media to stop the presses, but his disappearance was big news on 2 October for Arab mass-media outlets such as al-Jazeera, the Qatar-owned broadcaster. Khashoggi publicly supported greater freedom of expression in the Middle East and saw the Muslim Brotherhood as a symptom of a popular demand rather than as a terrorist organisation whose very existence was nefarious like al-Qaeda or Daesh/Isis.

On the point of the Muslim Brotherhood not only Qatar and Turkey agreed with Khashoggi. Rex Tillerson, Donald Trump's secretary of state, former CEO of ExxonMobile and hardly a barn-storming hippy, concurred. Rejecting the classification of the brotherhood as a terrorist organisation as 'problematic', Tillerson stated on 14 June 2017 that elements of the organisation had become a legitimate part of governments 'by renouncing violence and terrorism.' He used Turkey and Bahrein as examples.

When Putin spoke out on 3 October, the Turkish and international media still imagined that Khashoggi might be alive, but Riyadh officials knew better. There was a reason why none of the frantic phone calls that Turkish authorities made to their Saudi counterparts from 5.50pm the day before were answered.

9
Plotting

A private Gulfstream jet with tail markings HZ-SK2 touched down at Istanbul's Atatürk Airport at 3.13am on Tuesday 2 October and taxied to the private-jet terminal. It was owned by Sky Prime Aviation, a company whose shares had reportedly been transferred to the Saudi government after MBS's shakedown of his royal relatives a year earlier while they were locked up in the capital's most exclusive hotel, the Ritz Carlton. The jet had come from Riyadh carrying nine military operatives from the elite Tiger Team squad, Saudi Arabia's expertly-trained extraordinary rendition team, and included two colonels and a general. While the nine headed for customs to gain entry to Turkey, the jet idled stationary on the tarmac awaiting further instruction. Queuing for the single officer on duty at the private-jet terminal, they looked at their phones. Two of them wore suits, a few of them rolled up hand luggage. Two hours earlier an advance team of three elite Saudi soldiers had flown to the same airport, and the day before another forward trio of operatives, including another general and a major, had arrived midday in Istanbul. The two smaller teams had taken scheduled commercial flights – the first from Jeddah and the second from Riyadh – and had strolled in dressed like tourists in casual clothes.

All fifteen men checked in until Friday at two five-star hotels in Istanbul's Levent business district on the European side of the city – the nine-strong Gulfstream team at the Mövenpick Hotel and the two forward trios at the Wyndham Grand.

They were all caught on (subsequently leaked) CC-TV, passing through airport security and at their hotels' front desks. Both luxury tower-block hotels are close to one another and just a few minutes' drive away from the plain five-storey Saudi consulate, which is tucked away on a quiet street. At the consulate, the day before, Saudi secret-service agent Muflis al-Musleh, stationed at the consulate under diplomatic cover, had made bookings for the team, asking for 'seaviews'. From the sea-side of the Mövenpick hotel, the squad would have a clear eye-line to the consulate.

Later that day a second Sky Prime Aviation Gulfstream IV jet, with tail marking HZ-SK1, would touch down at around 5.15pm at Atatürk Airport's private jet terminal where security was tailored to meet the low tolerance for delays of its privileged clientele. It would immediately sweep up six of the fifteen-strong hit-squad, taking off again at 6.20pm. The flight did not have diplomatic clearance, but three of the men carried passports with diplomatic 'free passage' and their luggage passed on to the plane unopened.

The idling Gulfstream jet HZ-SK2 would take off four hours later in the evening at 10.54pm under diplomatic clearance with seven of the fifteen-strong hit-squad and whatever luggage they had with them. The remaining two members of the hit-squad would leave on a scheduled flight from the main airport terminal just after midnight. Meanwhile, there was another exodus. The Saudi secret-service chief-of-station of the consulate left for Riyadh on a commercial flight at 9.35pm with his family as well. Three of his Saudi secret-service officers stationed at the consulate would also disappear. All this would be reported by *Sabah*.

It is evident from the flight details that Jamal Khashoggi had already been tailed in London by Saudi operatives. The Gulfstream with the nine Saudi soldiers had departed from Riyadh at around 9.40pm (UK time), 35 minutes before take-off of Khashoggi's Turkish Airline flight from Heathrow. The Gulfstream's lift-off timed exactly with passengers boarding the Turkish Airlines Airbus 321 in London and the flight closing to push off its stand. No one could get on or off while the plane taxied to its Heathrow runway for its scheduled 10.15pm time slot. The UN Inquiry established that the Riyadh jet's flight plan and nine-strong passenger list were filed under diplomatic clearance as late as 9:23pm (UK time). As the jet took off a mere seventeen minutes later from Riyadh after filing, it was ahead of the departure of the Airbus in London which had a similar flight time to cover to Istanbul.

The timing of the operation was very tight, but on paper it left time for the soldiers on the Gulfstream to just about cross paths with Jamal Khashoggi at the front of the main airport hall where, clad in a yellow dress shirt, he would pull a small suitcase through the main arrivals hall to the taxi rank in front of the building.

Everything went according to plan and Turkish airline flight TK1984 was the last flight out of Heathrow to Istanbul at 10.15pm, and it landed at Atatürk Airport at 4am, half an hour after the nine operatives in the Gulfstream.

That half hour left plenty of time for the Saudi squad to go through security in the private arrivals hall and to the main Atatürk Airport arrivals hall for commercial flights to confirm that Khashoggi had arrived and gone through customs in Istanbul. Given the military precision of the operation, it is almost inconceivable that they did not do so. In any event, the arrival of their mark meant that the next stage of the major covert choreography involving over thirty people distributed across Britain, Turkey, Saudi Arabia, as well as the US, locked into place.

10
Caught

Although Saudi Arabia is immensely wealthy from oil money, its consulate in Istanbul is far from impressive. Over-shadowed by Levent's financial towers, it is a far cry from the modern Saudi Arabia dreamt of by its *de-facto* leader Crown Prince Mohammed bin Salman with his vision of skyscraper cities in the desert and luxury coastal-holiday resorts for sun-seekers around the world. Behind security barriers and razor wire, the plain, squat yellow-cream building with a huge specimen conifer, terracotta roof tiles crowned by a Saudi flag, and an air-conditioning unit flung against its masonry, is rather more Florida-utilitarian. It has the air of a worn, but well-maintained 1970s office, with light-blue painted metal window grills in elegant Islamic patterns and CC-TV cables slung over them. What is a little odd is the mysterious assortment of discreet electronic equipment dotted around the walls and windows. The ceilings of the harshly-lit public area facing the front entrance are low, while the help-windows are sealed with bullet-proof glass. On the desks, stacks of papers wait to be rubber-stamped in a jumble of passport photos and visa applications. It is also an unlikely murder scene.

Jamal Khashoggi, the fifty-nine-year-old *bon vivant*, Saudi man of mystery and royal insider, editor, writer and journalist, arrived at the consulate at 1.14pm for his appointment. In self-imposed exile in Virginia, USA, he needed Saudi documentation prior to his forthcoming marriage in Turkey. Unlike Saudi Arabia, Turkey did not recognise polygamy and in order for him to marry Turkish law required a certificate of celibacy stating whether he was single, divorced or widowed. He also needed an authorised copy of his birth certificate. Without it he could not marry his thirty-six-year-old fiancée Hatice Cengiz.

Khashoggi was wary of consular and embassy visits. As a former palace official, he was well acquainted with the furtive Saudi method of interrogations and extraordinary renditions. Inside the kingdom, troublesome Saudis were simply placed under government control to discourage repeat behaviour. Beyond Saudi borders, there were always a few privileged princes who misbehaved, or had become too Western and liberal in their opinions. It was a long-standing practice to capture them at diplomatic missions and then smuggle them back home. He had worked for five years at the two largest Saudi embassies – the one in London and the other one in Washington, DC – and he knew exactly what took place behind diplomatic walls. It hadn't bothered him then, but now he was at the receiving end of Riyadh's secret policies.

The Saudi consulate in Istanbul's Levent district, Akasyalı St entrance. Visible in the background are the towers of the Wyndham Grand and the Mövenpick Hotel where the Saudi operatives had rooms overlooking the consulate.

Not all diplomatic missions were the same, though. They were safer in certain countries than in others. Khashoggi had not hesitated to visit the Saudi embassy in Washington, DC, in the late winter of 2017. He had been recognised by Saudi embassy staff and the ambassador had immediately invited him up for a visit. The ambassador, aged thirty, was extremely important in the kingdom. He was MBS's younger brother, Prince Khalid bin Salman, abbreviated as KBS, and a son of the king with the same wife as MBS, the crown prince. He and Khashoggi chatted amicably for about half an hour in his spectacularly grand top-floor office and he offered him something to drink and eat. This was notwithstanding Khashoggi's strained relationship with MBS's government. KBS was charming to Jamal, with whom he was to develop a friendly exchange of Whatsapp texts – over time Khashoggi sent KBS several messages expressing his loyalty to the kingdom. 'We just had a nice chat, and he was quite nice', Khashoggi told a friend after meeting KBS.

How safe was the Istanbul consulate though? Would the Saudi government dare cause trouble in defiance of the Turkish government, if not international treaties? Riyadh would never contemplate doing so in Washington, where kidnapping a US resident from US soil would be the equivalent of poking a bull at the Capitol. But was he safe from Saudi rendition in Turkey?

On Friday 28 September, Jamal Khashoggi had first picked up the courage to go to the Istanbul consulate in the moneyed district called Beşiktaş ('cradle stone', after a stone taken from the stable in Bethlehem where Jesus was born). As a precaution, he had not made an appointment and just walked in at 11.50am.

As described above, he had bought a unit in a secure apartment complex in Istanbul's Zeytinburnu ('cape olive') district after Hatice agreed to marry him and her father asked for it to have her name on the deeds before agreeing to the marriage. Located well south of Beşiktaş, it was a jumble of traditional nineteenth-century six-story textile and leather factories with modern apartment blocks built like cliffs among them. Though architecturally lawless, it faced the Marmara Sea at one end and it adjoined historic Istanbul. It was only 15 minutes from Atatürk Airport and the apartment itself was a quick 30 minute drive from the consulate.

Khashoggi had been deeply apprehensive about the Friday visit. At the very least, he thought, they might refuse to help him with sorting out the documentation he needed to get married in Turkey. He had mooted to his fiancée Hatice Cengiz beforehand, 'maybe it's better if I don't go', she recalled.

Deep down he thought he would be safe in Turkey, but he reckoned that he might be questioned by the consulate's secret-service staff he knew would be stationed there, and this he feared most. 'Because he was a very emotional and delicate person, he was uncomfortable with tension', his fiancée later told Turkish TV about Khashoggi's hesitation to enter the consulate.

But without the two certificates there could be no marriage in Turkey and that Friday Khashoggi had decided to risk it. As he did not announce his visit, Riyadh would have little time to get organised. Moreover, he had to catch his flight to London in the afternoon and brought his luggage to the consulate. If he was being watched, taking a taxi with his suitcase and fiancée would throw them off the scent.

Three months later, Cengiz recalled in her book that she had been at least as apprehensive as he was and had urged her fiancé to use his political connections in Ankara to get the papers instead of going to the consulate and doing it in person. Khashoggi, however, wanted the marriage to take place within days rather than weeks as he had a busy travel schedule ahead in October. To the extent that he considered using his political contacts, he decided to go into the Istanbul consulate in person anyway.

It turned out, he told Cengiz with relief, that the consular staff had no prior warning that he might be paying a visit and that they were pleasantly surprised to see him. In fact, they were very warm in their response and compatriots had come up to him for a chat. The official helping him had said 'they would do it for him'. Khashoggi was relieved he had worried for nought that the consulate might refuse to supply the documents, Cengiz said.

Khashoggi had waited for almost an hour on Friday to get the papers. But then he apologised and said he had to leave for his afternoon flight. Perhaps it was one reason why he picked that Friday of all days. He had an excuse to leave quickly without risk of confrontation. His London talk the next day was well-advertised on the web and, if necessary, he could tell his presumed interrogators that his absence at the conference would promptly cause a big stir.

The consular staff in turn told him regretfully 'there is no time' to certify the paperwork against the civil registry in Saudi Arabia before he had to run off to the airport.

Cengiz had meanwhile been waiting outside the consulate roadblock for a little less than an hour. She was getting anxious because his flight was close to boarding. Another fifteen minutes and he would have missed it, she reckoned. She took Khashoggi straight to the terminal, where he checked in with just his carry-on but without his large suitcase, which he asked her instead to drop off at their apartment. Later leaked CC-TV coverage showed her taxi turning into the apartment complex's security gate at 1.50pm and Cengiz getting into the elevator to the floor of their future home at 2.04pm with the suitcase and talking to a worker at the complex. The large suitcase may have been another decoy Khashoggi had planted. He would only be in London for three days.

Cengiz felt relieved, too, despite all the tension of the day. She said Khashoggi was cheerful and thrilled with the 'nice treatment and hospitality' at the consulate. It had been an emotional experience and he felt less homesick after the visit among his country folk. It had made a weight fall off of his shoulders and at least some of his yearning for his mother land had abated. He had come out smiling and said, '*Inshallah* [God willing] I will get the papers after I return from London'. It had been 'unnecessary to worry' and 'everything was fine', he reassured his fiancée. He had told the consular staff that he would be back in Istanbul on Tuesday, 2 October, and they had said they would have all the papers ready by then.

TK197 is Turkish Airlines' last afternoon flight to Heathrow on Fridays and scheduled for take-off at 2.40pm. Khashoggi made it in time as Cengiz went up the elevator. Khashoggi's trip to London was to speak the next day at a conference at the Wellcome Collection on the Euston Road on Saturday 30 September. It was organised by the Middle East Monitor and attended by several well-known people. Other speakers included Tony Blair's outspoken former secretary of state for international development, Clare Short, and Sir Richard Dalton, consul-general in Jerusalem under John Major's government.

Khashoggi's London friends were deeply concerned about his safety in their city and worried about Saudi spies tracking him. They had offered to put him up at a low-key hotel rather than the four-star one arranged by the organisers.

But Khashoggi had airily waved their offer away. He felt 'relaxed and calm' after the visit to the consulate. A PLO friend at the conference even saw how Khashoggi left his smart phone – full of contacts and private messages – unattended on a table during the conference; the friend decided to keep an eye out until Khashoggi returned.

That evening he had dinner with Daud Abdullah, a former editor and translator at the Abul Qasim Publishing House in Jeddah and the director of the

Middle East Monitor which had organised the conference, as well as other colleagues and attendees of the conference, in a Turkish restaurant in Bloomsbury. When Abdullah, asked Khashoggi whether he thought the Saudi authorities might withdraw his passport, Khashoggi replied he didn't think 'they would go that far.'

Jamal Khashoggi speaking at the 'Oslo at 25' conference at the Wellcome Collection, London, 29 September.

Khashoggi's stay in London over the weekend was taken up with friends all day Sunday and Monday, despite his cold. There was the Arafat-family lawyer Saad Djebbar. Djebbar had been a friend since 1996 and Khashoggi helped him fix 'matters regarding Saudi institutions'. They met for an hour on Motcombe St at the Fine Cheese Company.

On Monday, Khashoggi spent the day with his friend Azzam Tamimi – a broadcaster on an Arab channel and reformer of the Finsbury Mosque in London after its radicalisation by the one-eyed, hooked, militant-Islamist cleric Abu Hamza who had since been jailed in a supermax facility in the US – and told him about the consulate visit. He had been received warmly, 'very warmly' he also told Tamimi. The people working there were just 'ordinary people'. He no longer had any fear. There would be no problem visiting again to pick up the certificates.

Despite feeling under the weather, Khashoggi had spoken with excitement about his plans to his friend and was full of ideas about the future. Tamimi confirmed this to the UK press. They had also spoken about Tamimi's interview of Khashoggi on his show on Thursday in Istanbul, and Khashoggi had talked about his forthcoming marriage and the apartment he had just purchased for Cengiz and himself at just over $250,000. He told the same to Waddah Khanfar, president of the al-Sharq Forum at which he and Cengiz had first met in Istanbul.

***

In actual fact, Khashoggi's initial fears were justified as we know. His visit had indeed triggered the tentacles of the well-oiled Saudi secret-service that reached through all Saudi government offices around the world. The UN report of July

2019 verified this. But it had not happened in the way Khashoggi imagined it would.

The member of staff who had first helped him at the window had quickly passed Khashoggi and his query on to one of the Saudi secret-service officers stationed at the consulate. The officer had pretended to be an ordinary clerk and given him his name as 'Ekrem Sultan' ('Saad [al-Qarni]', UN report detail 78) and had given Khashoggi his telephone number to call on Tuesday about the papers he needed. It was later leaked that telephone records showed that calls were made to Riyadh immediately after Khashoggi's Friday visit. The delay in providing the documentation and the return appointment to the consulate in Istanbul was the crucial bait for the Saudi trap to shut close.

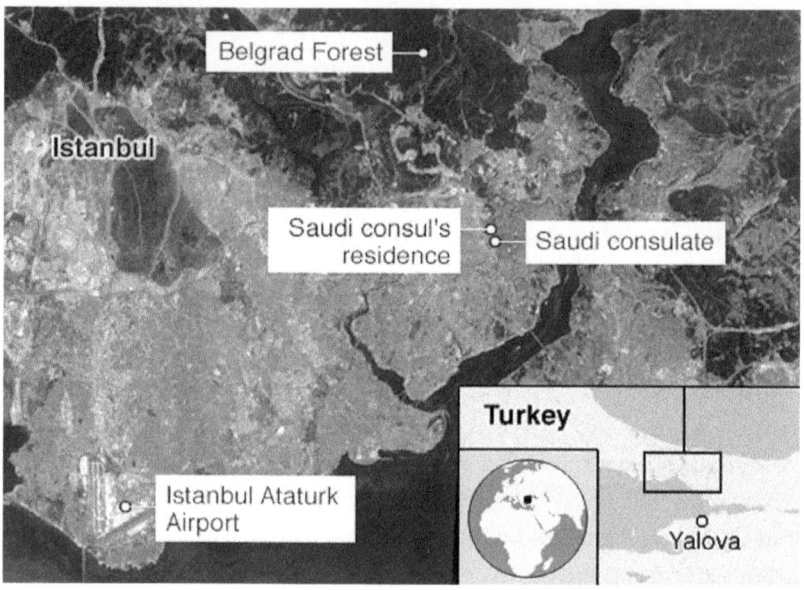

Topographical overview: the first trio of Saudi operatives arriving on 1 October drove to the Saudi consulate and fanned out from there to Belgrade Forest North of Istanbul and Yalova (inset) on the other side of the Bosphorus.

Callamard's UN report gave greater insight into the beehive of activity inside the consulate from telephone wiretaps of the consulate that Turkey shared with her UN team. At 2.22pm, while Khashoggi's plane was still waiting for clearance to take off for Heathrow, Riyadh-based top Saudi-intelligence agent brigadier-general Maher Mutreb confirmed over the phone to Istanbul secret-intelligence attaché Saad al-Qarni that his 'videos and images' were being appraised. At 2.27pm, in a follow-up call, five minutes later, Mutreb asked al-Qarni whether Khashoggi would return on 2 October (detail 78).

'Yes, we were all shocked. We just spoke. "I said how are you?" There isn't anything official but it's known that he is one of the people sought. However, we did not receive any letter from our service regarding whether there is any problem or not on him', said al-Qarni. The surprise and warmth by the consular staff when Khashoggi walked in was entirely feigned. At the same time – through the keen observance of generic watch-lists by consular staff – Khashoggi became a marked man despite the absence of a direct order to notify Riyadh.

Riyadh now knew that Khashoggi would be back inside the four walls of their Istanbul consulate. There were four short days to plan how to disappear him. For a dedicated special operations team who had a plan for what they wanted to do, it was plenty of time, however.

On Friday evening, just before Khashoggi landed in London, another Saudi attaché, Abdulaziz al-Ghumuzi, spoke to the consul-general Mohammed al-Otaibi. He said 'the head of state security called me and they have an assignment. They are asking for anyone from your delegation for... a top secret mission'. The assignment would last four-five days. Consul-general al-Otaibi then spoke to a staff member whom he told that security staff of the ambassador had contacted him to say that 'there is an urgent training in Riyadh... The issue is very important and developed rapidly'. They agreed their colleague would catch a flight at 8 or 9pm next day.

On Saturday 29 September, after Khashoggi's impromptu Friday morning visit, the Istanbul chief-of-station of Saudi intelligence Ahmed al-Muzaini (officially a military attaché at the consulate and a diplomat) and another attaché (Khashoggi's handler al-Qarni) flew straight to Jeddah from Istanbul's satellite Sabiha Gökçen Airport on the city's Asiatic side at 2.31pm for consultation with their superior, vice-president of Saudi intelligence major-general Ahmed al-Asiri. Other consular staff, involved two days before in a scheduled sweep of the consulate for bugs, also travelled to Saudi Arabia for a meeting according to *Sabah* newspaper.

Military attaché al-Muzaini flew back on Saudia flight SV263 ('SF263' in the UN report) to Istanbul afterwards on 1 October, going through Atatürk Airport customs lugging a large suitcase under diplomatic cover after his 48-hour trip and exited the terminal at 4.04pm, with his colleague, delivering Riyadh's orders to the Saudi consul-general Mohammed al-Otaibi. This was all captured on the airport's CC-TV leaked to the Turkish media. The first forward team of the Tiger Team squad also arrived on this Saudia flight from Riyadh that Monday 1 October. The forward trio of operatives went to the consulate at 7pm, an hour and a half after checking in, and returned to the Wyndham Grand at 10.40pm, shortly after take-off of Khashoggi's Turkish Airlines plane.

While Khashoggi was still in London with his friend Azzam Tamimi, the four men set to work immediately. They were joined by four further staff, including secret-service attaché Muflis al-Musleh. At 5.30pm al-Muzaini took a Saudi consular BMW on a reconnaissance trip to Belgrad Forest 25 minutes to the north of the consulate, caught on (later leaked) CC-TV footage at 6.28pm at its gated entrance in the woods. Reconnaissance was also made at Yalova, across the

Bosphorus on the Asiatic side of Turkey, 1 hour and 15 minutes south by car from the consulate. Near Yalova, in the city of Termal, one of MBS's friends, 'Ghozan', owned a palatial villa with a deep well in the garden.

Consulate secret-service chief Ahmed al-Muzaini arriving and at the airport pick-up rank at 4.04pm, 1 October.

Upon arrival at the consulate, the general among the trio of soldiers, major-general Mansour Abahussein – who travelled on a diplomatic passport from Riyadh and was caught on airport CCTV wearing a traditional white *thaub* robe and a patriotic red-and-white-blocked Saudi *ghutra* that covered his head – had made a preparatory call to this friend of MBS's. All these details were also leaked later and confirmed in the UN report of June 2019.

Abahussein asked Ghozan, 'how far the house was from Istanbul, and Ghozan responded "The bridge has been opened. It takes one hour and fifteen minutes to get there via highway. It takes forty five minutes from the airport." He asked "Is there anyone there?" Ghozan replied: "No, there is nobody. Just a caretaker"' (detail 84).

Attachés Abdulaziz al-Ghumuzi and Saad al-Qarni then briefed another at the consulate at 9.48pm, just as Khashoggi was heading to Heathrow Airport in London where it was three hours earlier on the clock. Preparing the consulate for the presence of the Tiger Team delegation, one of them instructed their colleague, 'They will have something to do on my floor in the office… Their work inside will take two or three days' (detail 85).

Oblivious of all this activity, Khashoggi arrived for the first time at the Istanbul apartment he had just bought early in the morning on Tuesday, a little groggy from his cold and the four-hour red-eye. At 4.58am he went downstairs again in a black t-shirt and faded jeans looped with a leather belt to wait outside for a minute or so to meet his fiancée. Just before take-off from Heathrow, he had texted her at 10pm, 'I'm on the plane right now, I'm coming home to you. In love, loving and passionate.'

Cengiz arrived in a long coat and with a purple traditional *hijab* wrapped around her hair and wearing fashionable but slightly severe glasses. In public and even personal photos of her and Khashoggi's she was never seen without her hair being covered, often with an elaborate purple or tan coloured shawl. Once, in traditional Kemalist Turkey, wearing a head-cover was seen as religious fanaticism and had been a reason for being denied access to schools and universities, working for the government, and even a passport. But in modern Turkey, it could be worn as a sign of political affiliation with Erdoğan's ruling AKP.

Jamal Khashoggi and Hatice Cengiz at their apartment building's lobby at 4.58am on 2 October.

Khashoggi let her in through the security door of the building while she carried a plastic bag in her left hand with some supplies. When they went out again together to go to the consulate he had changed into a blazer, shirt and grey trousers.

The Dillek branch where Khashoggi and Cengiz had breakfast on 2 October.

Earlier, during breakfast at around 11am in the Dilek restaurant downstairs, Khashoggi had called the number of 'Sultan', Saudi secret-service officer al-Qarni, at the consulate to say he wanted to come in that day for the paperwork. Some forty minutes later, around 11.50am, the officer, still masquerading as a consular clerk, called back and told him yes the papers were ready and he was welcome to come and collect them at 1 pm.

Cengiz, a PhD student at the Fatih Sultan Mehmet University, Istanbul, overheard Khashoggi on these calls. He hadn't yet shared with her that he intended to pick up the papers that day. She told him she didn't realise he meant to go to the consulate and asked who was coming with him? He was clearly unworried this time because he responded, 'I am going alone or with one of my friends', she recalled.

His response worried Cengiz and thereupon she decided that she would skip university that day and join him on this trip, too, as she had on the first one the week before. That way she could be certain he would not do the trip on his own after all. Together they planned to spend the rest of the day together and make some final purchases for their apartment after what they thought would be Khashoggi's brief appointment at the consulate to collect the marriage papers.

Hatice Cengiz and Jamal Khashoggi about to hail a taxi outside their apartment building, 12.43pm 2 October.

They returned from breakfast at 12:17pm, talking animatedly, holding hands and smiling, while Hatice was almost cradling Jamal's arm. Khashoggi briefly let her hand go to flip his card past the pad to open the door. Almost half an hour later they left once again hand-in-hand walking along the new plantings on the side of the internal road to the security gates of the complex. At 12:42pm they passed the tall glass-and-brown-metal guards' house, filing one by one by its yellow metal railing through a turnstile for pedestrians, where Cengiz briefly was caught off-balance. They both snaked past the gate and turned left and crossed the road to hail a taxi for the 30 minute drive to the consulate. All their movements on Khashoggi's last journey were captured on the CC-TV (later leaked) angled from the road at the frontage of the entrance.

While he was no longer 'that hesitant [about their] second trip', Khashoggi again did not think Cengiz should come inside the consulate with him. You were only allowed inside if you had business there, she recalled of their conversation. She was neither Saudi and nor were they yet husband and wife. On 28 September, the duty porter at the consulate's canopied entrance had sent Cengiz back to wait beyond the roadblock (as captured on CC-TV) during their first attempt to obtain the marriage documentation.

They agreed that she would wait outside until he came out. He handed her his mobile phones. They contained messages, information and numbers he didn't want to take into the consulate. If he didn't come out after a few hours she should contact 'the authorities', he told her. He wasn't more specific than that. As he entered the road block to the consulate, he didn't give her names and numbers to call she told Turkish TV.

Cengiz said she would wait outside, near a supermarket 20 yards from the roadblock and the entrance to the consulate. 'Fine, my darling', he replied, and turned towards the security guards, who frisked him briefly before he walked to the door of the covered walkway to the consulate's public area. It was the last time she would see him.

She circled around a little and bought chocolate and water for Khashoggi at the Migros supermarket two hundred yards from the consulate, waiting patiently for him to exit.

Jamal Khashoggi in front of the Akasyalı-Street security gates, saying goodby to Hatice Cengiz (top right), being searched (bottom left), and being greeted at the Saudi consulate in Istanbul (bottom right).

By 4pm her mood changed to panic and she called her friend Arzu who looked up the closing time of the consulate – 3.30pm. Cengiz immediately went up to the security gate and hailed the security staff – a Turkish man, she thought – who said he did not know who Jamal Khashoggi was and told her that there was 'no one inside and everybody had left'. She then looked up the consulate's number and rang from her mobile phone. The Saudi officer who had answered her call came outside after a few minutes and walked up to her. Speaking through the security gate he told her he had 'checked all the rooms and there was no one inside; so it was pointless for [her] to wait'.

This made no sense. Anxiously, Cengiz, later told Turkish TV, she remembered that eight or so days earlier Khashoggi hadn't felt well enough to attend a talk and was hospitalised. It had worried Cengiz and she had asked him whom to call in case of an emergency – Khashoggi had given her the number of a close friend who would help her. This time Khashoggi hadn't specifically given her a number to call, she said, but this number was the first she rang anyway.

The friend of Khashoggi's Cengiz called was Yasin Aktay, chief advisor to Turkish president Erdoğan as well as a former MP and deputy chairman of the ruling AKP. Erdoğan, in fact, was a friend, too, of Khashoggi's. Aktay said he knew the exact time she called because he took a screenshot at 4.41pm during the call that he showed on Turkish TV. Her name on his phone came up as 'Hatice Kaşikçi', the Turkish spelling of Khashoggi, and evidently not as 'Hatice Cengiz'.

Cengiz also rang a number of Arab friends of Khashoggi's in Istanbul, including Waddah Khanfar (the Palestinian organiser of the conference where she had met Khashoggi first) and Turan Kişlakçi, director of the Turkish-Arab Journalists' Association.

Though Khashoggi hadn't given specific instructions for her to call Kişlakçi, he was an old friend of Khashoggi's whom he had known for a decade and a half. Kişlakçi knew Cengiz as well and had attended the same conference where Cengiz first met Khashoggi (he would later tell the media he had first introduced the would-be couple to another). A lively, enthusiastically-gesticulating, bearded, bespectacled, serious-looking forty-five-year-old Turkish man with a Pakistani graduate degree, Turan dressed in stylish suits, and earlier in the month had gone to Hatice's father on behalf of Khashoggi to propose the marriage officially.

Turan Kişlakçi was in a meeting, however, and she couldn't get through. Khashoggi had not prewarned Kişlakçi that he was visiting the consulate that day to say he might be at risk. She persisted with Turan, calling 'four or five times', and was rewarded when she finally got to speak to him at 5pm.

'Turan', she said in distress, 'come to the front of the consulate, Khashoggi is missing'. He asked whether she had called Aktay, and then he also called Aktay in Ankara himself.

Cengiz's first call to Aktay had been a bull's eye. Aktay, fluent in English and Arabic, was based in Ankara and immediately got Saudi ambassador Waleed Elkhereiji to take his call. Elkhereiji replied 'that's awkward' and, asking for ten minutes, said 'I'll call the consulate and see what happened and will call you back'. When Elkhereiji didn't call back, nor responded to a text and another phone message, Aktay realised the ambassador could not help him as this 'was beyond his power' and that this was a far from ordinary problem.

Aktay instantly also understood that something catastrophic was taking place. He called a Saudi colleague of Khashoggi's for an assessment, who fumed that he had told Khashoggi 'many times' never to enter the consulate. This mutual

Saudi friend advised Aktay to call the president immediately. Aktay then left an urgent message for President Erdoğan at his office, as the president was tied up in a senior party-committee meeting in the capital. In less than half an hour Cengiz's call had the ear of Turkey's strongman.

Cengiz meanwhile had also called the police in Istanbul. She said that Khashoggi was being held or that 'something bad' had happened – as President Erdoğan himself would later tell the press.

The alert to the president sparked a tsunami of activity. Handed Aktay's message by a secretary during the top-level meeting, Erdoğan instantly grasped its significance and took Khashoggi's disappearance on Turkish soil very badly. Even though Khashoggi was not Turkish, he tersely ordered 'that all measures be taken' to locate 'his friend' – the word he used to describe Khashoggi in later press conferences. Aktay now contacted Hakan Fidan, the head of the Turkish secret service MİT, and his deputy, and passed on the president's urgent instruction. Turkey's security forces woke up with a sharp jolt to start a feverish search for intelligence on the matter. He also contacted the Istanbul police top, which in turn summoned Istanbul's chief prosecutor Irfan Fidan. In a matter of half an hour, he had mobilised Turkey's highest security officials on Erdoğan's personal orders. The president clearly considered Khashoggi's presence in Turkey a matter of overriding national importance.

The security services swiftly opened a cross-agency investigation at 5.50pm. This precise moment was disclosed by Erdoğan later on. His officials, he said, still thought Khashoggi was inside the consulate at this point.

MİT and other Turkish authorities urgently called their opposite Saudi numbers. No answer. They also feverishly started to go through masses of footage of the wireless MoBeSe system, a Turkish CC-TV network of over 4000 HD cameras around Istanbul alone, with close to 500 staff maintaining and analysing its data. The acronym stands for 'Urban Security Management System' and had been rolled out across Turkey from 2005 by the Erdoğan government. An Istanbul attorney said wryly in 2014, 'it is now possible for the state to follow someone from his home to virtually everywhere'. At least six CC-TV cameras were positioned at the front of the consulate and another seven covered the back entrance. Investigators traced back every car – there were twenty six of them at the consulate – and person entering or leaving the consulate that day.

As night fell, Cengiz was still walking up and down outside the consulate's roadblock at 5.33pm. And at some point after 5.50pm the police showed her a CC-TV security-still taken from the street at 1.14pm to confirm it was Khashoggi going into the consulate, asking her – 'is it him?' Next day, after a terrible night, Cengiz rushed back to the consulate and went to the police station in the Fatih district near their home to give a statement, and hand Khashoggi's iPhones over – he liked to use new technology – as well as his laptop, and some of his clothes and things that had traces of his hair for DNA.

However quick off the mark the Turkish secret service MİT and police had been after the presidential ukase, theirs proved to be a rear-guard action to catch up with the Saudi special ops team. Almost three quarters of an hour before Erdoğan's kick-off, Gulfstream HZ-SK1 landed at Atatürk Airport at 5.15pm. It had picked up the first six of the Saudi Tiger Team, including the leader involved in the decision to kill Khashoggi – brigadier-general Maher Mutreb.

At Atatürk Airport, the six and their luggage had gone through Genel Havacilik private-jet terminal's routine boarding procedure 5 minutes before Turkey's national investigation was opened. Mutreb was travelling on a diplomatic passport and two others on government passports, which meant that they themselves and their luggage were dealt with under the private-jet-terminal's diplomatic 'free passage' rules. Some of the luggage of the other four soldiers was opened for inspection by sight at the private-jet terminal. The men were relaxed and smiled at the attendant and headed straight to their Gulfstream IV, which spirited them away at 6.20pm. At this time, the Turkish authorities were still only half an hour into hastily getting their heads around Khashoggi's disappearance.

On 27 March 2019, al-Jazeera would show CC-TV of a partially obscured black Mercedes van driving up to a jet and claim that Mutreb and the operatives were inside the van, implying that Khashoggi's body parts could have been loaded up as they boarded their jet. But the Qatar channel didn't explain how airport security would have allowed the van, or its unscreened luggage, access to the airport parking tarmac for jets even if it had diplomatic status and even if the CC-TV captured the right moment.

The team-leader of the Saudi operation, major-general Abahussein (who had arrived among the first troops on Monday's commercial flight), was in a hairier spot by this time. He was still in Istanbul and would fly out on the second Saudi Gulfstream, tail mark HZ-SK2, with another six of the Tiger Team. He travelled on a diplomatic passport like Mutreb and his jet's flight plan had diplomatic clearance. Even so, by this time, it had become a race between the Saudi operatives who were still in Istanbul and the Turkish security services trying to figure out who were involved in the events at the consulate.

The police and MİT, the Turkish secret service, were on full alert from a standing start and getting up to speed. The Saudi team-leader knew this because the operative at the consulate who had taken Cengiz's call at 4pm and told her to go home had given him the first warning that the clock had started ticking. The next wire to be tripped for the Saudis was the call a few minutes after 4.41pm by the Saudi ambassador, Waleed Elkhereiji, to consul-general al-Otaibi inquiring about Khashoggi in order to report back to Yasin Aktay. It rang the alarm bell for the operation to wrap up.

A few minutes after the ambassador's call, brigadier-general Maher Mutreb and forensics expert professor Salah Tubaigy promptly left the consul-general's residence at 4.53pm (caught on CC-TV). Mutreb and five operatives went straight to the airport, going through security an hour later between 5.44 and 5.49pm to board the getaway jet. On the other hand, the forensics expert went from the consul-general's private residence to the consulate to check on progress there. Two Tiger Team members – al-Hawsawi and Khalid al-Otaibi – were still cleaning the consulate after having come down from the consul-general's residence. The three of them would leave the consulate at 9.40pm for the second jet at the airport. Meanwhile members of the Tiger Team coordinating the operation from Saudi Arabia had a plan in place on how to stall Turkish officials and diplomats asking for clarification. Their colleagues were told not to return calls or emails, just as the Saudi ambassador ghosted Yasin Aktay.

As night fell, at the Genel Havacilik private-jet terminal Turkish officials were by now on high alert. Airport officials were told Khashoggi was being kidnapped and could still be on the second Saudi jet – the June 2019 UN report revealed this. Airport officials had not inspected the first jet and it had by now left Turkish airspace. Officials demanded to see the passenger manifest of the second jet and followed diplomatic protocol beady-eyed, while meticulously searching the non-diplomats and their luggage. The jet itself, flying under diplomatic clearance, was also inspected by sight for Khashoggi by intelligence officers posing as airport staff.

Professor Tubaigy and the two operatives at the consulate arrived at Genel Havacilik at 7.40pm. They wouldn't get through security until 8.28pm. By then, the Turkish security services had pieced together the connection of their Gulfstream jet to the events in the consulate. At the consul-general's-residence, there were still four members left: operation leader major-general Abahussain, his three squad members al-Arifi, al-Bostani and al-Zahrani. This four-men detail disposing of traces of the operation at the residence would arrive at the terminal at 8.24pm and not go through security over an hour later at 9.44-46pm. By contrast, it had only taken Mutreb and the other five special forces on the first jet a few minutes after arrival at the private-jet terminal to get through security. Whisked through by non-suspecting airport staff, their plane had left the runway 35 minutes later.

What would Turkey now do with the seven operatives? Erdoğan had unleashed the full power of Turkey deep state in order to save Khashoggi. Would the country ground the Gulfstream jet that was still sitting on the tarmac and the seven suspects seated in the private terminal's reception area? Although, the jet was flying under diplomatic clearance and three of its seven passengers held diplomatic passports, airport authorities might delay take-off even longer as Turkey's secret service put together the pieces of what had happened? Nor would it cause a diplomatic incident if the jet's four regular passengers were not permitted to board and held in Turkey pending criminal investigations if the diplomats and their plane were given free passage.

In actual fact, despite Erdoğan's personal involvement in Turkey's counter gambit, nothing at all happened.

Since the Turkish visual search on board had revealed nothing ostensibly untoward connected to the diplomatic flight, airport authorities allowed the second Gulfstream to take off at 10.46pm.

The same evening, passing through the commercial terminal of Atatürk Airport, another contingent of six Saudis fled the country without obstruction. Four military attachés – the Saudi secret service agents stationed at the consulate who were involved in the special operation – also left unhindered on commercial flights, as did the final two Saudi Tiger Team agents. This couple of laggards departed leisurely from Turkish soil a little after midnight.

In less than 36 hours on Turkish soil, the Tiger Team had almost invisibly pulled off one of the most sophisticated assassinations in recent history. Not more than a few Russian secret agents had entered Britain in each of the infamous poisonings of former Russian spies Alexander Litvinenko and Sergei Skripal. By contrast, Saudi Arabia had moved the equivalent of two football teams around and successfully exfiltrated them all. As far as the dark art of spycraft was concerned, it was an exceptional achievement based on awe-inspiring skills.

There was only one known covert assassination operation on foreign soil that could claim to be even more devilish and numerous: 9/11. Nineteen men (fifteen from Saudi Arabia, four of whom were US-trained pilots), outwitted US intelligence in their stealth attack on the World Trade Tower, the Pentagon and the White House. How many other operatives were involved on US soil has remained unknown.

Khashoggi Plot operatives, it would turn out, had been US-trained, too. On 22 June 2021, the *New York Times* revealed that a license was granted in 2014 by the State Department for paramilitary training of the Saudi Royal Guard. Two of the operatives had trained in the US with Tier 1 Group from October 2014 to January 2015, just before King Salman ascended to the throne. In 2017, the year before Khashoggi's assassination, four of the operatives entered the US under this license for training by Tier 1 Group, Arkanas, a company owned by private equity firm Cerberus Capital Management. The programme included 'safe marksmanship' and 'countering an attack', but also surveillance and close-quarters combat.

11
The Attack

❦

When Jamal Khashoggi walked towards the front door of the consulate from the security road block for his 1pm appointment, he was a little late. It was 1.14pm when he entered. From the covered walkway, he expected to go right to one of the three windows in the public section to get his two marriage documents. There was a bench of three fabric-covered chairs with comfortable padding in case he still needed to wait in the small claustrophobically-lit room. The papers were ready, Sultan had said, and it wasn't going to take long.

Instead, however, as Khashoggi came in, he was asked whether he would come up to 'take tea' with the consul-general, Mohammed al-Otaibi.

Khashoggi accepted the invitation with an uneasy 'edge' in his voice, according to the UN report. It was not totally impossible that the consul was star-struck – the reception on Friday had been very warm. Khashoggi was used to special treatment, given his closeness to former and present king and crown princes. The same had happened when KBS, the US ambassador, had invited him up to his private office in the US embassy a little over a year before. If he upset the consul general at this stage, he might not get his papers today or for long time. There was only one possible answer. He had to accept the invitation or he might as well turn around and leave.

Khashoggi was ushered into the second-floor office of the consul general, a mahogany-parqueted and panelled room, with deep green leather club chairs and sofas, leather-covered tables, neon lights, and a very large green, pristine Saudi national flag. There was little reason to fear the man behind the desk. Al-Otaibi was an ordinary career diplomat charged with sorting out applications, other formalities, and the day-to-day running of the consulate.

Khashoggi, however, was not the only stranger in the restricted area of the consulate. As if in the opening sequence of a James Bond movie, ten of the fifteen operatives of the Saudi Tiger Team that had flown into Istanbul were waiting for him in the five-storey building. The soldiers had arrived separately in the morning between 9.50 and 11.03am in civilian clothes from their nearby hotels. In addition to brigadier-general Mutreb, professor lieutenant-colonel Salah Tubaigy, the head of forensics in the kingdom's secret service, was present in the building. The others were major Badr al-Otaibi, lieutenant al-Harbi, sergeant-major Waleed al-Sehri, operatives Turki al-Sehri, al-Balawi, Saif al-Qahtani, al-

Zahrani, and another major-general called al-Madani (UN detail 90).

Mutreb and Tubaigy were going over the afternoon's details as they waited for Khashoggi. Mutreb asked his team, has 'the sacrificial animal' arrived? At 1.13pm, the answer finally came – 'He has arrived' (UN detail 91). The trap closed.

Most of the fifteen soldiers had taken part in the operations of the Saudi 'Rapid Intervention Group', *Firqat el-Nemr* or Tiger Team, a group of fifty specialist soldiers acting as 'field operatives' formed in 2017 to kidnap, detain, or even torture, Saudi citizens after MBS's appointment as crown prince. Those caught by the group were forced to sign non-disclosure agreements about what had happened to them, on penalty of 'full responsibility'. The 'tigers' were drawn from very different parts of the Saudi secret service to bundle specialist areas of expertise for maximum efficiency of its special ops, some members of the team, for example, were trained in the latest spy technology.

The fidelity of the Tiger Team members had been repeatedly tested and rewarded in previous assignments. The team derived its tiger name from the nickname of their leader, the 'Tiger from the South', major-general al-Asiri. Arguably, the team should have been restyled after their leader received a new moniker – 'The Beast' – earned from being the spokesperson of the Saudi-led coalition in the ongoing Yemen War. Crown prince MBS himself had chosen 'The Beast' to form the 'spinal cord' of the Tiger Team. He had also attached a further five whom he trusted most from his personal security detail.

The Istanbul assignment given to fifteen of the Tiger Team was different from any they had done before. Contrary to Saudi law, custom and Islamic observance, today's target was not meant merely to disappear to Saudi Arabia. The hit-squad was going to assassinate him.

Every detail was organised with tight military precision. No sooner had Khashoggi entered the consulate at 1.14pm in Istanbul than in Riyadh the second Gulfstream HZ-SK1 took off at 1.47pm, flying directly to Istanbul. Its purpose was to remove from Turkey the first members of the hit-squad and evidence of the special operation. HZ-SK1's flight path had been prepared at 10.30am, close to the time when Khashoggi first rang 'Sultan', consulate secret-service agent al-Qarni, to confirm that he would visit the consulate. It was filed at 1.30pm after the consulate had swallowed up Khashoggi. The jet arrived empty in Istanbul and the pilot only stepped out of the cockpit briefly while the jet refuelled – as captured on CC-TV leaked to Qatar's al-Jazeera TV station on 27 March 2019.

Step two of the Saudi Khashoggi Plot was to deal with the forty four non-Saudi staff at the consulate and the nearby consul-general's residence. Some had already been told not to report for work that day. Lunch hour was normally the same for everyone who worked at the consulate, and started at 12.30pm. Of those at the consulate, some were given the afternoon off with the plausible-sounding reason that an important visitor would arrive. Others, such as Turkish drivers of the consulate's 26 cars, were told to stay in their rooms as there would be an inspection from Riyadh. Those in the consul-general's residence were either told not to come in or not to leave because of an engineer visiting. The least of the Tiger Team's worries were the loyalties of the Saudi staff in the buildings. They could be relied upon. With families back in Saudi Arabia, any Saudi member of staff would be too terrified to speak out of turn or leak information to outsiders. A number of staff members were then instructed to clear their offices on the second floor. This floor would remain out of bounds over the following days for cleaning the consulate's interior from 11am on Wednesday.

It was also a simple matter to disable the hard disk of the Saudi-operated (but Turkish-installed) CC-TV within the consulate, which they did – President Erdoğan would officially say they 'destroyed' it, intelligence officers used the word 'removed' in leaks to the media.

Despite this precaution, Mutreb and his team had been filmed by thirteen cameras planted outside the consulate as they were walking towards the door of the building. This footage from Turkey's nation-wide (MoBeSe) CC-TV cover would later be leaked to the world press by 'anonymous official sources'. Brigadier-general Mutreb arrived at 9.55am in a tailored suit, wearing it straight-backed as if it was a uniform. Another tall and big team member bounded in smiling at 11.03am in a loud blue check shirt and jeans with two smaller team members – one with a hoodie and another with a white-red jumper and dark jacket.

Taken on its own, that early-morning footage was hardly suspicious to any Turkish security staff of the MoBeSe programme monitoring it. The team members had filed in independently over the course of two hours and were indistinguishable from ordinary Saudis coming in between 9am to 3.30pm during the consulate's weekly walk-in hours.

***

Sealed behind closed doors in a secure building surrounded by Saudis, Jamal Khashoggi's fate had ceased to be his own. A diplomatic mission is territory whose boundaries the host nation is not permitted to 'penetrate' under diplomatic law, and it is blind-sided if the guest nation so wishes – which it invariably does – to anything that goes on inside. The British government's inability to access the Ecuadorian embassy, for example, kept Julian Assange from being arrested by British police for seven years until Ecuador's president finally decided to expel him on 1 May 2019. What was about to take place at the Istanbul consulate would never be known to the outside world.

Or so, at any rate, Riyadh and the elite Saudi hit-squad thought. In Turkey, and elsewhere, diplomatic missions manage to have foreign ears determined to listen in and spy diplomatic secrets. But before their arrival the consulate had been swept for bugs by a Saudi tech team and the assassination operatives assumed that they were out of earshot of all but themselves.

It proved to be a catastrophic miscalculation. While Khashoggi's body was never found, unbeknownst to the Saudis, their tech team had failed to uncover a number of hostile bugs hidden inside the building. Intelligence officials from at least one spy agency were recording almost every sound and every word of the Saudi operation, from the first telephone call to Khashoggi's fateful last day alive inside the consulate. How these recordings ended up in the hands of Turkey's government itself became a comedy of errors as we will see. Ultimately, the Turkish secret service MİT ended up patting itself on the back – but it was not entirely clear whether they deserved it. Either way, without these recordings we would not have known about Khashoggi's fate and this book could not have been written. History would have run a different course.

From these recordings we know that after Khashoggi entered the office of consul general al-Otaibi on the first floor, one of the Tiger Team grabbed Khashoggi's arm. He exclaimed, 'Release my arm! What do you think you are doing?'

Khashoggi now recognised brigadier-general Maher Mutreb. He knew him well as a former London-embassy colleague. When they were both stationed in London they had been friendly. Without a doubt, he had since seen the multiple coverage of Mutreb in the entourage of crown prince MBS during his trips abroad.

In London, Khashoggi had been personal advisor to MBS's uncle Prince Turki bin Faisal when Turki was Saudi ambassador to the United Kingdom (2003-5, and subsequently to the United States from 2005-7). Those years were fraught for Saudi Arabia. The secret links between Saudi's toxic, ultra-conservative Wahhabi brand of Sunni Islam and 9-11 were becoming public knowledge as first detailed in Craig Unger's *House of Bush, House of Saud* and Michael Moore's prize-winning documentary Fahrenheit 9/11 that was in part inspired by it. Fifteen of the nineteen 9/11 suicide hijackers were, after all, Saudis. Like the planes presently deployed in the Tiger Team's Khashoggi plot, the three planes that carried out the 9/11 attacks had been coordinated with breath-taking military precision.

In London Mutreb had been first secretary of the embassy, doubling as station-chief of the Saudi secret service, and Khashoggi and he had worked together further to the fall-out of 9/11 for Saudi Arabia. Mutreb would at times join Khashoggi and other staff for Friday prayers and tea afterward in Mayfair.

Jamal Khashoggi now realised that his worst fears were about to come true. Cengiz had asked him the week before, what exactly might happen if they held him at the embassy. He said he didn't worry about being arrested as he had never been accused of a crime. But he reckoned he might be 'interrogated... asked to return home, or maybe… pressured to return home'.

In the morning, over breakfast in Dilek, Khashoggi had however said confidently to Cengiz, 'they can't do something like that in Turkey.' His body language had been relaxed this time, Cengiz recalled. It had none of the anxiety of the previous Friday. Another time he had told her – 'If I were an undesirable, they would have cut-off my pension'.

Yet Khashoggi – a survivor of the religious rip currents at the Saudi royal court – lacked the foreboding that, in fact, MBS considered him so urgent a liability that even his death was an acceptable outcome of the operation. Lulled into a false sense of security, the one-time insider had completely misread the signs.

Mutreb took the lead and told Khashoggi curtly that he had to return to Saudi Arabia: 'You are coming back'.

Mutreb tried again, bluffing, 'We will have to take you back. There is an order from Interpol. Interpol requested you to be sent back. We are coming to get you.' Khashoggi simply replied that 'there isn't a case against me. I notified some people outside; they are waiting for me.' '[A] driver is waiting for me', he lied.

'Let's make it short', Khashoggi was told repeatedly while he admitted that it was really only his fiancée Hatice waiting outside (UN detail 94). There followed 7 minutes of quarrelling and a heated Skype call to Saud al-Qahtani, one of crown prince MBS's closest aides, known in dissident circles as the 'Saudi Steve Bannon'. His other nickname was 'Lord of the Flies', after the swarm of social media trolls he commanded to attack adversaries. The Skype call streamed on for 7 minutes to Riyadh.

Khashoggi also knew al-Qahtani well. Shortly after his self-exile from Saudi Arabia in the summer of 2017, al-Qahtani had called him in Virginia and given praise for his public statements in support of the crown prince's reforms, including the decision to let women drive. This surprise reform was first announced on 26 September 2017. 'Keep writing and boasting', al-Qahtani had added in October. He had offered a high-level job in the royal court, at a Saudi think tank, or heading a major Saudi media network – Khashoggi could take his pick. Al-Qahtani had said suavely 'Oh, Jamal, come home, you miss being here'. Al-Qahtani had called him again about this not long after.

Mentioning these tempting offers luring him back to Saudi Arabia to friends, Khashoggi had said, 'I won't fall for that… I don't want to end up in jail.' He was right. It was feigned by al-Qahtani on behalf of MBS. Khashoggi was right. MBS was furious about Khashoggi's first piece in the *Washington Post*. It was in September 2017 that the crown prince told Turki Aldakhil, Khashoggi's one-time colleague, the CEO of Saudi broadcaster al-Arabiya, in confidence that he would go after Khashoggi 'with a bullet' (leaked by the CIA in February 2019).

During the call, Khashoggi had politely challenged al-Qahtani about his Saudi colleagues who had been rounded up or arrested. However, he was deeply agitated underneath the surface. A friend who was in the same room witnessed how tense Khashoggi was despite the cordial tone of the conversation with al-Qahtani, 'I saw how Khashoggi's hand was shaking while holding the phone'.

This time, al-Qahtani dropped all pretence of charm. Jamal Khashoggi was told he was being kidnapped and would be taken back to Saudi Arabia by force.

'You can't do that,' Khashoggi replied again apprehensively, 'People are waiting outside.' 'People' was a generous term, as at this point only Cengiz stood between him and the hit-squad.

At some point following the conversation with al-Qahtani four officers attacked Khashoggi. During a further 4 or 5 minutes, the soldiers held him in a vice and restrained him. Jamal Khashoggi groaned and repeatedly pleaded, 'I can't breathe'.

While this happened, Mutreb shouted 'Traitor! This is what you deserve!'

***

Meanwhile in Riyadh, Gulfstream IV jet HZ-SK1 took off at 1.47 pm for Istanbul where it would swoop down at 5.15pm to exfiltrate the first six Tiger Team operatives. It meant that the Saudi death squad at the consulate had less than four hours to achieve what they had been instructed to do. After killing Khashoggi they needed to remove all traces of the crime and of his body as fast as they could.

Some two hours after Khashoggi had entered the consulate, Turkey's MoBeSe CC-TV picked up six vehicles leaving the consulate's compound ostensibly going in different directions on different routes. Two arrived at 3.09pm on MoBeSe's time clock at the residence of consul-general Mohammed al-Otaibi, who lived only a few hundred yards away. Four travelled into Istanbul as MoBeSe CC-TV decoys, being shown to buy large suitcases.

The CC-TV camera (number 4) mounted on the consul residence's security cubicle (right).

The consul-general's private home was a far more imposing affair than the consulate itself. It was built like a miniature palace, its pediment crowned with the

Saudi emblem of golden crossed swords and a palm tree like the gates of the consulate. A Saudi flag flew outside and it was flanked by two guard cubicles, one next to a ramshackle tall car port. A tall wall with dark green heavy metal inserts traced with big golden rivets, like those on the doors of the consulate, screened the residence from prying eyes.

The largest of the consular vehicles, a Mercedes Vito van with tinted windows and plates 34 CC 1865, pulled into the consul-general's garage. Three of the operatives were captured on the leaked MoBeSe CC-TV carrying two very big round light plastic bags, and rolling five large and heavy suitcases through the front door of the consul-general's home at 3.19pm. The other consular car, an Audi with number plates 34 CC 2464 parked in its place in between the two guard houses flanking the garden wall. Up to eight of the fifteen operatives were now in the consul-general's residence. In fact, the total number of operatives earlier in the morning five other Tiger Team operatives had driven up in consular Mercedes 34 CC 3071 at 11.08am and installed themselves in preparation for what would happen in the afternoon – they were major-general Abahussein, major al-Arifi, and soldiers al-Bostani, al-Hawsawi, and Khalid al-Otaibi.

The first team of five secret agents, headed by team-leader major general Abahussein, arrives for preparation at at the consul-general's residence, 11.08am.

That afternoon, neighbours of the consul general's home, which is situated next to the popular Pizza Raffaele and the restaurant's outside garden, reported that for the first time ever the smell of roasting meat came wafting over from the pool area in the large fenced-in garden of the residence. Some had wondered whether the consul general was having a barbecue in the middle of the day on a Tuesday, it was subsequently reported in the Turkish press. Six months later further revelations would follow about the origin of the smell.

On 4 March 2019, a documentary by Qatar's al-Jazeera network would reveal leaked information that the consul-general had had a Tandoori oven installed in the garden of his residence in the middle of September 2018. Tandoori ovens can reach temperatures of 1000 degrees, the top temperature commonly used to cremate human remains. A Turkish newspaper leaked the next day on 5 March that a report from the Istanbul police stated 32 portions of raw meat had been ordered by the consulate that day. When the in-absentia murder trial started on 3 July 2020, Turkish consulate employee Zeki Demir said he was called to the consul-general's residence at 2pm to light the gas in the garden's new barbecue oven. 'It was as if they wanted me to leave as soon as possible. I left after lighting the oven', he testified.

At 3.21pm big black bags are carried inside (top right) from the Mercedes Vito minivan parked inside the compound by team members arriving from the consulate.

At 4.51pm – ten minutes after Yasin Aktay took an iPhone screenshot of his call with Khashoggi's fiancee – a relaxed brigadier-general Mutreb was captured on MoBeSe CC-TV leaving the consul-general's residence with two men. An hour later he went through airport security at 5.58pm, 22 minutes before taking off in Gulfstream HZ-SK1.

As mentioned earlier, three hours after Mutreb left and into the investigation by Turkish security forces that the Tiger Team now assumed was taking place, two men left the residence in a Mercedes at 7.37pm, followed ten minutes later at 7.48pm by several others who climbed into the Mercedes Vito van. They all headed to the Genel Havacilik private-jet terminal at Atatürk Airport where Turkish authorities were waiting for them at Gulfstream HZ-SK2, whose arrival early in the morning they had connected to what went down with Khashoggi at the Saudi consulate. Three came through security at 8:28pm and four followed three quarters of an hour later at 9.44pm.

Aerial photograph of the consul-general's residence between Meşelik Street (front) and Faruk Nafiz Çamlibel Street (back), next door to Pizza Raffaele (left) and university crammer Elips Academy (right, two doors down).

The Saudi operation had run smoothly and, as the last operatives were exfiltrating, the hit-squad would not be needing their hotel rooms after all. They had paid their hotel bills and cancelled the reservations for the rest of the week before heading to the airport. Only the first trio who arrived on Monday had actually stayed the night in their hotel rooms. The other twelve had merely used them as a parking space for their gear.

HZSK1		HZSK2		
2 OCT	3 OCT	1 OCT	2 OCT	3 OCT
Riyadh: 13:23 Istanbul: 17:15	Istanbul: 18:40 Cairo: 20:32	Cairo: 23:31 Riyadh: 01:45	Riyadh: 23:40 Istanbul: 03:13	Istanbul: 22:54 Dubai: 02:48	Dubai: 22:08 Riyadh: 23:35

Gulfstream IV HZ-SK1 with six operatives headed to Cairo after its 6.20pm lift-off. After spending twenty-five hours on the ground there, it flew on to Riyadh. When Gulfstream HZ-SK2 was finally cleared for take-off at 10.20pm with another seven Saudi operatives on board, it skirted the border between Iraq and Iran, favouring the Iraqi side, and crossed the Persian Gulf, landing in Dubai at 2.30am. The following morning, it flew on to Riyadh. The final two operatives would leave Turkey on Turkish Airlines flight TK144 to Riyadh, going through security at 0.18am for boarding through the main terminal and a scheduled take-off at 1.20am.

The audacious plan to disappear Khashoggi had been pulled off like clockwork by the team of highly skilled military, right under the noses of the Turkish authorities. It was the Saudi equivalent of operation Neptune Spear in which US navy SEALs captured and killed Khashoggi's former intelligence friend Osama bin Laden on hostile territory of frenemy Pakistan. That was where the similarity ended, however. Unlike widely televised operation Neptune, the strike against Jamal Khashoggi was meant to remain a deep secret, known only to the death squad and a small number of top officials in the Saudi capital Riyadh. Nor had Khashoggi ever killed anyone, or plotted like bin-Laden to terrorise Saudi Arabia and strike fear into the hearts of its citizens. Even so, he had been taken out with overwhelming force as if he was a vital threat to Saudi state security.

12
'Is he facing charges?'

~

Only a few years older than MBS, Saud al-Qahtani was nonetheless the long-standing Riyadh mastermind behind the use of new technology in the palace's defences. A lawyer and Saudi air-force captain, he had been hand-picked by King Abdullah's most powerful civil servant to lead an electronic intelligence army as early as 2012, acquiring sophisticated tools and spyware for the government – money being no object.

With permission of the (then) Crown Prince bin Nayef, al-Qahtani had also started managing 'lawful intercepts' of private information in Saudi Arabia. Where the 2005 MoBeSe CCTV scheme rolled out across Turkey had an old-school Erdoğan flavour, al-Qahtani's civil-vigilance army was very twenty-first century, like the computer-games played by MBS and Saudi Arabia's young and social-media addicted population. Any Saudi of interest to al-Qahtani's Center for Studies and Media Affairs would be monitored any which way with cutting-edge hacking technology.

Ironically, the fifty-eight-year-old bin Nayef would fall victim of his own decree. The 'lawful intercepts' for which he had authorised al-Qahtani, came in useful after the latter caught the eye of King Salman's upwardly-mobile son MBS. In 2015, the year of King Salman's accession to the throne and two years before MBS's replacement of bin-Nayef as crown prince, al-Qahtani was promoted from 'advisor to the royal court' (the same rank that Khashoggi reportedly had under King Abdullah) to the rank of 'minister'. With al-Qahtani's digital soldiers under his command, MBS knew everything he needed to know: bin-Nayef's conversations and movements were an open book to him ahead of the coup he was planning.

Though Jamal Khashoggi had gone into self-imposed exile, his children and former wife and extended family had not. They remained in the kingdom. Apart from Salah (the same age as MBS) and Abdullah, both given travel bans after Khashoggi left the country, there were his daughters Noha Khashoggi (b1991) and Razan Khashoggi (b1995), as well as his divorced wife Dr Alaa Nasief and the other relatives of the Khashoggi clan.

When Abdullah rang his family back home on 10 September to tell them that he had met Hatice Cengiz, his father's new fiancée, and that Khashoggi was going to marry her and was about to buy a house to live with her in Turkey, they were clearly not the only ones to learn about Khashoggi's intentions to change his life.

It was around this time – late August/early September – that Saudi officials began to exchange ideas about Khashoggi's extraordinary rendition according to US intelligence intercepts that were later leaked to the *Washington Post*. GCHQ in Cheltenham, Britain's cryptography and digital intelligence agency, also picked up intel that 'something was going' at this time.

In fact, by the end of September quite a few people in the US intelligence community were aware of the Saudi plans to capture Khashoggi. The secret intercepts had been digested and disseminated to relevant US government agencies and were contained in reports that were routinely available to people working on US policy toward Saudi Arabia. This immediately imposed a legal duty on the spooks in the US. As Khashoggi was a US resident under standing government order ICD19-'Duty to Warn', US intelligence services were obliged to warn him of impending danger.

'Capturing him, which could have been interpreted as arresting him, would not have triggered a duty-to-warn obligation', a former official told the *Washington Post*. 'If something in the reported intercept indicated that violence was planned, then, yes, he should have been warned.'

Did the Saudis intend to arrest Khashoggi – which would be lawful, and there would be no duty to warn incumbent on US intelligence personnel – or plan violence, torture, or to kill him – all of which unlawful? Officials under the Trump administration who reviewed the intercepts decided not to tip off Khashoggi about the developing Saudi plans. Given Khashoggi's *Post* connection and the military-aspect of the planned Saudi rendition, it was difficult to see what persuaded the Trump administration to spread the news to its own agencies but not to include Khashoggi himself in their alert if only to err on the side of caution regarding the fourth estate. But that is what they did.

As to the legal point whether he might be arrested during a consular visit to obtain certification of his marriage documents, Khashoggi had addressed this point with his friend and fellow member of the Turkish-Arab Journalists' Association, Turan Kişlakçi. They had met on Wednesday and Thursday the week before his first consular visit in order to prepare for a talk the next Friday at the association's premises.

Khashoggi had no fear of criminal prosecution. 'I'm not afraid, because there is no official investigation against me.' He cited the job offers that had started rolling in again from Riyadh over the past few months. 'On the contrary, recently, [Crown Prince] Mohammed bin Salman asked me to be his adviser, and I refused, saying this is against my country and region's interests.... The most they can do is interrogate me. And I can give them answers, I have nothing to hide.'

In actual fact, on 3 October when asked by Bloomberg, 'Is he facing any charges in Saudi Arabia?', MBS's own answer to the question was surprisingly evasive about the man assassinated the day before in his consulate.

Pressed by the Bloomberg team, 'So he might be facing charges in Saudi Arabia?', MBS ignored the question again and repeated what he had said before about Khashoggi's whereabouts, 'If he's in Saudi Arabia I would know that'.

There was a good reason why MBS was carefully hopping between his answers. In a later leaked conversation he had with top White House staff in daily contact with Trump – who would be keeping up with what he said on Bloomberg around this date – MBS told these officials Khashoggi was a 'dangerous Islamist', evidently a crime in Saudi Arabia carrying a prison sentence since King Abdullah. That very week, for example, economist Essam al-Zamil, a friend of Khashoggi's and a critic of the crown prince's proposed sale of 5 per cent of Aramco, Saudi's oil company, was charged with joining the Muslim Brotherhood, providing information to foreign diplomats, and inciting protests.

PART 2

A movable feast

I
3 October

∾

The second part below focuses on a different type of fact (its chapters are numbered with roman numerals). The facts here are the 'leaks reported by journalists' about the Khashoggi Affair that the UN investigation decided to ignore unless these leaks agreed with what it had found out independently. While the truth of these 'leaks' remained unverifiable to the media who reported them (unlike those verified by the UN team half a year later), their first appearance in a news story was itself clearly a fact. As these stories didn't appear out of thin air, someone sought to manipulate the news cycle at that moment in time.

One should also consider that these leaks and rumours may well have reported actual facts apart from their moment of entry into the news machine and that the UN investigation team simply had no access (or were not given access) to the evidence that established them. Often, months later 'anonymous officials' denied the truth of 'leaks' in this section in the same way that 'anonymous officials' had introduced them. At either end, they relied on the ostensible authority of officialdom and the plausible deniability of anything said by anonymous attribution.

In 2018, Turkey never officially released footage of its MoBeSe CC-TV network to the media and instead leaked these clips through individual journalists. The Callamard UN team was given full official access in 2019, however. This 'unofficial' distribution approach in 2018 had the benefit of creating both a feeding-frenzy for leaks by Turkey's 'anonymous officials' among the media while underlining, at the same time, the impression that all leaks were as solidly grounded, worthy of reporting, and as irrevocable as the clips provided. (And indeed, as mentioned, even though they were later retracted they may still be true.)

The Khashoggi Affair is, therefore, also a vivid illustration of how totalitarian regimes undermine the very existence of 'facts' with rumours that they will not allow anyone else to challenge. That is not to say that countries that do have a free press have saintly government officials who are above such deception through a rock-solid moral compass that keeps them on the straight and narrow. Rather it is that the temptation to be opportunistically economical with the truth is dampened by the knowledge that if (when) lies are found out, there will be real consequences for the deceiver. The Watergate Affair and the Clinton and Trump Impeachments are but some well-known examples of facts being dramatically tested independently. If such a threat does not exist, facts – real or imagined, which one only some officials will know for certain – become a movable feast.

If the leading world media in the US no longer thought their role was to parse facts by verification and instead considered themselves merely as an indiscriminate hatch for news, it is *unlikely that the Khashoggi Affair would have dominated the news agenda for any amount of time. Where facts are merely items of propaganda or entertainment, whether something is true or not hasn't got much excitement value.*

As it was, the unfolding facts certainly had an effect on US politics. This proved to be low-hanging fruit to Turkey, a country where the AKP regime fights investigative journalists with the full force of the state. The Erdoğan regime also laid its hands on the largest trove of Khashoggi facts (after Saudi Arabia) that it could produce, spin and withdraw as desired. Saudi Arabia's responses are equally illuminating, as indeed are those of the US and other Western governments.

Even so, it should be borne in mind that the core forensic question behind this part is – did Khashoggi die around 13.25pm or much later. If much later, it is virtually certain that he was brutally tortured before being assassinated.

* * *

Those standing outside the Saudi consulate, including Turan Kişlakçi, knew next to nothing on 3 October. Kişlakçi said, 'We believe he's still inside. There was no sign that he was taken out in a black car or something. Maybe they are interrogating him'. According to Kişlakçi, 'His fiancée's father pressured him to get the relevant documents to initiate the official marriage process in Turkey. His trusted Saudi friends in the US gave him assurance. He was confident in what he was doing.'

But al-Jazeera, the TV station based in Qatar, was now reporting that Khashoggi had been abducted. Some seventy thousand tweets were discussing his disappearance – though many said they doubted Saudi involvement, alleging a conspiracy between Turkey and the Muslim Brotherhood to defame the kingdom.

Others, though, were already pointing the finger at MBS. One commentator wrote: 'If news of abducting Jamal Khashoggi is true, it will be one of the biggest follies of Mohammed bin Salman. The man has an international standing and reputation. It will not go unnoticed.'

Another, quoting a source who claimed to be close to the royal court, said that Khashoggi had indeed been abducted and was smuggled into Saudi Arabia arriving there in the early hours.

'If it is true, it would be difficult to imagine Turkey standing idly by while Mohammed bin Salman is playing with its sovereignty before the world,' the tweet read.

Hatice Cengiz was now beside herself with worry and spoke to the media.

'I don't know what has happened to him,' she said. 'I can't even guess how such a thing can happen to him. There is no law or lawsuit against him. He is not a suspect, he has not been convicted. There is nothing against him. He is just a man whose country doesn't like his writings or his opinions.'

The Turkish government still had no answers to what had happened with

Khashoggi either. A Turkish security official was quoted as saying they were in discussion with the Saudis and believed that Khashoggi was still being held in the consulate.

Further to the questions, Saudi Arabia sent a statement to Associated Press, saying 'Mr. Khashoggi visited the consulate to request paperwork related to his marital status and exited shortly thereafter. The government of Saudi Arabia follows up diligently on any reports related to the safety of any of its citizens and will continue to follow up on these reports'.

Turkey's concept of what had happened in the consulate was confirmed by President Erdoğan's own office and contradicted the Saudi statement. 'According to the information that we have, this Saudi citizen is still in the Saudi Arabian consulate in Istanbul,' said Ibrahim Kalin, Turkey's presidential spokesperson on 3 October at a press conference.

'We don't have any information to the contrary. We continue to follow this issue closely.'

Echoing MBS's statement to Bloomberg on 3 October, Saudi authorities issued a statement flatly denying Khashoggi was being detained, and claiming that he 'visited the consulate and exited shortly thereafter'. It was technically true.

Meanwhile the *Washington Post* issued another statement concerning the fate of its blogger in the night of 2 October.

'We have been unable to reach Khashoggi today and are very concerned about where he may be,' said Eli Lopez, a senior Global Opinions editor at the online newspaper. 'It would be unfair and outrageous if he has been detained for his work as a journalist and commentator.'

Press calls and emails to Saudi missions in London, Washington, and Istanbul yielded no further information about Jamal.

After the Saudi radio silence to inter-government telephone calls on the evening of 2 October, the Turkish government tried to apply pressure behind the scenes.

Hakan Fidan, Turkey's powerful secret-service chief rang the 'head of the Kingdom of Saudi Arabia', demanding Khashoggi's return. Non-aligned Turkish website jonturk.tr would report in March 2019 the rumour that Fidan and MBS had had a stormy exchange during which Fidan asked for Khashoggi's body and MBS abruptly ended the call saying that he would put Fidan on his black list.

The official stance of Saudi Arabia slightly shifted, with the state-run Saudi Press Agency providing an official update at 5.14am in the morning of 4 October: 'The consulate has confirmed that it is co-ordinating with the brotherly local Turkish authorities in the follow-up procedures to reveal the circumstances surrounding the disappearance of citizen Jamal Khashoggi after having left the consulate building.'

Next Saudi ambassador Elkereiji was summoned to the Turkish foreign ministry to clear up the matter. Despite Aktay's call to him on 2 October Elkereiji told the

Turkish deputy foreign minister that he had no information about the missing journalist. 'We are investigating,' he said. 'I will convey any information we get.' In Riyadh a Saudi under-secretary spoke to Turkish ambassador Erdoğan Kök.

The Saudis used the situation to cause further confusion. Some Saudi officials leaked that Khashoggi never entered the consulate. Others claimed he entered and then left. In effect, they were implying that Hatice Cengiz, who had dropped him off at the consulate, was confused at best or at worst making it all up to cause trouble.

The Turkish police continued their work on the case. 'The missing persons department has launched an investigation upon the application of Jamal Khashoggi's family,' reported the Kemalist opposition newspaper *Sözcü* ('the advocate'). 'Police teams have launched a broad investigation to find Khashoggi, primarily analysing city surveillance footage.'

There was still the suggestion of sweeping access to the Saudi consulate sanctioned by the palace. In the wide-ranging Bloomberg interview of 3 October MBS had already given his personal promise to allow such access. Calling Khashoggi a friend to indicate his close personal interest in the matter, MBS said, 'Yes, he's not inside.' This was not a lie, as revelations in the case would prove. But what followed would neither happen according to the letter nor the spirit of cooperation his words promised. He guaranteed that, though the 'premises are sovereign territory', he would 'allow [the Turkish government] to enter and search and do whatever they want to do.'

Social media users were not convinced, however, and continued to say – as the Turkish government did – that Khashoggi was being held at the Saudi consulate.

Others speculated he had been smuggled back into Saudi Arabia. Khashoggi's personal website, to which Cengiz had access, bore a banner headline saying: 'Khashoggi has been arrested at the Saudi consulate in Istanbul!'

The Saudi Arabian authorities issued an official statement denying (truthfully, albeit economical with the truth since Kashoggi had been assassinated the previous day) he was being detained at their Istanbuli consulate. Supporters and bots continued arguing on Arab social media that the whole story had been made up to smear the kingdom.

Cengiz was adamant, however, saying: 'We want to know his whereabouts. Where is Jamal? We want him to come out of the consulate safe and sound.'

She subscribed to the theory that he had been kidnapped. 'If that's not what happened, where is Jamal?' she asked. 'Right now we have no information. As a missing person, he is in danger.' She said that the Turkish authorities were working hard to locate her fiancée and wanted to believe that he had not been smuggled out of the country.

'I want to be positive, I want to be hopeful,' she said. 'I hope that Khashoggi is in Istanbul.'

Karen Attiah, Khashoggi's editor at the *Washington Post*, said the newspaper had still not been able to reach him.

'We have inquired about Jamal's whereabouts, and expressed our deep concern, to both Turkish and Saudi officials,' she said.

On Friday 5 October, the *Post* printed a blank column in the paper to show solidarity with their missing blogger. It bore Khashoggi's byline and photograph, and was headlined: 'A missing voice.'

A note from the editor read: 'Jamal Khashoggi is a Saudi journalist and author, and a *Washington Post* Global Opinions contributing columnist. Khashoggi's words should appear in the space above, but he has not been heard from since he entered a Saudi consulate in Istanbul for a routine consular matter on Tuesday afternoon.'

Clutching at straws given Turkey's and Saudi-Arabia's stance on investigative journalism, the *Post* called on the crown prince to 'do everything in his power to ensure that Mr Khashoggi is free and able to continue his work'.

In an editorial, the newspaper said: 'Mr Khashoggi is not just any commentator. Over a long career, he has had close contact with Saudi royalty and knows more than most about how they think and function. His criticism, voiced over the past year, most surely rankles Mohammed bin Salman, who was elevated to crown prince last year and has carried out a wide-ranging campaign to silence dissent while trying to modernise the kingdom. Among those in his prisons for political speech are clerics, bloggers, journalists and activists. He imprisoned women who agitated for the right to drive, a right that was granted even as they were punished.'

The *Post*'s editorial board also made a direct appeal to MBS: 'The crown prince has been all over the US preaching his vision of a more modern Saudi society, breaking out of the stale old religious codes and practices, opening up to foreign entertainment and investment. If he is truly committed to this, he will welcome constructive criticism from patriots such as Mr Khashoggi.'

Journalists from Turan Kişlakçi's Turkish-Arab Journalists' Association meanwhile staged a protest outside the Saudi consulate in Istanbul.

'We demand the immediate release of Jamal Khashoggi, who we think is being "hosted" at the consulate building in Istanbul, or the revealing of his whereabouts,' said Kişlakçi. 'If they do not release him we will stand here for weeks and months. We will stage the same demonstrations of solidarity not just here but everywhere in the world.'

The New York-based group Human Rights Watch took a keen interest. Middle-East director Sarah Leah Whitson said: 'If Saudi authorities surreptitiously detained Khashoggi it would be yet another escalation of Crown Prince Mohammed bin Salman's reign of repression against peaceful dissidents and critics. The burden of proof is on Saudi Arabia to produce evidence for its claim that Khashoggi left the consulate alone, and that Saudi agents have not detained him.'

At this point, however, MBS seemed to hold all the cards. Without further information the media cyclone would soon pass.

II
'Friends'

In the Bloomberg interview of Wednesday night 3 October, Crown Prince Mohammed bin Salman had volunteered part-definitive part-vague information on Khashoggi's whereabouts.

'If he's in Saudi Arabia, I would know that,' MBS had answered confidently. It was impossible to verify.

Yet, contradicting the words of Khashoggi's fiancée who had been waiting outside the consulate's front door, MBS said, 'My understanding is he entered and he got out after a few minutes or one hour'. But he also equivocated about this, adding, 'I'm not sure'.

'We are investigating this through the foreign ministry to see exactly what happened at that time'.

Amiably, he directed subtle responsibility for the fate of his 'friend' (his own words) Khashoggi at Turkey. 'We hear the rumours about what happened,' said MBS. 'He's a Saudi citizen and we are very keen to know what happened to him. And we will continue our dialogue with the Turkish government to see what happened to Khashoggi there.'

The crown prince used the rest of the Bloomberg interview both to brandish his profile as a new broom and as a conservative, while dispatching any criticism of him personally as a consequence of the machinations of the kingdom's enemies.

'I didn't call myself a reformer of Saudi Arabia,' he said. 'I am the crown prince of Saudi Arabia and I am trying to do the best that I can do through my position.'

He addressed the arrest of women's rights activists in his kingdom and accused them of espionage. It was the same blame-the-foreigner strategy that the profiles in support of him used on social media.

'They have connections with agencies of other countries,' he said, naming Iran and Qatar. 'They have a network, connection with government people, leaking information for the sake of these other governments.' The activists, who had been calling for women's right to drive, had not been formally charged and were denied contact with their families following their arrest five months earlier, or so he said.

MBS also spoke about Donald Trump.

This was interesting with hindsight The interview took place a day after Saudi operatives moved against Khashoggi: a journalist for a major US newspaper; a US resident; and a US-citizen applicant. MBS's deep commitment to a close and productive relationship with President Trump was a public secret after Trump's extravagant first presidential visit abroad to King Salman and MBS. While Riyadh was never going to tip off frenemy Turkey of the plot, it was possible but not exactly probable that the move across Trump's bow was made without at least partial sounding out of the White House powers that be that Khashoggi was a person of interest to the Saudi state.

On exactly the same day Khashoggi was lured into the consulate and assassinated, the US president himself had, in an extraordinary statement, brought up his new Saudi friends. He said at a political rally in Mississippi:

'We protect Saudi Arabia. Would you say they're rich? And I love the king, King Salman. But I said "King – we're protecting you – you might not be there for two weeks without us – you have to pay".'

Donald Trump's statement was so curious and out of place that it became instant global news. Like Vladimir Putin's unscripted reflection on 'traitors' the next day, it was an uncanny coincidence.

In response to Trump's outburst, MBS was adamant to Bloomberg that the Saudi royal family were no puppets of the US. He smoothly brushed off Trump's comment.

'We believe that all the armaments we have from the United States of America are paid for, it's not free armament,' said MBS, focusing on Trump's suggestion that the US paid for the Saudi military. 'So ever since the relationship started between Saudi Arabia and the United States of America, we've bought everything with money.' Warmly MBS went on to express his delight with fellow billionaire Donald Trump to Bloomberg's journalists.

Trump was no stranger to Saudi Arabia. He had registered eight companies in the home town of Khashoggi's family, the Saudi beach resort Jeddah, after MBS's $500 billion bonanza to turn Saudi Arabia's Red-Sea coastline into a holiday destination and shortly after launching his presidential campaign. Trump already had a hotel bearing his name in neighbouring UAE.

'I love working with him,' MBS gushed about his new-found billionaire friend of March 2017. Like Khashoggi, Trump was a critical friend, though, and MBS observed smoothly, 'You know, you have to accept that any friend will say good things and bad things. If you look at the picture overall, you have 99 per cent of good things and one bad issue.' He had sounded a lot more measured about 'friend' Jamal, but the Bloomberg journalists left it at that.

Then, on Friday night 5 October at around 11pm, everything changed with a media leak to a young PhD student at Brown University's Watson Institute in Washington, DC. It was the first semi-official sign that, whatever had happened to Jamal Khashoggi, it was not good – 'and by not good, I mean terrible.' Selim Sazak, a smiling, pleasant-looking, round-faced, well-dressed 2015 Fulbright scholar and researcher at NATO, posted these words on Twitter ('studies things that blow up', according to his handle until May 2019). He said that a senior Turkish official had gave him this information about his friend and neighbour in Tysons Corner.

Instead of a hostage situation or a rendition of Khashoggi, his words placed the events at the consulate in an entirely different class. They were taking on the appearance of a secret execution by a state of one of its citizens on hostile soil of the kind that had happened almost seven months ago to the day in Britain when Russian secret-service agents sought to assassinate Sergei Skripal and his daughter. Britain had not been able to prevent the attack in Salisbury, and nor had Turkey known about the strike against Khashoggi it seemed from Sazak's words. Many more leaks by Turkish officials would percolate hereafter, all similar in that they were highly suggestive but not necessarily forensically detailed.

Who else knew more, the media was keen to know? US intelligence knew at least as early as the beginning of September that Khashoggi's rendition was being mooted, the *Washington Post* reported. So did GCHQ in Cheltenham. Had either of those two shared information with others?

'We were initially made aware that something was going in the first week of September, around three weeks before Mr Khashoggi walked into the consulate on 2 October, though it took more time for other details to emerge', a 'highly placed' intelligence source leaked to the long-standing and well-connected security editor Marco Giannangeli at the *Sunday Express* on 29 October.

Either way, the GCHQ intercepts of the rendition left little to the imagination that force would be used against Khashoggi by the Saudis. 'These details included primary orders to capture Mr Khashoggi and bring him back to Saudi Arabia for questioning. However, the door seemed to be left open for alternative remedies to what was seen as a big problem', the senior British intelligence source leaked.

III
Five Eyes

⁓

What did these intercepts actually mean to people working in British intelligence – or US intelligence for that matter? Intelligence gatherers are 'in pursuit of information, rather than evidence'. They don't find a neat email with a blue-print, arrows, operatives and goals. It is a game of inferences and statistics. 'There is rarely a definitive point at which "enough" intelligence has been harvested.' 'There comes a time when an intelligence service or operative simply has to make a stab at assimilating what all this means.' These quotes were the conclusions by Callamard's UN delegation after having gone through all the Khashoggi intelligence intercepts Callamard had been given (detail 39).

GCHQ had intercepted Khashoggi's rendition information in early September from the 3 quintillion bytes flitting around the world every day. It had caught GCHQ's fine-grained cyber net to identify threats to the UK that it shared it with the nations who were part of the Five Eyes Alliance, the intelligence-pooling club formed in 1941 by the US, UK, Canada, Australia and New Zealand. 'Five Eyes coverage of the world is pretty impressive. The alliance is electronically promiscuous – if I can put it like that. It hoovers up gigabytes of stuff each day that is then fed through their computers looking for patterns,' said a former senior security expert with experience of No 10-level clearance and daily assessment of intelligence reports who was interviewed for this book.

In other words, intelligence services have to act 'in anticipation of an event' as the UN report stated. British intelligence had to anticipate and pursue information that predicted behaviour that would need to be pre-empted. British intelligence wasn't going to let the Saudi government undertake a clandestine special operation on its territory.

It is clear that the contents of the intercepts raised fears that London could be targeted as a location for Khashoggi's abduction in the way the Russians had used London for their unfinished business with former KGB colonel Litvinenko and Salisbury for former GRU colonel Skripal. Although it might never happen in the case of Khashoggi, this was the event it worried about. Khashoggi had made his self-exile very public on 18 September 2017, and wrote critically about the Yemen war in which the UK arms industry supplied billions worth of weapons to Saudi Arabia (£4.7bn-worth would be stopped by the Court of Appeal on 20 June 2019). After his intelligence posting at the Saudi embassy in

London and years of writing for London-based Arab publications, Khashoggi was a regular visitor to the UK. He had stayed for weeks when he was first contemplating moving to the US or Turkey in April 2017 and also in July that year when having dinner at central-London's Clos Maggiore restaurant.

While some intelligence fears and patterns may prove to be chimaera, such as the Weapons of Mass Destruction in Iraq, the Saudi rendition plot of Khashoggi would turn out to be, in fact, real and trigger-ready. In Riyadh, the Saudis were actively looking for a suitable foreign location to deploy their rendition team against Jamal. 'The fact that a team was put together and operational within 48 hours tends to point to a "Special Operation" scenario, with core team members already appointed and in place, ready to act whenever the order comes. Such a level of preparation is unlikely to have occurred otherwise.' This is what the UN delegation concluded in its report having reviewed the forensic evidence and interviewed experts (detail 199).

The first red flag for British intelligence was hoovered up as early as 24 September when the Middle East Monitor put on the website of its PLO conference, 'A late addition to the line-up of speakers is Jamal Khashoggi, Saudi journalist and the former editor-in-chief of al-Arab News Channel'. Khashoggi's presence at the high-profile conference could not do anything else but lock London into the rendition matrix GCHQ had uncovered earlier in the month.

Was this, then, the moment British intelligence assimilated all the information at its disposal and decided to act and prevent another Skripal-style attack from happening? According to the senior security expert interviewed for this book, it would have prompted an immediate interdiction. 'I have no doubt that our people would have known that something by the Saudis might be going down in London and suggested that the dirty work should be done elsewhere. That's how it works.'

British intelligence continued to be on high alert about a possible cloak-and-dagger operation on British soil. Anything could happen during this four-day visit. First, Khashoggi flew into Heathrow in the late afternoon on Friday. This would have raised another set of flags. Since four fifths of the 9/11 attackers were Saudi, special attention was paid to who goes where when. From Khashoggi's Turkish Airlines flight details and his hotel reservation at the Ambassador Bloomsbury hotel by the PLO conference organisers, it was clear that he would be in Britain for four days from Friday to Monday evening. 'Air travel is subject to a whole load of checks since 9/11. Saudi spooks would alarm the system pretty damn quick', said the senior expert interviewed for this book. Given the high profile of the British attendees at the conference, it seems likely MI5 agents covered the conference. If so, it would also be likely they were aware of any Saudi agents tracking Khashoggi's movement from his arrival on Friday.

More flags soon appeared like poppies in Spring. As the UN team observed, intelligence services are not omniscient. What they spy is unusual details which they then try to interpret together with other snippets and details. While GCHQ/Langley don't make the data they gather a matter of public record, we can nonetheless reconstruct what the unfolding plot looked like from their end with the information gathered in the 2019 UN report.

The first movement was of two Saudi secret-service personnel travelling to Riyadh on Saturday at 3.15pm, shortly followed by others at 5.15pm (UN detail 81; *Sabah* reported in 2018 that al-Muzaini, the Saudi chief-of-station in Istanbul, had travelled back to Riyadh from Istanbul's Sabihah Gökçen Airport. The Turkish government paper had CC-TV grabs of him arriving at the departures lounge at 2.33pm).

Everything remained peaceful, however, on the London-front from Friday to Sunday. Nothing untoward happened to Khashoggi while he was attending the conference. But things started moving again on Khashoggi's last day, Monday 1 October, when he was due to fly out at 10pm in the evening on Turkish Airlines.

To start with there was al-Muzaini's flag. His flight back to Istanbul was booked for Monday.

But on his scheduled Saudia flight SV263 (leaving Riyadh at 11.10am and arriving at 3.25pm in Istanbul, ten hours before Khashoggi's arrival) were also three members of MBS's personal Tiger Team – major-general Abahussein, lieutenant al-Arifi and intelligence officer al-Zahrani – with at least one additional consular security staff member who had left for Riyadh on Saturday (detail 82, flight S'F'263 there) as well.

There were also three more of MBS's Tiger Team operatives on flights from Riyadh. They were scheduled to arrive two hours before Khashoggi's Turkish Airlines plane touched down at 4am in Istanbul – lieutenant al-Bostani, al-Hawsawi, Khaled al Otaibi.

As British intelligence feared, the Saudis had pressed the nuclear button after all and were now now in pursuit of Khashoggi, who was still in London.

'On 1 October we became aware of the movement of a group, which included members of [the Saudi secret service] to Istanbul, and it was pretty clear what their aim was', the highly-placed British source also told Marco Giannangeli, the defence and diplomatic editor of the *Sunday Express*.

MI6's response was immediate. 'Through channels we warned [Saudi intelligence] that this was not a good idea', the source said. The attack plans, whatever they were exactly, would have to be stopped was the message.

Nothing happened and Khashoggi left Heathrow unharmed. But suddenly a massive alarm bell went off while Khashoggi was heading for Heathrow.

A flight plan and passenger manifest with nine Tiger Team operatives on a private jet heading to Istanbul was filed with the European Organisation for the Safety of Air Navigation at 8.30pm UK time. It was amended an hour later at

9.23pm to insert diplomatic cover subject to Eurocontrol rules (UN report detail 86).

The passenger manifest included two people who were linked to Khashoggi through his work for Saudi intelligence – brigadier-general Maher Mutreb and major Badr al-Otaibi (detail 87) – and four linked directly to MBS.

By the time of Khashoggi's departure, it was virtually certain that Saudi Arabia was flexing its intelligence muscle and that Khashoggi was the intended target. While a Saudi plan to move against Khashoggi on British soil had been stopped in its tracks, he was now likely going to be intercepted somewhere in Istanbul.

As indeed proved to be the case. 'Subsequent events show that our warning was ignored', the *Sunday Express*'s intelligence source observed drily.

The UN delegation's audio access in 2019 to secret recordings of secure telephone calls inside the consulate made transparent what the plot looked like from the Saudi organisers point of view.

Seizing the moment, Saudi intelligence was indeed poised to strike. The theatre of its rendition plot was picked on Friday afternoon just before Khashoggi headed for Heathrow.

The selection of the moment and the location was, however, down to sheer chance.

The first call to alert Riyadh of Khashoggi's consular visit was made by Istanbul Saudi security attaché Saad al-Qarni without orders precedent to do so that Friday 5 October.

He said, among other related things, to Maher Mutreb at 2.27pm while Khashoggi's plane for London was still taxiing, 'we did not receive any letter from our service regarding whether there is any problem or not on him' (detail 27).

When questioned in the UK Parliament on the 29 October report in the *Sunday Express*, foreign secretary Jeremy Hunt replied, 'But, I did not know about this attack.' He had previously said 'It is not possible for a foreign secretary or indeed any minister to comment on intelligence matters.'

British intelligence's decision to inform the Saudis but not their US colleagues would have been congruent with the decision of Trump administration officials not to forewarn its resident of the impending plot. If GCHQ had shared that 'alternative remedies' for 'a big problem' had become a fact on the ground, the Trump administration would almost have no escape from its duty to warn Jamal. At least from September, Trump intelligence staffers were sailing into potentially very tricky legal territory by not sharing with Khashoggi its internally widely circulated intel that Saudi Arabia was about to make a move.

The decision to keep information from a US resident would look curious if something did happen and it ever came to light – even if no one would ever believe that President Trump's verbal attack on Saudi Arabia the day after the rendition was somehow connected through real-time knowledge. The US excuse wrote itself if Khashoggi vanished without a trace after his rendition – which is after all the point. In case of a lawful arrest, there was no duty on the US intelligence services to pre-warn a US resident. And who would know for sure in the case of a ghostly disappearance?

But the optics would be less convincing if the rendition came to light. At worst, it would start to look like tacit approval of the extraordinary rendition of a US journalist and resident by the Trump administration.

As the latter situation obtained, Trump officials were in the end forced to defend themselves from breaching US government order ICD19. Their excuse, cast in serpentine language, boiled down to the argument that it wasn't clear whether Khashoggi would be lawfully arrested or illegally detained or killed. Khashoggi himself had repeatedly asked Saudi officials in the US whether there was a Saudi warrant for his arrest, which suggests that he had a good grasp of the far-reaching implications of such a warrant had on his safety abroad.

Apart from many other things, there was no upside for US intelligence to share its August/September intercepts with NATO ally Turkey. Nor in embarrassing MBS, an otherwise enthusiastic ally of the US and President Donald Trump, who was nurturing an order book of $350bn with the kingdom.

On NBC's Meet the Press on 26 June 2019 Donald Trump would inflate this figure to '$400 to $450 billion over a period of time' and diminish the importance of the Khashoggi affair by saying 'It has been heavily investigated... I have seen so many reports', prompting the presenter to say 'you'll overlook some of this behaviour'.

There was also the Kurdish situation in Turkey's neighbour Syria where Trump and their NATO ally Erdoğan were on opposing sides. And there was the fact that President Erdoğan had seriously irked Trump by not releasing Andrew Brunson, a US pastor Turkey had held captive since the military putsch against Erdoğan in the summer of 2016. He had been charged with being a member of the Gülenist Terror Group (FETÖ) in Turkey's Izmir province and with spying for them and convicted to three years imprisonment. Brunson's wrongful arrest was a cause célèbre among Trump's religious conservative supporters.

Following Trump's angry tweets against Turkey on the subject of Brunson, there was little love lost in Washington for the obstinate Erdoğan who refused to release the pastor. Earlier Trump had imposed drastic sanctions that made the Turkish lira plummet by 45 per cent in August 2018.

One suggested reason (by *Forbes* writer Melik Kaylan) for Erdoğan's intransigence in the Brunson case was the corruption file the US was gathering for sanctions against specific Turkish people under the 2012 Magnitsky Act. They included Erdoğan's confidants and family members. More to the point, the file included phone-taps of President Erdoğan himself telling his son to stash away millions of Euros around the house. The phone-taps had been certified as admissible evidence in a 2017 court case against a Turco-Iranian trader called Reza Zarrab. According to the *Forbes* writer, Erdoğan had no intention of budging until his associates and family members were taken off the US sanctions list which made them financial pariahs. It was worth infuriating Trump as Brunson was Erdoğan's bargaining chip.

IV
Who Benefits?

ஒ

Karl Marx asked the question 'who benefits?' – as indeed did lawyers in ancient Rome, *cui bono* – when reconstructing the causes of historical events. Setting aside the question whether or not they interfered with events around Jamal Khashoggi's rendition, the leader of one particular country certainly benefitted from the furore that ensued. He also had a long-standing very effective policy of causing the US to tailspin.

When Vladimir Putin spoke about the Khashoggi case at the Valdai Discussion conference of 18 October in the Black-sea beach resort Sochi, he had echoed Donald Trump's own official response to the murder mystery. Vladimir Putin declined to promise action or sanctions against Saudi Arabia when asked this question by Raghida Dergham, a former colleague of Khashoggi's at *al-Hayat* where he had his column until 2016. Putin agreed with Trump that more facts were needed about Saudi governmental involvement before taking measures against the kingdom as a whole.

'We first need to wait for the results of the investigation' to conclude who is behind the assassination, Putin said.

'How can we, as Russia, start to harm our relationship with Saudi Arabia without knowing what really happened?'

Putin went on gleefully to draw a comparison between Khashoggi and the poisoning in Salisbury with *novichok*, the top-secret state-of-the-art Russian chemical nerve agent, of Sergei Skripal, his daughter, detective sergeant Nick Bailey, Charley Rowley, as well as the agonising death of Dawn Sturgess, a little over two months earlier in Britain.

Complaining bitterly about US and European sanctions against Russia over the Salisbury *novichok* attack he argued, 'There's no proof with regards to Russia, but steps are taken.' The *novichok* sanctions against Russia were unfair, unjust and unfounded in other words. There was no solid proof that either he, his associates, or Russia, had anything to do with the top-secret state-of-the-art poison. Or at any rate, not more proof than there was in the Khashoggi case.

The facts in Jamal Khashoggi's case were really no different from the Skripal one, he claimed. 'Here, people say that a murder happened in Istanbul, but no steps are taken [against Saudi Arabia]. People need to figure out a single approach to these kinds of problems', he said exquisitely needling the West. It wasn't equitable for the US and UK to blame Russia for the deployment of a secret Russian-state nerve-agent on foreign soil. 'Enough evidence' was required, Putin said, pleading for fair treatment of Russian behaviour.

Other countries without a free media formed a chorus line behind Putin's complaint that the Skripal sanctions against Russia were unjust. A Chinese media outlet helpfully connected the dots made by the Russian president. Eager to make clear that 'citizens' rights' were no more than a cudgel of West democracies to bully other countries around the world, the Chinese outlet commented sourly that it 'shows that there are double, even multiple standards for the West's human rights diplomacy'.

In a further dig Putin went on to say that, 'the US bears a certain responsibility' for the assassination of Jamal Khashoggi.

Putin clarified that he really did mean genuine responsibility rather than merely moral responsibility: 'we can see that complicated processes are also taking place within the US elites', he spelled out. He had evidence, in other words, that the US was not blameless either in what had happened to Jamal Khashoggi.

Drily he concluded, 'I hope America will not go as far as Saudi Arabia did.' If it wasn't a slip of the tongue, it was a peculiar throwaway comment.

He had said moments ago there was 'not enough evidence' that Riyadh was behind Khashoggi's assassination, whereas now he seemed to imply he knew that Saudi Arabia was the culprit.

There were other reasons why Putin cared deeply about the way Turkey saw the Khashoggi Affair and would want to influence the outcome in a way favourable to Russia.

Erdoğan was more than Putin's Black Sea neighbour. He also controlled Putin's one and only warm-water shipping and naval route. It ran from Ukrain's Crimean ports through the Bosphorus to the Mediterranean. This maritime route was so strategically important to Russia's defence and commerce that Putin didn't think twice about occupying Ukraine's Black-Sea ports when the EU got within an inch of bringing Ukraine into its fold in 2014.

Erdoğan was also a member of NATO. Putin would do anything to peal him away from that military alliance and draw Erdoğan ever closer into his own orbit. Rossatom, owned by one of Putin's oligarchs, was already building Turkey's first nuclear reactor in Akkuyu.

As, the *Moscow Times* wrote on 15 April 2019 in a candid appraisal of Putin's most recent handiwork, 'Without firing a single shot, deploying a single tank or using a single internet troll, Moscow can soon destroy the unity of NATO by removing a key country from its military network.'

The prize the *Moscow Times* referred to was Turkey's out-dated air-defence system.

As part of its upgrade, Turkey had committed itself to buying 100 F-35 fighter jets from Lockheed at $70 million each. It was only because its air defence was wired into NATO that Erdoğan could make the purchase.

A few months before October 2018, the Turkish air force had taken possession of the first one on 17 June, though their F-35 wasn't allowed to leave the US just yet. But it was available for training Turkish fighter pilots. The deal was worth $8bn and up to 7 per cent of F-35 parts would be made in Turkey since it was one of the eleven countries investing in the state-of-the-art fighter jet. Turkey's upgrade within the NATO pact seemed a done deal.

But Erdoğan was at the same time looking to update Turkey's antiquated anti-air missiles and had ordered China's FD-2000 missile defence system in 2015. Since its integration with the F-35 would be tantamount to handing secret fighter data to China, the Obama administration had kiboshed the Chinese deal and forced Turkey to reopen its air-defence tender.

Aggravating his NATO partners, Erdoğan had thereupon picked Putin's long-range s-400 system. It meant that secret F-35 data would now be shared with Russia instead of China once Turkey got the fighter jets.

As the Khashoggi Affair began, the Trump administration was pressuring Turkey to cancel the order for the s-400 system and pick a NATO supplier: either the US Patriot system or the Franco-Italian Eurosam. But, unlike the Obama administration, it would be spectacularly unsuccessful in making Erdoğan leap through this hoop.

Three weeks after Turkey started the drip-drip of fly-on-the-wall details of Khashoggi's assassination, Erdoğan's defence minister Hulusi Akar all of a sudden confirmed that Turkey's order for four s-400 units at $2.5bn from Rosoboronexport, Russia's main arms-export agency, would go ahead. The s-400s would be on Turkish soil from October 2019.

Was there a sweetener that Putin shared with Erdoğan during this time that clinched the deal? Was it connected to the Khashoggi Affair? It seemed like it.

As a countermove, the Trump administration halted the delivery of all F-35s to Erdoğan in April 2019 and removed Turkey entirely from the F-35 programme in July the same year and kept the $1.3 billion Erdoğan had already paid.

In a widening of the rift with its NATO ally, Biden imposed sanctions on Turkey under the Countering America's Adversaries Through Sanctions Act (CAATSA) in 2020.

Was it detailed knowledge of what happened to Khashoggi in the consulate that he shared with Erdoğan? It would certainly explain Turkey's sudden confidence in setting demands on Saudi Arabia over the first weekend after Khashoggi's assassination.

If Putin did have such knowledge, trading it to Erdoğan would have another side effect. Given Khashoggi's US-Saudi connections, strengthening Erdoğan's hand would also aggravate the dysfunctional relationship between the Trump administration and Congress, and put pressure on the US relationship with Saudi Arabia.

Putin was a master at such intrigue. The Mueller investigation laid bare on 18 April 2019 how astutely Russia operated with regards to the US.

Russia had gathered secret intelligence on Hillary Clinton which it filtered to the Trump campaign via Julian Assange's Wikileaks on 16 March 2016. This occurred promptly after Donald Trump asked for it publicly during a campaign stunt on 3 March.

Russia's swift response to Trump's request undermined the US's political stability for three years: not least once again through the publication of proof of Russia's actions detailed in the Mueller Report of May 2019. Donald Trump himself reignited the issue on 13 June that year as to whether he would accept damaging information on a Democratic candidate from a foreign power: 'It's not an interference. They have information. I think I'd take it.'

V
Thunderbolt

◊

On 6 October, at 11pm the Turkish government followed up its leak to PhD student Selim Sazak with the first climactic leak to international-news agency Reuters. Turkey's 'we don't have any information' stance was replaced from one day to the next with 20/20 vision. How was that possible?

'The initial assessment of the Turkish police is that Mr Khashoggi has been killed at the consulate of Saudi Arabia in Istanbul,' two anonymous Turkish officials told the news agency. 'We believe that the murder was premeditated and the body was subsequently moved out of the consulate.'

Suddenly the fact that Turkey thought (and therefore had precise information on what had gone on inside the consulate) that Khashoggi's fate was premeditated murder hit the international media like a thunderbolt.

Hatice Cengiz was aghast and found the new twist to the story hard to believe. She tweeted, 'Khashoggi was not killed and I cannot believe he was killed!' She later added that she was waiting for official confirmation from the Turkish government of the leaks by its officials.

The *Washington Post* editors gave the news report credence in Saturday's paper of 6 October. 'If the reports of Jamal's murder are true, it is a monstrous and unfathomable act,' said Fred Hiatt, the *Washington Post*'s editorial page editor. 'Khashoggi was – or, as we hope, is – a committed, courageous journalist.'

Suddenly, over the course of a few hours, Saudi Arabia was on the back foot. Saudi officials continued to claim that Khashoggi entered the consulate but left shortly afterwards. But they released no CC-TV footage to back up the claim.

'Entries and exits into the embassy, airport transits and all camera records are being looked at and followed. We want to swiftly get results', President Erdoğan officially told Reuters himself on Sunday 7 October. But he also moved his language away from Khashoggi being detained at the consulate – the version his spokesperson Ibrahim Kalin had previously presented. 'I hope we will not be faced with a situation that we do not want,' he said, describing Khashoggi as 'a friend' and 'a journalist I have known for a long time' – it was not clear whether they could communicate in the same language since Khashoggi spoke no Turkish.

He had added, 'My expectation is still positive'. Erdoğan's words allowed Turkey to step back from the information Turkish officials had leaked 'unofficially' to Reuters. He was not truthful in hindsight. There was no 'positive' outcome for Khashoggi and Erdoğan knew it when he spoke those words.

Erdoğan's personal advisor, Yasin Aktay, however, heralded to the Saudis what would later become Turkey's new public version of the events at the consulate. That Sunday, he presented a hunch to CNN Turk – no longer owned by CNN but bought in March 2018 with a state loan by AKP-cheerleader, the Demirören group, also owner of Turkish newspapers *Milliyet* ('nationality') and *Hürriyet* ('liberty') – 'My sense is that he has been killed. The Saudis are saying we can come investigate, but they have of course disposed of the body.'

He threatened, 'There is concrete information; it will not remain an unsolved case. If they consider Turkey to be as it was in the 1990s, they are mistaken.'

The information leaked to Khashoggi's friend Turan Kışlakçi of the Turkish-Arab Journalists' Association who was a further degree removed from Ankara officialdom, went yet another step further in contradicting what Ankara had said so far.

'It is certain that he was killed,' he said on the same day as Aktay, reporting that 'lower officials' had leaked to him that Turkey had evidence that his friend had been murdered in a 'barbaric' way, made to 'faint', and 'dismembered'. The officials had told him, 'make your funeral preparations'.

The Turkish authorities had not yet officially produced any statements to support claims that Khashoggi had been assassinated. Unofficially authorities were leaking, however, that details of their investigations would be made public in the days ahead.

Nor had President Erdoğan publicly challenged Riyadh. Turkish diplomats were trying to keep the fallout 'under control' behind the scenes. Saudi Arabia and Turkey could still find a solution together. That is to say, Ankara would agree to sweep the new information Turkey had about Khashoggi's assassination under the carpet as long as the terms reached with Saudi were right.

VI
Meticulous Planning

At this stage, Saudi Arabia had to assume Turkey knew certain things for a fact. Security officials would have access to all available surveillance data from 5.50pm on 2 October: CC-TV, airport data, consular phone records, consular car movements, etc.

But they also knew the Saudi attack itself had been operationally brilliant. Everything had depended on avoiding those disparate pieces of information from Turkish intelligence sources coming together too soon to stand in the way of the Tiger Team's objectives and before all Saudi operatives, including the local secret service staff tainted by operational knowledge, had safely been exfiltrated from Istanbul to Riyadh.

It was hardly suspicious for consulate intelligence chief al-Muzaini to fly to Riyadh for a briefing on a Saturday and back on the Monday. It was also perfectly normal for six Saudi men to fly in from Riyadh. Every day some 147 flights passing through both Riyadh and Istanbul off-loaded Saudis.

Even if Turkish intelligence had made a point of tracking the Saudi-consulate's intelligence chief's movements in real-time, it would still have been impossible to connect the six commercial arrivals to him – or indeed to Khashoggi himself. It would only be obvious if you possessed the cyber capabilities to connect the dots that the UK and US shared through the Five Eyes Alliance. 'The difference in reach and analytical power between Five Eyes and the next best is huge', said the senior security expert interviewed for this book.

For Turkish officials, the nine men on the Gulfstream would be as invisible as if they had arrived on one of the many scheduled flights from Riyadh. The arrival of Saudis on a private jet run by Prime Aviation, the largest private jet company in the Middle East with 70 per cent of the market, was hardly a reason for anyone to sit up and take notice. Still, it was important to cover all angles. Since there was a theoretical possibility that the six earlier Tiger Team arrivals might already be tracked by MİT, the Saudis checked in at different hotels to make it more difficult to make a connection between the three sub teams.

What was clever was to keep the jet on the tarmac at Atatürk Airport's Genel Havacilik private-jet terminal. Its manifest of passengers and IDs was waiting to be discovered. Planned as a 'sitting duck' it diverted attention away from the more important getaway jet. Whatever incriminating evidence had to be got out of the country could be loaded on to the latter without much risk of detection.

Furthermore, as the decoy jet had flown in under diplomatic clearance, it was almost impossible for Turkish airport authorities to prevent the plane itself and those with diplomatic clearance from taking off without good cause – unless Turkey wanted to wanted to create an international incident.

The second private Gulfstream landed in the afternoon and took-off almost immediately. It was invisible to anyone but Five Eyes, and they clearly didn't tip off Turkey either that a second jet was on its way. Without Five Eyes' help, Turkey couldn't know about the function of this jet until it was boarded for take-off by members of the Tiger Team who it had linked to the operation by having arrived on the 'sitting duck' earlier in the morning.

Invisible to the Turks until such time, this second Gulfstream IV bought time for a safe escape. Passenger manifests at Atatürk's Genel Havacilik private-jet terminal were provided on a form in hand-writing, and last-minute filing provided additional time cover. Once the operatives' passports were scanned at airport security an alert might be tripped, but Turkish authorities would still not know which plane they were on until the hand-written manifest was entered into the airport's databases.

Many incriminating items were taken back home on this jet, Turkish authorities later leaked unofficially. According to these leaks the team's luggage contained scalpels, two syringes, scissors, three staple-guns, two defibrillators, one signal jammer, ten telephones, five radios and wireless intercoms for the radios.

Even boarding a private jet with such items might cause delay if it is just a standard flight, but not if you are a diplomat and have safe passage. Brigadier-general Maher Mutreb, the man who had made the decision to kill Khashoggi at the consulate, was on this jet and travelled on a diplomatic passport.

At 5.49pm Maher Mutreb, travelling on a diplomatic passport, is frisked at Genel Havacilik's luggage-check before departure; Abahussein, al-Zahrani, al-Arifi, and al-Bostani, the last Saudi operatives leave the residence at 7.48pm (the first three have by then spent almost nine hours in the residence from 11.08am).

Certainly the getaway jet with the 'interrogation team', the operatives who had assinated Khashoggi, beat a hasty retreat. The hand-written flight manifest was filed at 6.30pm, 10 minutes after the flight's departure, thwarting detection of the operatives on board by Turkish officials – as did the Cairo destination. The jet took one of the shortest routes out of Turkish airspace from Atatürk Airport in no more than 45 minutes. Mutreb was clearly rattled by Cengiz's call and feared the possibility of being challenged by Turkish air control as the jet also 'revised its flight plan to flag the flight as diplomatic' (UN footnote 192). The 'sitting-duck' jet idled for another four hours on the tarmac, made a stop at Nallihan between Istanbul and Ankara, and then skirted along the longest flightpath through Turkish airspace for almost two hours heading for Dubai. In that lazy arc, Saudi intelligence almost thumbed its nose at MİT as the seven support operatives were ferried away.

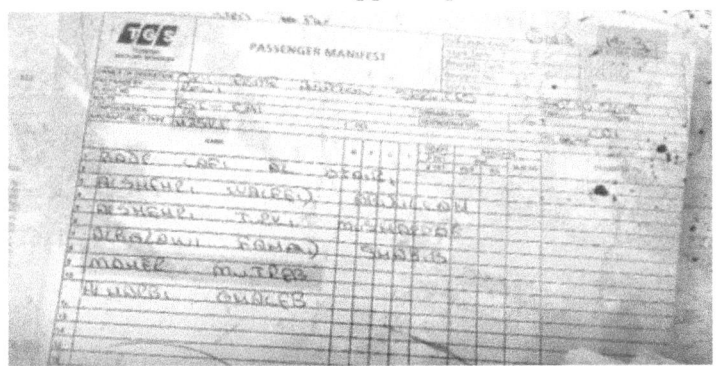

The flight manifest of HZ-SK1, timed at 6.30pm, listing:

Badr al-Otaibi, Waleed al-Sehri, Turki al-Sehri, Fahad al-Balawi, Maher Mutreb, Thaar al-Harbi.

The fact that, once Turkish intelligence had made the first match through CC-TV around the consulate to the arrival jet, they also knew that all nine men on the Gulfstream IV were hostile operatives had another consequence. It also meant that they would start to track all their movements around Istanbul against the visual data of MoBeSe CC-TV.

Isolating an operative's face on MoBeSe CC-TV didn't mean confirmation of their identity. The names of the six operatives who had arrived on commercial flights the day before would only reveal themselves with certainty once they boarded the 'sitting duck' jet to travel back at night. There was only one operative who had arrived in the morning on the jet and flew back with them – forensic pathologist Salah Tubaigy. And he was in possession of a government passport and could make an appeal for diplomatic immunity. In any case, judging by the fact that these six 'commercial flight' operatives arrived at the airport in drips and drabs in the evening at the private-jet terminal, the Saudis clearly weren't worried.

The Saudi timing worked optimally in favour of their tight operational schedule for the getaway jet, however. The six including Mutreb had gone through security 5 minutes before MİT's Khashoggi investigation started at 5.50pm. This gave the men 35 minutes to take-off and another 45 minutes to get out of Turkish airspace.

It was enough – Turkish intelligence hadn't yet connected all the dots on the evening of 2 October. The Gulfstream IV that had left Riyadh when Khashoggi called at 11 in the morning to confirm his consular appointment was treated like any business jet at Atatürk and took off without problems.

There was one loose end. Nine men had arrived on the decoy jet in morning. Six departed on the getaway jet and one – Tubaigy – flew back on the sitting duck. That meant MİT would conclude that two operatives were still at large after both jets had left Turkey.

These men left for Riyadh on a commercial flight, going through customs at 0.18am after midnight apparently without receiving any special attention from Turkish authorities. Turkish airport authorities acted only to prevent Khashoggi from being smuggled out of the country as opposed to stopping these stray Saudi operatives from leaving the country.

In fact there were four more pieces of the puzzle. Hidden among all the Turkish data was also the departure of an additional team of four conspirators propping up the operation. The consulate's secret-service chief al-Muzaini left on a commercial flight for Riyadh at 9.32pm, an hour before the 'sitting-duck' jet. Three more accredited secret-service staff at the consulate left the same evening. None would ever return to Turkey. None were prevented from leaving Turkey.

As soon as Turkey had reviewed the consulate's MoBeSe footage of thirteen cameras – how long could it have taken to review a few hours of recordings? – and had figured out that a strike team of at least fifteen men had descended on Istanbul, Turkey would also know for a fact that Khashoggi had never left the consulate from the footage. But such a negative was difficult to summarise in a concise piece of evidence.

The CC-TV footage from outside the consulate also captured a lot of car movements by consular vehicles. The same was true of the footage in front of the consul-general's residence. Both buildings had carports screened from the street, but the MoBeSe street-camera aimed at the consul-general's home also looked over the wall straight at his front door. The footage captured numerous large suitcases and bags being brought inside his home.

All this was also known as soon as the MoBeSe footage of two of the cars led Turkish analysts to the consul-general's residence. The Turkish government gave the UN investigators comprehensive access to the official footage of its MoBeSe system in 2019. In 2018, however, instead of releasing relevant clips officially to the Turkish and world media, they were given to *Sabah* newspaper only in the first week after the assassination. This made it seem to the outside world as if the paper had done its own investigation and that this explosive scoop was based on original research rather than being planted by officials. It was a strategy of divide and rule the media that all governments wishing to set the news agenda commonly use, and it proved extremely effective on this occasion.

VII
Cat and Mouse

୬

Before 11pm on Saturday 6 October, the unspoken assumption was that Khashoggi was alive. Ömer Çelik, a spokesman for AKP, the ruling Justice and Development Party, still said, as if Khashoggi had not been assassinated, 'A journalist disappearing like this in a secure country like the Republic of Turkey is something that will be followed up with sensitivity.'

Yet, while he said that publicly, Turkey certainly knew on Friday that Khashoggi was dead. On that day, Turkish officials offered in secret their version of what took place at the consulate for inter-governmental eyes only. They met with Saudi diplomats in Ankara and presented to them their conclusion that Khashoggi had been murdered at the consulate.

How do we know?

Turkey would leak this meeting to the *Wall Street Journal* three weeks later. The Saudi diplomats, the article reported, promised to relay the information to Riyadh. Even as Çelik still talked about the old version to the press that Erdoğan's spokesperson had put out there on 3 October, Turkey was waiting for the response from their Saudi counterparts.

While this made sense when it was first reported by the *Journal*. All this was, in fact, very strange.

If Erdoğan had a recording of the assassination on Tuesday, why did Turkey pretend that Khashoggi was alive only to change its mind completely to complain to Saudi diplomats on Friday. It made little sense.

Riyadh was clearly underwhelmed, too, by Turkey's mixed messages. It decided to strike back.

To the consternation of Turkish authorities and Erdoğan's fury Turkey discovered on Saturday that they weren't being taken seriously. Consul-General Mohammed al-Otaibi had invited Reuters on a televised tour of the five-storey premises at 8.17pm that day.

'The Saudis were making fun of us', a person close to Mr Erdoğan told the *Journal*, 'It was insulting'.

But was it an act of Saudi arrogance? Or was Riyadh merely convinced by now that Turkey lacked the know-how to penetrate the consulate's cyber umbrella and that Turkish officials were on a fishing expedition? In other words, was al-Otaibi instructed to call Turkey's bluff because the Friday version was different from what Turkey told the world and had, over the previous days, communicated to Saudi authorities through diplomatic channels?

'We are worried about him,' al-Otaibi claimed on camera. The consul-general acted theatrically like an exceptionally well-dressed cartoon character. He took the Reuters TV-crew on a guided walk-through, opening cupboards, the women's bathroom, small glass-doors in library cabinets and large solid doors covering shallow electrical equipment and air conditioning units, walking through the Spartan hallways in his consulate. It might have been meant to inspire the viewers' confidence, but he appeared testy instead. 'But look, he is not here', he told the camera.

He complained that 'The idea of kidnapping a Saudi citizen by a diplomatic mission is something that should not be put forward in the media.' While the consulate was equipped with security cameras, al-Otaibi said he couldn't provide images of Khashoggi on his way out, because the Saudi cameras only provided a 'live-stream' that wasn't backed up anywhere. He did not address the fact that all the CC-TV footage outside his consulate would have made it clear that Khashoggi never left the building.

He also showed the Reuters camera-crew around one of the attic offices with tall cream-coloured leather desk chairs as well as his own office, dominated by paintings of King al-Saud in the centre, King Salman to the right and Crown Prince bin Salman to the left. They looked over his shoulder when he was seated behind his desk.

The consul-general, a tall, moustachioed man dressed in a grey, slightly shiny suit with a small pin-stripe, white Windsor-collared shirt and blue discreet paisley-style silk tie, had one further observation about the man whom he knew first-hand had been assassinated by Saudi government operatives four days earlier in his consulate.

The suggestion that Jamal Khashoggi had been abducted in the building was based on 'rumours that have no proof', 'talk of his kidnapping was baseless'. Hopping between the facts like MBS, he was in a very technical sense telling the truth. He also offered that such rumours were 'disgusting'.

This Reuters visit became the trigger for Turkey to advance their new version in public. Officials leaked the first details of other facts they had established. But – in what would be the theme of Turkey's changed campaign – officials would only speak on condition of anonymity and refuse to disclose their evidence. It meant that Turkey could plausibly deny what had been leaked or tack to a different story line if that suited them better.

Washington-based PhD student Selim Sazak, who had that evening tweeted the first scoop on Turkey's new version, was also given an additional scoop – that Khashoggi was no longer in the consulate but had been taken out of the building, based on CC-TV footage in Turkey's possession.

'They don't know that Jamal Khashoggi was murdered,' Sazak still said in an interview to the *Independent* further to his Twitter post.

'They know that he came in, didn't come out. They saw unusual personnel activity, including uncredentialled personnel, coming to the embassy almost immediately after Jamal Khashoggi's first visit so they think they were dispatched from Riyadh, and they speak of an unknown staffer, acting like he was moving out the embassy, packing stuff into his trunk, and leaving at the end of business the day Jamal Khashoggi disappeared. So they add up the pieces to infer that Jamal Khashoggi was incapacitated and spirited away.' This Reuters report also first mentioned that it was a team of fifteen Saudis that had arrived on 2 October and was suspected of having been sent there to seize him.

To Turan Kişlakçi, president of the Turkish-Arab Journalists' Association officials again leaked the full scope of Turkey's knowledge. 'They followed the cars, and they know what happened. We [Turkey] have all the details, and he was killed', he said.

The Middle East Eye news site was handed another inflammatory scoop on Turkey's new version of events. An anonymous Turkish official leaked to them that 'everything was videotaped to prove the mission had been accomplished and the tape was taken out of the country'. A person 'briefed on the matter' would leak on the same day to the *New York Times* that MİT had 'obtained' a copy of the video. But this additional claim, published on 9 October, that there was a video in MİT's possession was never repeated or confirmed by Turkish authorities after that date.

Fred Hiatt, editorial-page editor at the *Post* summarised the stand-off between MBS and Erdoğan succinctly: 'If the story that was told about the murder is true, the Turks must have information and videotape and other documents to back it up. If the story the Saudis are telling, that he just walked out… after half an hour, if that's true, they ought to have facts and documents and evidence and tapes to back that up.'

It was a cat-and-mouse game, with the facts about Khashoggi in the middle. Turkey's economy was wilting under the Turkish lira freefall. The fall itself had made moving to and buying a flat in Istanbul an easy proposition for Khashoggi himself, but it made the cost of a fight by Erdoğan with trade-partner Saudi Arabia higher. Yet the events also handed Erdoğan unexpected opportunities.

Intense diplomatic discussions continued in secret. Despite the new information Saudi Arabia continued to stonewall Turkey.

VIII
The Mood in Riyadh

❦

What was on MBS's mind when his embassy in Ankara passed on Erdoğan's allegation that an assassination had taken place in the Istanbul consulate? By this time, if not earlier, his staff would have prepared a detailed report on what exactly had taken place for the crown prince. In ordinary circumstances, the easiest way of countering any speculation of state involvement in the Khashoggi's disappearance would have been to release a security video of him leaving the consulate. But in the absence of such a video – a curious blemish in an otherwise painstakingly-prepared operation of MBS's special forces that will be discussed below – a decision had to be made on how to handle the kingdom's response to Turkey.

Only months earlier MBS had completed his charm offensive as his country's new leading face and had softened Saudi Arabia's austere image abroad. Potentially being linked to a murder plot had disastrous media optics in the US.

None of this can have escaped MBS, who was far from a party prince in real life. In many ways, he was a carbon copy of King Salman. Before becoming king, Salman was not just the governor of Riyadh. King Fahd, his Sudairi brother, had appointed him as custodian of the Saudi royal family. As the 'prince of princes', he was the impartial referee in family disputes and, in a private jail, disciplined Saudi royals who abused their status.

Salman deserved this role as a family judge. As governor, he arrived for work at 8am in the morning and took it very seriously. Riyadh's municipal offices had no princes, all contracts were overseen by a non-Saudi lawyer from the West, and his civil servants, who could otherwise not be fired as Saudi citizens, were informed at regular intervals that embezzlement would lead to life imprisonment. In effect, he ran a non-tribal, Western style bureaucracy. When he became king, he replicated his style of municipal government to Saudi Arabia's eight major cities.

In MBS, Salman recognised a fellow workaholic. MBS worked long hours, was extremely well-prepared in meetings and, it was said, did not gamble, drink or womanise. Meetings lasted no more than forty five minutes and, though he could keep underlings waiting for hours, he was always on top of his brief. He was practical. Like his father he studied law at the ibn Saud University. When he became minister, he hired the top student in his year.

Interestingly, Riyadh evidently decided that it was not necessary to come up with a credible explanation to Turkey. Nor, in the weeks ahead, to create the impression of a more Western-style leadership that would have improved Saudi Arabia's chances of pushing forward its new image as well as nuclear agenda.

One could be forgiven for thinking that MBS was the only one who decided how Saudi Arabia would respond to Turkey. However, while MBS was *de facto* ruler, his father remained in charge as king.

It would be a mistake to underestimate the final word of King Salman in the kingdom. He was if anything a planner. As early as 2008, when the poor health of his older Sudairi brothers Nayef and Sultan became clear, he had started drawing up a blueprint to run the country when he would be king.

The idea was simple. He would run the country like Riyadh. It meant that when he ascended the throne, Saudi Arabia became the only Arab country where anti-corruption was driven from the top. Elsewhere only the Arab Spring had that effect, which was a popular uprising against the crippling corruption by Arab leaders who siphoned off public money into their private bank accounts. In January 2015, royal princes got their Arab Winter.

Ultimately, MBS was no more than the right-hand man executing the king's wishes. Months before MBS's Ritz coup, for example, Salman had privately collared the worst known offenders, shown them how much they had made from corruption, and suggested that they pay back two thirds. Subsequently, 3 days before the coup, Salman terminated the last independent power base left in the kingdom – the National Guard traditionally run by the Abdullah-branch. On the same day, he created the anti-corruption committee chaired by MBS that executed the Ritz Carlton arrests on 7 November.

As the Saudi royal family's policeman, Salman knew every transgression and was used to forcing royals to behave and limiting privileges. It is no surprise that everyone detained at the Ritz Carlton lost a lot of weight, one fell to his death, and another returned deaf in one ear.

The Trump White House may have had a transactional outlook that was unusual in US politics, but the al-Saud kings were masters at checkbook government, starting with founder ibn Saud. Salman was cut from the same cloth. They were consummate dealmakers and knew that money always won in the long run, particularly if you produce 11% of the world's daily oil supply.

How effective Salman was at the kingdom's transactional-style of government was clear from the extent of his anti-corruption drive at home. Princes, civil servants and business men were not Salman's only targets. Previously untouchable Wahhabi clerics were in his sight, too. They had grown rich as a result of the money poured in their direction after 1979. This was the year that several hundred extremists occupied Mecca's Great Mosque. To end the siege, the Wahhabi top had agreed that it was permissible for the Saudi government to use 'all measures'. Carnage ensued, but the problem was solved. The clerics even got religious attaches at embassies who began propagating its extreme form of Islam throughout the world with limitless funds to build mosques and madrasas outside Saudi Arabia.

In November 2017, no senior clerics were held at the Ritz Carlton by MBS. Nor did they have to hand over their enormous land holdings to MBS's anti-corruption committee. But the king did extract a corruption price for not having MBS touch their private estates.

In 1979, as part of their moral support of the king's attack on the mosque terrorists, the senior clerics also extracted the closure of mixed-gender swimming pools, movie theatres, music stores, and an exclusion of women on TV and from driving cars. Even dolls were forbidden. In 2017, in exchange for not being prosecuted for corruption by MBS, the clerics agreed to women driving, gender-mixing and movie theatres, and more. It was a valuable bargain for the clerics as land is extremely costly in Saudi Arabia.

Behind the scenes, King Salman had ended the 1979 Wahhabi pact as the Ritz Carlton coup took place. To *New York Times* columnist Thomas Friedman, MBS explained: we are 'restoring' Islam to its origins — and our biggest tools are the Prophet's practices and [daily life in] Saudi Arabia before 1979'.

Whatever Erdoğan wanted in exchange for keeping the Khashoggi Affair quiet was not a bargain King Salman or MBS thought beneficial for the kingdom.

* * *

From the king's point of view, evidently, nothing about Turkey's blackmail seemed compelling. Remarkably, the palacesaw no reason to change its position over the weeks of media attention that followed. Any development on their side seemed to have been done more as a reluctant courtesy to MBS's friends in the White House than because the Affair required further attention.

It was almost as if Salman and MBS reckoned they had dealt appropriately with Khashoggi. They had no close ties to him anyway. The Sudairi-branch had never been a patron of his and, under Abdullah, Khashoggi had even been critical of Salman during the Afghan war. One detail, however, did get their full attention from day one. Riyadh was to make sure that every single forensic trace of Khashoggi's body was expunged from the consulate.

Salman and MBS knew, too, that for the Saudi population the death of one former courtier didn't register high on the list of priorities. It was probably seen as collateral risk of being part of the Saudi high flyers.

When Jamal Khashoggi was born in an elite family in 1958, Saudi Arabia had four million inhabitants. In 2021, there were thirty four million. In 1958, few Saudis were literate. But under the Saudi kings literacy for men and women had grown to 95 per cent in 2021. As imams had ceased to be the most learned people in their communities, respect had fallen in inverse proportion among the young over the same time. The religious fanaticism that had energised well-off students such as Khashoggi and bin Laden in the 1960s and 1970s held little appeal for the average Saudi pupil, perhaps because one third of the curriculum covered religious studies; nor did harassment for religious infractions by the *mutawa'a*, the Wahhabi police force that operated separate from the state police on Saudi streets. Satellite TV, social media and football, however, were hugely popular among Saudi youth.

This shift in demographics caused different kinds of headaches from the religious ones King Abdullah faced when Khashoggi was his advisor. The Saudis were using as much water as Canadians and three times more than Europeans in 2021. This volume of water – more than the rivers Tigris and Eufrates together – was produced in the Saudi desert by boiling sea water with subsidised oil. Similar subsidies kept fuel prices low for consumers. When Salman became king in 2015, 20 per cent of Saudi oil was consumed at home. At that year's rate, in fifteen years the kingdom would only export a third of its daily production. Salman's country was addicted to oil as if it was fentanyl.

Also, Saudis families had to be housed somewhere. But land not owned by clerics belonged to a few princes. Thus the Ritz Carlton arrests were largely about their land holdings, since these princes sold land only in small lots at the time to keep prices artificially high. Half of the $100 billion in property recovered in MBS's corruption deals with the detainees was paid out in such speculative land, which MBS was now free to develop into housing for the population at large. For example, under the Ritz Carlton settlements, more than half of undeveloped land in Riyadh and Jeddah (Saudi's largest cities, the former governed for half a century by Salman before becoming king) was returned to government ownership in exchange for the freedom of their princely owners.

Another headache of King Salman's was the Saudi work force. A third of Saudi Arabia's population were guest workers who sent a large part of their pay package abroad instead of spending it in Saudi Arabia. Meanwhile, his ten thousand royal relatives were not the only indolent Saudis. Saudi nationals had little incentive to work hard and the first law Salman changed when he became king in 2015 was the right to fire Saudi employees. In addition, native Saudis were mainly employed by the public purse. MBS's Vision 2030 was meant to get them back on the payroll of businesses rather than just the Saudi government. In addition, only 20 per cent of women were part of the work force because of religious strictures of 1979.

What King Salman set out to achieve with MBS was an administrative revolution, sweeping away decades of kleptocracy as well as the religious strictures introduced after 1979. MBS was obsessed with spreadsheets, performance indicators and business consultants. Over three years, he and his father eviscerated the budget independence of ministries and replaced most ministers with technocrats rather than princes. After meeting MBS, Thomas Friedman also commented, 'It's been a long time, though, since any Arab leader wore me out with a fire hose of ideas about transforming his country.' While religious funding was reduced, spending on education continued to rise. It was King Salman's bargain with Saudi youth under twenty five, who made up half the native population, and the nascent educated middle class.

So, no. The palace maybe didn't consider the fact that the Khashoggi Operation had come to light alarming in view of King Salman's ambitious goals. If anything, it focused the minds of their civil servants and courtiers on remaining loyal to their overlords. It also discouraged royals to disobey orders from the palace or sow dissension. Erdoğan could stew in his own juice. Donald Trump was a different matter.

IX
Pastor Brunson

What were the US goals on the other side of the Atlantic meanwhile in the first week of the Khashoggi Affair? Given Five Eyes, it is pretty clear that Langley (the CIA) had a good idea what had gone down.

The White House saw it as a great opportunity to get something from the recalcitrant Erdoğan. The Turkish president needed a third big brother who could act as a behind-the-scenes broker with Saudi Arabia. That meant he had a price to pay.

Here the fate of pastor Andrew Brunson was like a buoy floating on troubled water, tethered to intense Khashoggi-related diplomacy between Erdoğan and Donald Trump. The Turkish economy, once seemingly unstoppable, was sagging with 15.9 per cent inflation and Erdoğan needed the US both as a mediator and also to resume the influx of Western money. Khashoggi's disappearance was shaping itself into a key that would resolve a number of hitherto intractable problems between the two countries.

For Trump, Brunson's 2016 incarceration had been an election rallying cry aimed at his evangelical voters. His running mate Mike Pence was the Brunson-*cause-célèbre*'s poster child.

Despite persistent pressure from the US – where the Christian conservative lobby relentlessly agitated for his release and where Trump regularly tweeted about this 'great Christian' – Erdoğan had stubbornly refused sofar to release the pastor. Yet his release was a core 2016 election promise and when Turkey pulled back yet again from early release in August 2018, Trump had been furious. He had doubled tariffs on Turkish steel and aluminium, causing a further collapse of the Turkish lira.

The pastor's arrest was in itself curious as Brunson had had a flock of no more than twenty four congregants. But for Turkey, Brunson was connected with another cleric whom Erdoğan blamed for the 15 July 2016 putsch against him. This cleric, Fethullah Gülen, lived in longstanding exile in rural Saylorsburg, Pennsylvania, and was protected by US law from extradition. Ironically, Gülen had been instrumental in harnessing popular Islam at the beginning of Erdoğan's rise to power in what had been secular, Kemalist Turkey operating in the image of founder Kemal Atatürk. But that was then.

Three days after Khashoggi's assassination, Trump excitedly tweeted on

Friday 5 October: 'Working very hard on Pastor Brunson!' It was the day on which Turkey had had its meeting with the Saudi diplomats in Ankara about the affair and Erdoğan realised later in the evening that Riyadh wasn't going to budge.

In the heat of the Khashoggi stand-off with Saudi Arabia, Turkey decided to drop its refusal to hand the pastor over to the US. This was announced on Saturday and Erdoğan released Brunson within a week. The miraculous early release from the pastor's three-year prison sentence was officially because of 'good behaviour. Erdoğan merely said about the release that he was 'bound by Turkish law'.

Instead of a looming public-relations disaster regarding 'a certain responsibility' of the US (in Putin's gnomic words) flaring up around the disappearance of Khashoggi, a US resident under the 'genius' or O-visa, there were instead jubilant headlines for Trump.

It led to a triumphant photo opportunity for Trump with the now celebrity pastor in the White House beckoned. On 13 October the finally-free Brunson would tearfully pray for Trump to have 'supernatural wisdom' in the Oval Office. While he kneeled before the president, Trump remained seated. Other collateral damage of the 2016 putsch, such as a number of imprisoned US consulate workers and the holidaying NASA scientist Serkan Golge, were less fortunate than the pastor. These people remained locked up in Turkey – in the case of Golge in solitary confinement.

Four weeks later, yet more evidence of the sudden thaw in Turkish-American relations would emerge when both Turkey and the US, shortly after one another, started 'unilaterally' to roll back sanctions against black-listed government officials.

Later, on 19 February 2019, the US also announced that it would withdraw troops from Kurdish Syria, which had thwarted the Turkish army. On 21 May, Turkey complied with US oil sanctions against Iran after a 6-month reprieve given on 1 November.

What had changed on Friday that brought about such a quick and unexpected resolution to the Brunson impasse, and personal sanctions against those close to Erdoğan being lifted?

Erdoğan had told Reuters on Sunday 7 October that he was following the Khashoggi case 'personally' and that 'entries and exits into the embassy, airport transits and all camera records are being looked at and followed. We want to swiftly get results'.

Leaks surrounding Khashoggi's fate by Turkish officials started to gather more pace. Now that the word 'murder' was part of the discussion, rumours started swirling around social media that Khashoggi had been dismembered and removed from the consulate in several parts inside body bags, fuelling further shock, embellishment and still scepticism in the absence of any real proof.

'Turkish sources insist that Jamal Khashoggi was tortured, then killed and his body cut up,' tweeted Saudi whistle-blower Mujtahidd, who had over two million followers – many more than Jamal Khashoggi. He made subversive claims that Khashoggi himself would never have countenanced.

'All this was filmed and the video was sent to Mohammed bin Salman so he could enjoy the scene. If this is confirmed, then it seems like the news that he was removed from Turkey and has arrived in Saudi Arabia isn't true. Tomorrow Turkey should announce full details.'

Turkey was looking for more than that. Yasin Aktay told Qatari broadcaster al-Jazeera on Sunday 7 October: 'We demand a convincing clarification from Saudi Arabia, and what the crown prince offered is not convincing.'

Turkish daily newspaper *Hürriyet*, another government mouthpiece owned by AKP standard-bearer Demirören group, suggested that the Saudis had taken Khashoggi out of the building by cutting his body into fifteen pieces – the first time this number was mentioned.

The rumour mill soon got out of control with the Iranian channel IRTV1 reporting the unfounded but sensational claim that Khashoggi's corpse had been found in a neighbourhood in Istanbul five days after he had disappeared.

On 8 October, Khashoggi's friend and Erdoğan's chief adviser, Yasin Aktay, wrote in his column in Islamist *Yeni Şafak* ('new dawn') yet another government mouthpiece, owned by the AKP billionaire Albayrak family: 'Although we are still trying to maintain optimism, we were not able to prevent the abduction or brutal killing of Khashoggi, whose ideas and stance I have followed with great appreciation and approval.... I know that all precautions have been taken.'

'We never had the opportunity to protect him, to do something when he was still alive,' he said, by way of an excuse for Turkey's impotence in preventing what had taken place. He assumed in the piece Khashoggi was dead. They had talked the month before about the targeting of Saudis on Turkish soil. 'He voiced his concern about possible operations against Saudi citizens.... He was confident they couldn't conduct such operations in Turkey.'

Yeni Şafak also added some conspiracy theories of its own by blaming the PLO, Israel, the UAE, the US, apart from MBS.

The non-religious, traditional Kemalist-socialist, non-AKP *Aydınlık* ('enlightenment'), carried its own speculation on the affair and alleged that Khashoggi was a spy and had brought 'significant documents' from Saudi Arabia.

'It is known that Khashoggi had left the country with several files containing secret information. Some of them are thought to be in Istanbul while others are in Washington,' it claimed in its coverage close to bull's eye.

'The team and mentality that poisoned Yasser Arafat [the late chairman of the Palestine Liberation Organisation] to death is also behind the Khashoggi murder. Killers like Mohammed Dahlan [the former leader of Fatah in Gaza] are in the backstage. The Dahlan team studied Turkey a year before 15 July [Turkey's 2016 coup attempt] too! Although a journalist in opposition to Mohammed bin Salman has been killed, the signature belongs to Mohammed bin Zayed al-Nahyan [MBZ, the crown prince of Abu Dhabi]. He is Salman's patron. And the patron of both of them is US-Israeli intelligence.'

Nearly a week after Khashoggi had gone missing and on a Brunson-high, Donald Trump was ready to address the issue in public as well.

'I am concerned about it. I don't like hearing about it. And hopefully that will sort itself out. Right now nobody knows anything about it, but there are some pretty bad stories going around. I do not like it,' the US president offered.

US secretary of state Mike Pompeo asked for a thorough and open probe by Saudi Arabia into Khashoggi's disappearance.

'We call on the government of Saudi Arabia to support a thorough investigation of Mr Khashoggi's disappearance and to be transparent about the results of that investigation,' he said in a statement.

Giving a coy insight into US intelligence on the matter he added the vague words that he had seen 'conflicting reports' on what had taken place at the consulate.

President Erdoğan, on a trip to Hungary, stirred the cauldron further. 'There are some people who came from Saudi Arabia,' he said, part-confirming officially what had been leaked unofficially about a team arriving in Istanbul. 'The public prosecutor's office is looking into the issue.' He added that CC-TV footage from the airport was being studied.

As for Saudi Arabia's refusal to provide CC-TV coverage of Khashoggi leaving he said, 'Whose duty is it to prove that he left or not? The consulate's officials should. Don't you have cameras and other things?'

Senior officials in Ankara upped the ante and leaked that a convoy of six vehicles left the consulate two hours after Khashoggi entered, and that this was of particular interest.

They said that security camera footage showed objects being loaded into a black van which carried diplomatic number plates. After leaving the consulate, three cars turned left onto a main road while the remaining three turned right. Investigators said one of the vehicles, a van with blacked-out windows, had become the focus of the investigation. It had already been tracked to a nearby motorway where CC-TV showed it taking the D100, the highway leading to Ataturk Airport.

'There were some vehicles,' said Yasin Aktay. 'There were fifteen Saudi personnel inside. They were carrying bags and going to the airport. Turkish security cameras can follow up until the airport.'

Two of the vehicles were of particular interest according to the Washington-based PhD-student Selim Sazak. The first to confirm Khashoggi's fate was bad, he was now revealing to the *Independent* more information leaked to him.

'One, on the suspicion that it might have been used to carry Jamal Khashoggi out of the consulate. Another, on the suspicion that it might have been used to shuttle some of the people involved,' he said, citing a briefing he was given by unnamed Turkish officials.

Though used as the opening conduit by Turkey's government, the US-based Sazak did not seem to be part of the Erdoğan inner circle. He wrote in November in the US magazine *Foreign Policy*, part of the same stable as the *Washington Post*, about civil liberty in authoritarian states, 'What is an intellectual debate in the US is a daily struggle there. It gets you sued, fired, exiled, arrested, even killed'.

Turkish newspaper *Sabah* ('morning'), on the other hand, was unequivocally a government mouthpiece. Its morning edition led with speculation about the van that was involved: 'The black minibus will explain the riddle of the Saudi journalist.... [It] left the building two hours after Khashoggi entered the mission.' The paper said the police were looking for this suspicious vehicle.

The Turkish police now confirmed officially that they were examining the flight records showing that two private Saudi Gulfstream IV jets had arrived at Istanbul's Atatürk Airport on Tuesday and departed separately that same day, hours after Khashoggi was last seen. They already knew this on the day itself, but the Turkish government now went on the record with this information. If negotiations with Saudi Arabia had taken a different turn, it might, presumably, have never become public knowledge.

Finally there was a response. While Saudi authorities continued to insist they had played no role in Khashoggi's disappearance, they now acknowledged that a 'security delegation' had been sent to Istanbul. The weight of evidence from Turkish CC-TV required some response. But the Saudis did not offer a reason for the journey of this security detail.

In Saudi Arabia, however, where MBS had an even greater control over the media and thus the narrative than Erdoğan in Turkey, the statements arising from the disappearance took a very different turn.

Khashoggi's media peers who now headed Saudi outlets took care to block the rumours and leaks from abroad – as he would have done himself – and created a different story for national consumption.

The website of Saudi-funded al-Arabiya TV said that the Khashoggi family was in contact with the Saudi authorities over his disappearance. Khashoggi's eldest son Salah told the station: 'The issue is that a Saudi citizen has gone missing. We are co-operating with the Saudi authorities to discover the circumstances of the incident....' Obligingly he added, 'The whole thing is a personal issue and is completely unrelated to politics.' Though US citizens, both of Khashoggi's sons had been placed under house arrest after the murder and were barred from leaving Saudi Arabia.

After chairing a family meeting in the Saudi city of Jeddah, legal counsellor Muatassim Khashoggi also confirmed his faith in the royal family: 'We trust the government and the measures it is taking. All efforts being exerted in Jamal Khashoggi's case are being coordinated with the authorities and the embassy in Ankara.'

He accused foreign media of using his cousin's disappearance to 'attack our country for negative purposes'.

In a sidebar he added that they had never heard of Khashoggi's 'alleged' fiancée Hatice Cengiz.

'We don't know her and we don't know where she came from,' he said. 'She is not connected to the family in any way. Her tales and her existence could be part of her personal agenda.'

Salah, Khashoggi's oldest son from his first wife and a Saudi banker, agreed emphatically: 'I don't know this woman. I'd never heard of her before except from the media.'

Although Salah's brother Abdullah had told the Khashoggi family of his 10 September trip to Istanbul, when he met Cengiz and his father, and of their father's marriage plans, Salah and his uncle Muatassim, the head of the Khashoggi clan, professed not to know anything about her to al-Arabiya. To anyone listening inside Saudi Arabia, Khashoggi's family was implying that Cengiz, a Turk, was lying on behalf of her country and was intent on soiling the reputation of the kingdom. As we will see, they had more ground to complain when she celebrated what would have been Khashoggi's sixtieth birthday on 13 October.

X
Horse-Trading

On the evening of Sunday 7 October, the Saudi ambassador to Washington, the crown prince's brother, Prince Khalid bin Salman or 'KBS', joined the fray to counter the rumour of Khashoggi's assassination.

Fred Ryan, the publisher of the *Washington Post* had sent a letter to KBS asking for clarification. It was delivered via diplomatic channels to the prince, facilitated by the Trump administration. But the administration's responsiveness to help had quickly evaporated midweek following MBS's call to White House staffers to say that Khashoggi was a dangerous islamist. Presumably, the White House had also by then collated all its intelligence on what went down in Istanbul. After Saturday's shock news of murder in the consulate by Reuters, KBS had finally responded and agreed to meet at 9pm at Ryan's Georgetown home.

'Khashoggi has always been honest', KBS said, 'We have never perceived him as being an asset of [a hostile country] or anyone else'.

'It's impossible that this would be covered up and we wouldn't know about it', he assured the publisher.

Asked about the rumours of the two Gulfstream jets by Ryan, KBS said this was 'baseless', the consulate's CC-TV 'weren't recording', allegations of Saudi involvement were 'ridiculous', and 'Saudi investigators' were already at the consulate. It was the same line that al-Otaibi held during his Reuters walkabout in the consulate. Ryan would later call the ambassador a liar who should be 'shunned'.

The next day KBS also sent an unprompted WhatsApp message to a news reporter in the US at a different outlet.

'I know that many people here in Washington and around the world are concerned for his fate, but I assure you that all reports saying that Jamal Khashoggi vanished in the consulate in Istanbul, or that the kingdom's authorities detained or killed him are completely false and baseless,' the 30-year-old ambassador wrote.

He did, however, confirm both Khashoggi's importance to the palace and the unease of Saudi top royals about the fact that he lived outside the kingdom: 'Khashoggi has many friends in Saudi Arabia, and I am one of them. Despite differences on a number of issues including what he called his "self-exile", we kept in touch when he was in Washington.'

Echoing the recital by the Khashoggi family – whose members based in Saudi Arabia were under a travel ban – the prince painted a picture of 'Jamal' as someone 'who has dedicated a large part of his life to serve his country'.

KBS went a step further. He supported unreservedly the testimony of consul-general al-Otaibi and called the rumours about Khashoggi's fate 'malicious' and 'outrageous'.

His WhatsApp message went on to promise, 'Khashoggi is a Saudi citizen whose safety and security is a top priority for the kingdom, just as is the case with any other citizen. We will not spare any effort to locate him, just as we would if it were any other Saudi citizen...'

KBS flatly contradicted Hatice Cengiz's words that Khashoggi was nervous about his first visit to the Istanbul consulate on Friday 28 September. The ambassador claimed, 'This was not his first visit to the consulate in Istanbul, as he regularly came to the consulate (as well as the embassy in Washington) in the last few months for citizen services', though he did not provide evidence to back up this statement.

The ambassador also claimed incorrectly that 'Turkish authorities and the media were allowed to inspect the consulate building in its entirety.' All that had happened so far was that Reuters had been given a guided publicity tour by the consul-general.

There was subsequently speculation about the role of KBS in the assassination plot and that he had personally lured Khashoggi to either the embassy in Ankara or the consulate in Istanbul. Several friends reported that Khashoggi had told them he had made inquiries at the Saudi embassy in DC, fuelling the idea that MBS's brother was a co-conspirator. If true, it would be an additional explanation of the Saudi chatter about the rendition of Khashoggi that GCHQ and US intelligence had picked up in September, and also why Khashoggi was worried that consular staff in Istanbul might refuse to help him with the marriage certificates – Khashoggi feared he had pulled a trip wire by reaching out to diplomatic staff for marriage documentation.

But, when Khashoggi's fiancée Hatice Cengiz was asked about this by Turkish media, she made a point of clarifying to *Hürriyet* on 26 October that Khashoggi hadn't talked to her about having contacted the Washington embassy to sort out the Saudi certificates required under Turkish law. If he had, she thought, he would have told her. She herself had gone to the Fatih Marriage Office on 7 or 8 September to find out while Khashoggi was in the US.

It looked, however, as if Khashoggi hadn't shared all of his plans with Cengiz. The UN inquiry reported in June 2019 it had been given credible information 'that Khashoggi attempted to obtain the needed marriage documents online and within the United States but was told he needed to obtain them in Turkey' (detail 199, footnote 165). Presumably, this was an online response, logged on the computer Cengiz gave to the Istanbul police. Online Khashoggi could inquire under a pseudonym and, unless they had access to his computer, Saudi authorities would not be forewarned of his intentions.

The *Washington Post* now published the famous last known photograph of Jamal Khashoggi – a still from the leaked CC-TV footage – that they had been given by Turkish officials as a scoop showing Khashoggi entering the Saudi consulate at 1.14pm on Tuesday 9 October. It was probably also the one Turkish authorities showed Hatice Cengiz on Tuesday at the beginning of their investigation. Turkish officials said that if Khashoggi left the consulate he would have come out of the same door and would have been captured on the same camera (they also had cameras aimed at the back entrance of the consulate, but didn't yet disclose this).

The last public sign: Jamal Khashoggi entering the Saudi consulate at 1:14pm, 2 October.

At 7.22pm on the same Tuesday, British BBC 24 published off-air audio from an interview Jamal Khashoggi gave in London, three days before he disappeared. Asked if he would return to Saudi Arabia, he replied: 'I don't think I will be able to go home again. When I heard of an arrest of a friend who did nothing, it makes me feel like I shouldn't go. The people being arrested aren't even dissidents, they just have an independent mind.' By way of apology for the broadcast the BBC said, 'We wouldn't normally release this conversation but we've decided to make an exception in light of the circumstances.'

The release of a private conversation was controversial and BBC was criticised on social media for airing the recordings without Khashoggi's consent and before there was any definitive proof of his death as opposed to mere rumours, however credible by this stage.

All this speculation was particularly upsetting to Hatice Cengiz. All she had to go on was leaked media information by anonymous Turkish officials. Turkey had still not given an official account of what happened to Khashoggi at the consulate according to the facts in its possession. In fact, officially Turkey still treated the diplomatic impasse as if her fiancée was inside the consulate.

'I no longer feel like I am really alive,' she said. 'I can't sleep. I don't eat. As his fiancée, as someone close to Jamal and in love with Jamal, I am waiting for information from my government about what has happened to him. Where is Jamal?'

While waiting for access to the premises, the Turkish police announced officially that it had formed a 'special team'. They would look for DNA belonging to Khashoggi inside the mission, using Luminol and infrared light to find bloodstains, as well as 'K-9' police dogs in the search, they said. It was waiting for the consulate's response to its request to search the place.

There was no official Saudi response. But it was clear that, behind the scenes, the Turkish government was negotiating with Riyadh.

Erdoğan's adviser and Khashoggi's friend Yasin Aktay suddenly seemed to pedal back from his earlier 'hunch' that his friend had been 'brutally' murdered and that Saudis had 'of course, disposed of the body'.

Aktay said in an interview to *Russia Today*, reported by the *Saudi Gazette*, that his friend's 'killing is not an official statement' and that 'the Saudi state is not blamed here'. It was even reported that he 'hinted at the possibility that Khashoggi was abducted by a third party, or perhaps by members of what he called the "deep state",' a reference to the 2016 putsch which – according to Erdoğan when his power was secure again – had been organised by many military officers, judges, journalists, and other professionals with affiliations he didn't like. Whether these were in actual fact Aktay's real words or ones liberally translated from Arabic by the Russian outlet and gratefully copied by Saudi-broadcaster al-Arabiya was unclear.

Turkey's willingness to compromise on the truth, however, was also flagged up by government-controlled paper *Sabah*. It said Turkish investigators were considering that Khashoggi had been transported in a van seen parked in front of the consulate on the last image of Khashoggi alive and smuggled out of the country on one of the two Saudi Gulfstream IV jets that had left in the evening of 2 October. Arab newspapers loyal to Saudi Arabia gratefully seized on *Sabah*'s new rumour.

Turkish investigators of course knew this wasn't the case from MoBeSe CC-TV coverage which they still kept a secret from everyone. At the same time, Turkish authorities told US and European officials that they were certain about the killing but that Ankara was willing to climb-down in exchange for concessions from Riyadh. It was unclear who did the leaking about concessions here, but the *Guardian* newspaper and others reported it.

Also, *Yeni Şafak* columnist Kemal Öztürk reminded everyone of the leak that 'there are claims that there is a video of the moments Jamal Khashoggi was killed.

I haven't seen it, it's in an interview on Turkish TVNET'. It was to be the last mention that such a snuff video of Khashoggi's assassination existed.

In Saudi Arabia, however, the press stuck to the story that Riyadh was entirely blameless of the disappearance. It hit back at its critics. It was now no longer Saudi enemies who were to blame for the brouhaha, but it was what they called an 'international media campaign that did not verify the incident but relentlessly contributed to tarnishing the image of Saudi Arabia'. Putin and China would repeat a similar argument later, both complaining about double-standards in Western sanctions.

The Saudi media also reckoned the 'campaign' was 'politicised by sides that aim at settling scores with the kingdom at the expense of the truth'. Foreign media were 'spreading poison in honey' said Saudi paper *al-Yaum* ('today').

Saudi Arabia's friendly Gulf neighbours also gave MBS full-throated support. The UAE's foreign minister tweeted that a 'fierce campaign against Riyadh is expected, as well as the coordination between its inciting parties.'

Bahrein's foreign minister added, 'The target is the kingdom of Saudi Arabia and not the search for any truth. Throw your masks away.'

Meanwhile Iran's state-run Channel One thought it could kill two birds with one stone and reported to its home audience without evidence that it was likely that Israeli Mossad agents had co-operated with Saudi Arabia in Khashoggi's murder.

Under mounting pressure, Riyadh finally opened the door a crack, however. On Tuesday it reportedly gave permission to Turkish investigators to inspect the consulate.

This was a small but significant break-through and a highly unusual if not unheard-of deviation from the immunity of diplomatic missions and it appeared to be the first indication that Turkey's campaign was gaining serious traction. Saudi Arabia seemed to be paying attention.

Three Turkish investigators would be given access to all parts of the Saudi consulate, but not to the residence of the consul-general. Reuters' guided tour had been a light-touch media inspection, theirs would be a more full-flavoured one. They would, however, only be allowed a 'visual' survey and not a forensic probe. In a repeat of the Reuters tour, the Turkish trio of officials would, by *reductio ad absurdum*, confirm that Khashoggi had left the building and thus be delivering the second best to CC-TV footage of this fact that President Erdoğan had been asking the Saudis for.

XI
Dr Death

⁕

Following Riyadh's grudging concession to allow for a visual inspection only, Ankara ordered a quick, unofficial leak of more new facts to the media. In its Wednesday 10 October morning edition (which was available towards midnight the night before) *Sabah* published a big front-page splash with the names of all the fifteen men of the hit-squad, giving the year of their birth, and printing face pictures as they passed through passport control or checked in at their hotels. They were aged between thirty and fifty-seven. Mostly moustachioed, the men were dressed in anything from a red T-shirt to a smart dark blazer and open white dress shirt. Twelve were shown guiltily looking away from the camera and three at it with insolence.

Meshal al-Bostani, Mustafa al-Madani, Mansour Abahussein, Maher Mutreb, Waleed al-Sehri, Fahad al-Balawi, Thaab al-Harbi, Salah Tubaigy, Saif al-Qahtani, Khalid al-Otaibi, Naif al-Arifi, Abdulaziz al-Hawsawi, Mohammed al-Zahrani, Badr al-Otaibi, Turki al-Sehri

Sabah reported that the nine people arriving on the first jet HZ-SK2 checked in at 5:51am at the Mövenpick Hotel, within walking distance of the consulate.

They booked rooms until Friday. The six others, the paper catalogued, arrived in two batches on 1 and 2 October and checked in at the five-star Wyndham Grand, also within striking distance of the consulate.

Both trios of Saudis who had arrived at Atatürk Airport on commercial flights – one in the late afternoon of 1 October and the other in the early morning of 2 October – left on the last private Saudi jet out at 10:46pm. *Sabah*'s article therefore surmised that they formed part of one and the same group and were a Saudi hit-team sent for Jamal. The thin veneer of the official leak was that the piece was a result of *Sabah*'s own investigations team.

The entire fifteen crew of the hit-squad left again within twenty four hours, in a rush despite their three or even five-day reservations, *Sabah* revealed to the public in its front-page scoop. It was noted that two Saudis who had arrived on the first private jet did not leave on either jet HZ-SK1 or HZ-SK2. Instead, they mysteriously left Turkey separately at 18 minutes past midnight on a scheduled flight.

On the heels of the *Sabah* revelations, Erdoğan's government launched a second shot across Riyahd's bow for the Wednesday morning news bulletins. Grainy video detail from Turkey's CC-TV footage was leaked to Turkish channel 24TV. The clip was short, damning and thrilling.

It showed one of the two Saudi Gulfstream jets that had landed in Istanbul the day Khashoggi vanished. Marked 'HZ-SK1' and 'HK-SK2' an info banner said, the jets were reported to have come from Riyadh. The former landed at 3.41am with nine men and the latter in the afternoon at 4.29pm, after Khashoggi's disappearance.

HZ-SK1 landing under diplomatic cover on 2 October at 3.29 am, 30 minutes before touch down of Jamal Khashoggi's Turkish Airlines flight from London (part of the 24TV clip).

The leaked footage next showed two men in summer clothes in the dark of night, and said six of them had left their hotel in small groups between 9.40am and 9.55am on 2 October. The same morning other crew members, the clip reported, bought large suitcases in Istanbul's Grand Bazaar, a 30 minute drive from the consulate.

The footage then cut to frantic parking activity by four Mercedeses with green diplomatic license plates in front of the consulate an hour before Khashoggi entered at 1:14pm. One of them was a Mercedes Sprinter van with green consular number plates, though the footage was too blurry to read the license plate number. A later leak feeding the news cycle would make it clear it had number plate 34 CC 2342 ('34' for Istanbul and 'CC' indicating consular staff).

One hour and 54 minutes later, the clip said, the Mercedes van and a sedan with license plates 34 CC 1865 and 34 CC 1248, respectively, were seen being let through the roadblock in front of the consulate.

These two were shown speeding away in different directions while the van parked a few minutes later, at 3.07pm, on leafy Meşelik Street in front of the tall cream-coloured wall of the consul-general's imposing home about a mile or so away from the consulate. While the driver chatted to the guard at the home, an Audi sedan parked as well. At least half a dozen people then entered the house while the van itself pulled into the enclosed driveway.

The clip showed short stills only at double the speed and all one could make out was that people arrived and went into the house, but not how many or what they were doing. The fast-moving images conveyed furtiveness more than what was exactly on them.

If Riyadh was unconcerned about the negative publicity, the practical consequence of Turkey's release was that the anonymity of these fifteen members of MBS's elite Tiger Team was blown. If the team's total strength numbered around fifty, the cover of almost a third of its highly-trained operatives had been unmasked in the *Sabah* article.

Saudi Arabia's response to Erdoğan's unveiling was furious and swift. The permission for the three Turkish investigators to do a visual inspection of the consulate was promptly withdrawn that morning.

For the international media, Erdoğan's team had prepared its own blitz. On Tuesday 9 October, at 10.30pm Turkish time, when *Sabah* was first available, the *New York Times* published leaks by Turkish officials to its reporters that one of the fifteen men was an 'autopsy expert', Khashoggi had been killed during a 'quick and complex operation' and dismembered with a 'bone saw brought for the purpose'. One of the anonymous Turkish officials summarised to the paper what they had discovered in a quotable phrase: 'it is like Pulp Fiction'. He was applying pressure where it mattered. If all that was true – and one had to assume Turkey had the evidence – the Khashoggi operation was pre-meditated murder.

Yet, the paper also still didn't discount that the truth would never come out in favour of 'a face-saving story blaming Mr. Khashoggi's disappearance on some third party, on rogue elements of the Saudi security forces, or on an accident during an interrogation that went wrong'. Erdoğan flagged to the Saudis that his olive branch was still an option if they agreed to his demands.

'Turkish officials left things murky enough – speaking on condition of anonymity and refusing to publicly disclose their evidence – that such possibilities cannot be ruled out. Some pro-government news outlets even reported that the police were still investigating the possibility that Mr. Khashoggi was abducted, not killed.'

Yet, later in the day on Wednesday, President Erdoğan's personal adviser Yasin Aktay backtracked full circle and claimed that he had never said Khashoggi could have been 'abducted by a third party, or perhaps by members of what he called the "deep state".' He blamed trolls for misquoting him the day before. The olive branch was on its way of being withdrawn.

The conflicting leaks regarding a third party who might have been involved were brushed aside in yet more unofficial leaks explaining that these versions of the truth were the result of a snafu between different agencies in Turkey. The fact that there were wrong-and-right leaks to the media was, so anonymous Turkish officials claimed, because of limited sharing of information between these different agencies.

'They flew away with their secrets,' *Aksam* ('evening') yet another newspaper close to the government mused in its evening edition at the end of the day.

'It seems that a period of headaches is about to begin for Saudi Arabia. A big crisis could break out between Ankara and Riyadh.' Hopefully it added, 'The horrible "extermination" of a journalist could also bring about the end of Crown Prince Salman.' *Aksam*'s owner Ethem Sancak, was ranked in Turkey's top 50 rich list and gave his media outlets AKP-favouring editors.

By now even Hatice Cengiz's optimism was dimmed by the deafening silence from her government. Officially, Turkey's position had still not changed from the week before – Khashoggi was missing and they were waiting for proof that he had left the consulate.

'Although my hope slowly fades away each passing day, I remain confident that Khashoggi is still alive,' she said. 'Perhaps I'm simply trying to hide from the thought that I have lost a great man whose love I had earned.'

Writing this in Wednesday's *Washington Post*, she said her fiancé had told her that he missed his native Saudi Arabia and homesickness had taken its toll on him. He had told her: 'I miss my country very much. I miss my friends and family very much. I feel this deep pain every single moment.'

'We were in the middle of making wedding plans, life plans,' she wrote. 'After the consulate, we were going to buy appliances for our new home and set a date. All we needed was a piece of paper.'

Despite being worried about a wave of arrests in Saudi Arabia, she said, he did not fear anything would happen to him on Turkish soil.

'I implore President Trump and first lady Melania Trump to help shed light on Khashoggi's disappearance,' she said. 'I also urge Saudi Arabia, especially King Salman and Crown Prince Mohammed bin Salman, to show the same level of sensitivity and release CC-TV footage from the consulate.... Khashoggi is a valuable person, an exemplary thinker and a courageous man who has been fighting for his principles. I don't know how I can keep living if he was abducted or killed in Turkey.'

Later she wrote in the *New York Times* of Saturday 13 October: 'I keep asking the same questions to myself: Where is he? Is he alive? If he is alive, how is he?'

'Had I known it would be the last time I would see Jamal, I would have rather entered the Saudi consulate myself.' According to her, he had had no idea that he was putting his safety on the line by going into the consulate.

Her *Washington Post* statement about her fiancé's unpreparedness twisted the knife into the US intelligence community. In a way that was never meant to happen, it now was an issue why Khashoggi had not been warned of the impending threat despite being a US resident.

Sabah had already published the names of the fifteen suspects of the hit-team and their movements and airport data. The next day it revealed in another scoop more background information on two members, one of them the 'autopsy expert' teed up by the leak to the *New York Times*. Mohammed Tubaigy, *Sabah* revealed was the President of the Saudi Fellowship of Forensic Pathology and an expert in post-mortem examinations. He had perfected the seven-minute autopsy and invented a mobile unit for this purpose to be on hand during the Hajj when millions of pilgrims visit the city of Mecca for six days and once many thousands of luckless worshippers died as a result of a stampede. Mohammed al-Zahrani was a royal guard.

Using the names and head shots *Sabah* had published, the global press also started filling in the CVs of the fifteen-strong hit-team. The *New York Times* noted that Tubaigy was a 'figure of such stature that he could be directed only by a high-ranking Saudi authority'. Tubaigy had learnt his trade at Glasgow University, where he took a master's in forensic medicine, and he had spent three months with the Victorian Institute of Forensic Medicine in Australia. He was being dubbed 'Dr Death'.

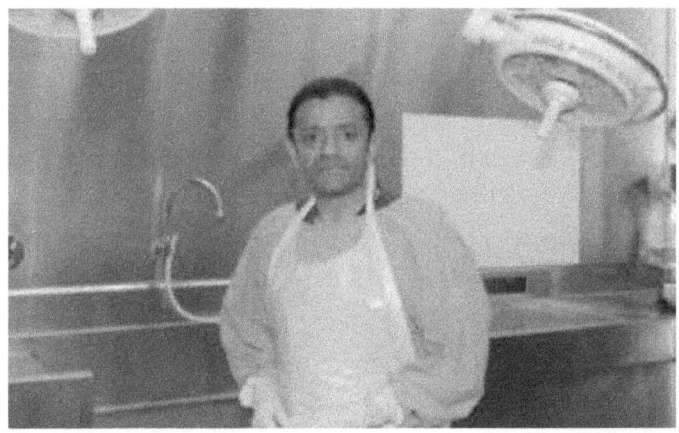

Professor Lieutenant-Colonel Salah Tubaigy, Dr Death.

Other jet passengers were also being identified by the international and Turkish media. Taken together, the background information made clear beyond doubt that these were Saudi special forces.

Brigadier-General Maher Mutreb in MBS (far right)'s world tour entourage, with KBS (third from right) in Washington DC.

They found there was a lieutenant-colonel in the Saudi civil defence force; a major and lieutenant in the Saudi air force; a lieutenant in the service guarding the crown prince's palace; and Maher Mutreb was quickly identified as a member of the Saudi intelligence community and former first secretary at the Saudi embassy in London where he was a former colleague of Khashoggi's. They had been identified via open source internet tools by Oslo-based Palestinian researcher Iyad al-Baghdadi.

On Thursday 11 October *Sabah* also published a picture of royal guard Mohammed al-Zahrani, hobnobbing with Mohammed bin Salman, while Mutreb was with the Crown Prince's entourage during his trip to the US in April 2018. The *New York Times* was to confirm their names and trace their closeness to MBS through its own research. Al-Zahrani was the first link of one degree of separation between an operative and MBS himself.

CC-TV coverage was leaked by Turkish officials on 18 October showing Mutreb checking in at his hotel at 5.05am on 2 October, arriving at the consulate at 9.55am, outside the Saudi consul general's residence on Meşelik Street at 4.53pm and clearing airport security at 17.49pm.

Brigadier-General Maher Mutreb entering the consulate's road block at 9.55am on Tuesday 2 October.

And yet officially it still remained unclear what had actually happened to Jamal Khashoggi, while anonymous Turkish authorities leaked they had pulled up the X-ray images of the operatives' luggage that had been scanned by airport security officials to check for body parts.

The scans of the first jet were merely routine ones before the Turkish police and intelligence services had opened their investigation at 5.50pm. But they had monitored the seven Saudis in the airport waiting room while they checked their luggage for the second flight that departed in the evening. As with all Turkey's visual evidence, none of it was on the record and this would be important months later.

As assassination allegations mounted, the optics of the situation were increasingly bad and the Trump administration was obliged to say something more in view of the fact that Khashoggi was both a US resident and part of the *Washington Post*.

US press releases started rolling in that Thursday. A statement from the White House said that several members of the Trump administration – John Bolton, the national security adviser, secretary of state Mike Pompeo and Jared Kushner, Donald Trump's son-in-law and senior adviser – had spoken to the crown prince by phone and asked for more details regarding the disappearance of the missing journalist.

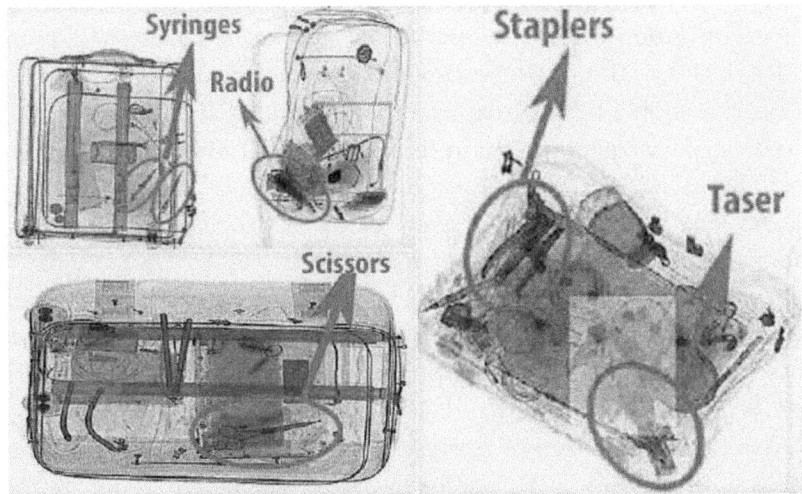

The luggage X-rays leaked to the Turkish media.

Asked what advice he gave to MBS, Jared Kushner said: 'To be fully transparent. The world is watching.... Take this very seriously.' According to Kushner the crown prince's response was an off-hand sounding, 'We'll see.'

'The reports that a Saudi-Arabian journalist may have been tragically murdered in Turkey should be deeply concerning to everyone who cherishes freedom of the press and human rights across the globe,' weighed in vice-president Mike Pence who could at the same time look forward to pastor Brunson's surprise release that week. He promised Washington was ready to 'assist in any way' with the investigation.

'We cannot let this happen, to reporters, to anybody.' This surprising statement was from Donald Trump and an unusual reversal from his 'fake news' approach to members of the press. 'It's a very serious situation for us and this White House. I want to see what happens and we're working very closely with Turkey and I think we'll get to the bottom of it.'

But his eye was trained on the deal that he had been negotiating with MBS all along in the background.

'We don't like it even a little bit', he said a few days later. 'But as to whether or not we should stop $110bn from being spent in this country, knowing they have four or five alternatives, two very good alternatives, that would not be acceptable to me.'

Leading Republican on the senate foreign relations committee, Senator Lyndsey Graham, however blamed the crown prince, not pulling his punches on Fox News: 'Nothing happens in Saudi Arabia without MBS knowing it. I've been their biggest defender on the floor of the United States Senate [but] this guy is a wrecking ball. He had this guy murdered in a consulate in Turkey, and to expect me to ignore it, I feel used and abused. The MBS figure is to me toxic. He can never be a world leader on the world stage.'

A bipartisan group of twenty-two US senators signed a letter to Trump that triggered a US government investigation and determination whether human rights sanctions should be imposed over the Khashoggi affair. The provisions for this mandatory investigation were in the 2012 Global Magnitsky Human Rights Accountability Act.

This Act was one of the biggest eye sores of Vladimir Putin, as its broad injunctions against foreign individuals had been passed by US Congress further to the brutal killing of a Russian lawyer in Russian custody in 2009 who was trying to expose Russian corruption. It required the US president to determine whether a foreign individual was 'responsible for extrajudicial killing, torture, or other gross violation of internationally recognised human rights against an individual exercising freedom of expression'. If so, sanctions had to be imposed. A lot of Russian officials and oligarchs had been sanctioned under the Act.

'Our expectation is that in making your determination you will consider any relevant information, including with respect to the highest ranking officials in the Government of Saudi Arabia,' the letter said.

Asked about suggestions in Congress that arms sales to the desert kingdom be blocked, however, Donald Trump replied that such a move would hurt the US economy.

'Frankly, I think that would be a very, very tough pill to swallow for our country'.

In Istanbul, further leaks burbled up as President Erdoğan authorised the release of additional evidence to put pressure on Saudi Arabia. They were still sitting on masses of secret MoBeSe footage around Istanbul that could be released anonymously in small nuggets.

But his team was still careful not to cross the line and circulate evidence that was conclusive proof as to what had really happened with Jamal Khashoggi. It was still the case, as the New York *Observer* put it, that 'the Middle-Eastern rumour mill can't agree whether the unfortunate man was murdered or merely abducted.'

Turkish investigators turned their attention, they said in release to the press, to the issue of the missing security camera footage at the Saudi consulate. Turkish authorities leaked that they believed that the hard drive was removed when Turkish staff at the consulate were abruptly told not to come back after lunch, and then taken on board one of the jets. All the leaks bolstered the notion that the Saudi government itself was involved in Khashoggi's disappearance.

Under pressure now that the odds that Khashoggi was dead were rising, US secret-service authorities were also leaking some of their own intel that showed that something was up with Khashoggi and Saudi Arabia – but that they didn't know what exactly it was. The *Washington Post* now cited secret American intercepts showing that the crown prince had ordered a repatriation operation targeting Jamal. The paper reported unnamed US officials saying the Saudis had been heard discussing a plan to lure the journalist from his home in Virginia and detain him.

The White House finger prints on what Vladimir Putin termed 'a certain responsibility' were quite well marked by now. In addition to the earlier chatter US intelligence had gathered, the NSA had picked up intel by 1 October that something odious was about to happen to the *Washington Post* journalist. This was the same date by which GCHQ spotted the Tiger Team flights, though the NSA's 'big ears' intercepted Saudi communications on the matter rather than flagged-up flight data.

An NSA official leaked to the New York *Observer* that this latest 'big ears' intel was relayed to the White House through the official intelligence channels, as part of the NSA's duty-to-warn procedure. 'Odious' did not seem like a non-violent arrest, but the White House didn't explain why it had not acted on the NSA's 1 October alert.

Several of Khashoggi's Washington friends now confirmed to journalists that, for four months, senior Saudi officials close to the crown prince had called Khashoggi to offer him protection, and a high-level job working for the government, if he returned to his home country, but that Khashoggi had refused.

XII
'Regular tourists'

Although Riyadh had cancelled the Turkish viewing of the consulate on Wednesday morning 10 October, the rest of the day had crashed over the news wires like a hurricane. The names of the fifteen men of the hit-squad was the *coup de grace*. It was only a matter of time before it became public knowledge that the fifteen men belonged to MBS's elite Tiger Team. It was time, according to the US, for damage control.

On Thursday 11 October, after holding out for nine days that there was no case to answer and still calling the rumours of Khashoggi's disappearance 'baseless', Riyadh finally conceded defeat. In the evening Ibrahim Kalin, President Erdoğan's spokesperson announced, 'Upon the suggestion of the kingdom, a joint-working team between Turkey and Saudi Arabia will be formed to investigate the case of Khashoggi in all its aspects.'

Although Kalin's wording was respectful of King Salman's high status as 'Custodian of the Two Holy Mosques' as one would expect from a populist-Islamic government, their essence left no doubt that the kingdom had caved in and had accepted, in principle, the widest possible brief for the team. Earlier in the week, behind the scenes, Jared Kushner had spoken to MBS and applied US pressure by mentioning the need for a 'working group' to move forward on the Khashoggi matter.

Another official close to the negotiations now also leaked, after Saudi Arabia's 'invitation' to Turkey, that the kingdom was close to 'accepting that a major crime took place at the consulate'. The source also mooted unofficially that 'Saudis intend to blame elements within their country's "deep state",' the story line Yasin Aktay had floated earlier on and withdrawn the next day. It seemed that the diplomatic horse trading about what had happened continued apace behind the scenes, but without reaching agreement.

As Saudi Arabia's original 'baseless' claim had changed to 'a question that needed investigating', MBS's brother KBS, the US ambassador, unexpectedly left Washington DC for Riyadh. The US state department's spokeswoman said, in response, 'we expect some information when he gets back', but he would not be back in the US until December.

So far, Erdoğan's team had anonymously leaked CC-TV footage as well as flight and airport data. But this was all information from outside the building.

Yet already on 6 October, 'lower officials' had leaked graphic details of the manner of Khashoggi's death inside the building to his friend Turan Kişlakçi of the Turkish-Arab Journalists' Association.

On 12 October an anonymous 'senior' Turkish official, speaking to the Middle East Eye, lifted the shadowy lid a little further and warned that 'investigators knew in which room of the consulate Khashoggi was killed and where the body was taken to be dismembered.'

How did Turkey know all, became the key question?

Now that Riyadh had officially agreed there was a case to answer, Turkey finally launched its most convincing piece of evidence, or leaked it anonymously at any rate. Presumably, this was the evidence the Saudi diplomats had chosen to ignore when it was presented to them behind closed doors on Friday 5 October in Ankara.

Turkey's decision to go public with this secret piece of information was curious. So far Erdoğan seemed to have no principled interest in establishing the truth and sought to negotiate instead. Now that Riyadh was signalling its agreement that a 'major crime' had occurred at the consulate, what more could be achieved?

'We never had the opportunity to protect him', Yasin Aktay had plaintively told the readers of conservative-religious AKP paper *Yeni Şafak*. Regardless, it was not a sign of strength that on AKP's watch the country was treated like a killing ground by an adversary. There was some evidence of this. Erdoğan's AKP would lose two important local elections in Istanbul and Ankara over half a year later which broke the party's uninterrupted string of success under his leadership.

Turkish officials explained the decision anonymously. Turkey had been surprised by the 'unprecedented international outcry' and the wave of positive international attention for the country.

Instead of appeasement Erdoğan as going for the jugular. The *Washington Post* was given the scoop that would transform everything some eight hours after the official Turkish-Saudi-Arabian announcement of a joint-team investigation.

Khashoggi's US paper said it had new 'shocking' and 'gruesome evidence'. Turkish officials who insisted on anonymity told its journalists that their government had made contact with the Trump administration and had described to US officials that they had a 'voice recording from inside'.

'You can hear his voice and the voices of men speaking Arabic', the Turkish official said. 'You can hear how he was interrogated, tortured and then murdered'. Another official leaked to the paper that you could hear 'beating'.

Now that the Turkish government had decided to cross the Rubicon and dispel any remaining public hope that Jamal Khashoggi was alive by leaking the existence of a murder recording, the media discussion once again changed direction. In view of Khashoggi's undoubted demise, the global press now charted the risks and perils of being a Saudi national.

Prince Khaled bin Farhan, a Saudi royal living in exile in Germany, told the *Independent*: 'Over thirty times the Saudi authorities have told me to meet them in the Saudi embassy but I have refused every time. I know what can happen if I go into the embassy.'

Only two thousand out of some fifteen thousand princes control Saudi Arabia's wealth and Khashoggi was, due to his closeness to the royal inner sanctum, considered an insider. Khaled bin Farhan added that there was deep anxiety among ordinary royals as to what had happened to Khashoggi.

'Around ten days before Khashoggi went missing they asked my family to bring me to Cairo to give me a cheque. I refused. Many, many princes are in jail right now in Saudi. Just five days ago a group tried to visit King Salman saying they were afraid for the future of the al-Saud family, they mentioned Mr Khashoggi's case. They were all put in jail.'

Khaled bin Farhan's story echoed the fate of another royal, prince Sultan bin Turki, grandson of Saudi Arabia's first king, ibn Saud. He had vanished on the way to Egypt in 2016 after criticising the Saudi regime.

'If I disappear you know what happened to me' was the last thing Sultan said to Bel Trew, the Middle East correspondent of the *Independent*.

Another of Sultan's friends said: 'I spoke to him before he got on the flight.... He actually joked that should he not make it, it was likely he was in Riyadh and I should raise the alarm.'

The prince was lured to Cairo, travelling on a royal private jet to see his father. But he was drugged and flown to Saudi Arabia instead. He was believed to be alive but under house arrest. His friends no longer had the means of contacting him. He had previously been kidnapped and drugged in Geneva in 2003 after calling for reforms under Crown Prince Abdullah's regency. Back in Riyadh, he was held under house arrest and only returned to Europe in 2015 for medical treatment.

Prince Saud bin Saif, a relatively minor prince who publicly backed calls for King Salman's removal, also went missing in 2016. Prince Khaled bin Farhan thought Saud had been tricked into getting on a Saudi-owned private jet which, instead of landing in Rome, flew on to Riyadh. Prince Turki bin Bandar, a one-time major in the police who took to publishing videos criticising the regime, disappeared in 2015 after applying for asylum in France. Khaled bin Farhan believed both Turki bin Bandar and Saud bin Saif could be dead, though he had no proof.

Prince Abdulaziz bin Fahd, the forty-five-year-old son of the late King Fahd, disappeared in 2017 amid rumours he had been put under house arrest. In January 2018, Prince Salman bin Abdulaziz, an expert fencer and graduate of the Sorbonne, was called to the royal palace in Riyadh with some of his relatives.

Soon after they arrived, a fight broke out reportedly between them and the bodyguards of the crown prince. The thirty-six-year-old Salman bin Abdulaziz was beaten unconscious. He had not been heard from since. His father, who was at the scene, was arrested two days later.

Non-royals fared no better. Ghanem al-Dosari, a Saudi satirist in exile in London, said he had not set foot in a Saudi embassy for nearly a decade, even though his passport expired in 2010.

'[The authorities] have a history of trying to lure people into embassies, they asked me to go inside the embassy in 2010 and I refused,' he said after Khashoggi went missing. 'I haven't travelled in years for fear of entering a country where I might be picked up. I know dissidents who are now scared to leave their apartments.'

He was attacked in a London street by men he thought were agents of MBS's regime. Dosari, who has refugee status in the UK, published footage of two men hitting him in the face in the Brompton Road on his YouTube channel that mocks the Saudi regime in August 2018. According to Dosari, they said: 'F*** London – the Queen is our slave.' He had received death threats in the past, including a threatening phone call, which he taped and published.

Major-general Ali al-Qahtani, an aide to Prince Turki bin Abdullah, the son of the previous king, King Abdullah, and a potential rival to MBS, died in government custody after being detained in MBS's Ritz-Carlton shake-down. The *Daily Telegraph* reported that the general's 'neck was twisted unnaturally as though it had been broken' and that his body had burn marks which appeared to be the result of electric shocks. General al-Qahtani was taken to hospital, but was reportedly returned to his interrogation after being seen by doctors. The palace did not offer an official explanation for how he died.

'People are very scared,' said a senior prince about the current situation. 'MBS is the reason people in my country are no longer sleeping.'

Days after the murder of Jamal Khashoggi, unconfirmed reports came through that a journalist had been tortured to death in the kingdom: Saudi authorities said Turki al-Jasser, the journalist, secretly ran a Twitter account called Kashkool. It exposed human rights violations by officials and the royal family in Saudi Arabia. He was arrested after Saudi moles in Twitter's regional office in Dubai unmasked him.

Amnesty International also reported that three female activists in prison in Saudi Arabia were subjected to electric shocks, torture, flogging and sexual harassment by officers. One of the men accused of involvement was Saud al-Qahtani, MBS's top intelligence enforcer.

There was also concern about Salman al-Ouda, a religious scholar detained after refusing to tweet in support of the Qatar blockade and who may face the death penalty.

Middle East Eye, however, argued that it was ever thus and MBS was no exception. It recalled the case of Nasir al-Sa'id, founder of the Arabian Peninsula People's Union (APPU). He was regarded as the first and most prominent opposition figure to the Saudi royal family. Having begun his opposition work in the 1950s, he ran an opposition radio programme. Sa'id then moved to Yemen to set up an office for the APPU before going to Beirut where he disappeared in 1979, the same year he praised the takeover of the grand mosque in Mecca by an armed group of citizens and called for the fall of the House of Saud.

Riyadh had a way of preventing people prying into its affairs. In August 2018, for example, Canada's foreign minister tweeted her alarm at the imprisonment of the sister of a Saudi blogger Raif Badawi, who was himself in prison for 'insulting Islam through electronic channels' and sentenced to a thousand lashes. Riyadh announced a suspension of diplomatic ties, expelled the Canadian ambassador, declared a freeze on new investment and withdrew Saudi students from Canada.

But the Brunson bribe to Trump was effective. Saudi Arabia couldn't bully it's main ally. Al-Arabiya TV reported on Friday at 4pm that the palace 'welcomes the Turkish response to the request to form a joint team into Khashoggi's disappearance', quoting an official Saudi source. The source added, 'We trust the ability of the joint team… to carry out its mission' as well as the mantra that KBS, the Saudi US ambassador, had WhatsApped a few days before, 'Saudi Arabia is concerned about the safety of its citizens.'

MBS's position in the kingdom was as unassailable as before. 'The bottom line is that the king has made it clear that despite the Khashoggi affair, he is not planning on removing his son,' a western diplomat told the *Sunday Times*. 'There is no group of people who are going to revolt against the king.'

MBS remained popular among ordinary Saudis who backed his social reforms. Apart from his great plans for the future, the palace didn't allow anything critical to appear in the Saudi media in any case. The death of Khashoggi, a member of the rarefied Saudi elite and intelligence establishment, did not have a huge impact on daily life. The diplomat said: 'In Saudi they say they're sorry it happened but my wife gets to drive and I get to go to the movies.'

There were some business consequences though. Richard Branson, for example froze business links with Saudi Arabia.

'I had high hopes for the current government in the Kingdom of Saudi Arabia and its leader Crown Prince Mohammed bin Salman and it is why I was delighted to accept two directorships in the tourism projects around the Red Sea,' he said. 'I felt that I could give practical development advice and also help protect the precious environment around the coastline and islands.'

'We have asked for more information from the authorities in Saudi and to clarify their position in relation to Mr Khashoggi. While those investigations are ongoing and Mr Khashoggi's presence is not known, I will suspend my directorships of the two tourism projects. Virgin will also suspend its discussions with the Public Investment Fund over the proposed investment [of $400 million] in our space companies Virgin Galactic and Virgin Orbit.'

Abahussain and al-Arifi, travelling separately from consulate secret service chief Ahmed al-Muzaini, but arriving on the same plane on 1 October (left); al-Hawsawi, Khalid al-Otaibi, and al-Bostani arriving on a commercial flight, landing at the same time as Khashoggi's London flight in the early morning of 2 October (right). They all roll large suitcases yet none of them will stay for longer than twenty eight hours in Istanbul.

Branson also pulled out of MBS's Future Investment Initiative conference in Riyadh – known as 'Davos in the desert' – along with World Bank president Jim Yong Kim, Uber chief Dara Khosrowshahi, Viacom's Robert Bakish, Steve Case, former head of AOL and Andy Rubin, the Silicon Valley entrepreneur best known for creating the Android smartphone operating system. Patrick Soon-Shiong, the owner of the *Los Angeles Times*, and the *Economist*'s editor-in-chief, Zanny Minton Beddoes, were no longer attending, and Arianna Huffington, the entrepreneur, media mogul and Uber board member, also pulled out of the conference, having previously served on its advisory board. The *Financial Times*, the *New York Times*, Bloomberg, CNN and CNBC withdrew as media sponsors. Ford and JP Morgan also pulled out, along with government officials from the UK, US, and other western nations where the media was not under state control.

In an echo of Russia's lament of 'innocent visitors' to Salisbury regarding the Russian Skripal *novichok*-poison squad, al-Arabiya now claimed that the fifteen-man team whose pictures appeared in the Turkish press were, in fact, 'regular tourists'. The argument was based on the fact that the last jet out had been thoroughly searched by Turkish security forces and that nothing untoward had been found on board.

Unfortunately, al-Arabiya also based it on the fact that a number of the fifteen men were photographed in the commercial arrivals hall (hence 'regular tourists') and the others in the airport's private-jet terminal, two kilometres away from the main hall. While this was true, al-Arabiya misunderstood the data.

After no more than between 30 and 20 hours in Istanbul the six men al-Arabiya claimed were 'regular tourists' on commercial flights flew out of Turkey on the less than ordinary second private Gulfstream IV jet. Outside the kingdom, the broadcaster was called out on its sloppy journalism.

Not long after the arrival of al-Hawsawi, Khalid al-Otaibi and al-Bostani from Riyadh, Jamal Khashoggi walked through the same customs corridor after flying in from London on 2 October.

The UN inquiry would reveal that the ground work for al-Arabiya's 'tourists' scenario had been laid well in advance by Riyadh. When booking rooms for the Tiger-Team members, the Saudi secret-service team in Istanbul, for example, could be heard using a tourism company and asked for rooms with a 'sea view' (detail 199).

XIII
Apple Watch – iCloud

With the leak to the *Washington Post* that it had a voice recording in its possession, the Turkish government had introduced the knock-out proof of its (still unofficial) allegations. But for Turkey to have a voice recording of what went on inside a diplomatic building would require at least some explanation of its origins to be credible to the media – quite apart from the fact that it potentially constituted a breach of the Vienna Convention, which stipulated that a designated diplomatic space must not be penetrated by the host country. Erdoğan couldn't very well insist on 'human conscience' in the Khashoggi case and at the same time rely on a flagrant breach of the law.

Ironically, therefore, the consequence of crossing the Rubicon was that it made clear that Ankara's pattern of behaviour in its handling of the affair was as underwhelming as Riyadh's. It gave the Khashoggi news story a continued lease of life. But from this moment, leaks were increasingly manipulated by Turkish officials in the way the news was orchestrated inside the country – as an opportunistic fantasy rather than as steps towards the truth. As will become clear, the Turkish government would start to contradict its own 'facts' as much as Riyadh whenver it was more convenient.

Once jolted by Erdoğan's terse instruction in the afternoon of 2 October 'that all measures be taken', the Turkish secret service MİT had retrieved the situation by following up with some urgency on Hatice Cengiz's and Turan Kişlakçi's catalytic calls to Yasin Aktay that Khashoggi was missing.

Yet no one could call MİT's performance stellar before 5.50pm that day. Yasin Aktay had said that 'all precautions' regarding Khashoggi's safety were taken but, unlike the US and UK, for example, Turkey had no idea that an attack was imminent. Furthermore, once they did know, they had had at least six of the perpetrators corralled in one place, and yet let them all go.

Not that there was any great dishonour in this. Despite the brute global reach of Five Eyes and GCHQ, MI5 and MI6 had been blind-sided in the Salisbury-Skripal attack, too. The Russian team had flown in and out of Britain without any hindrance as if 'regular' tourists. The same had happened in the 2006 case of Alexander Litvinenko's assassins, Andrey Lugovoy and Dmitri Kovtun, and in the case of an estimated fourteen further murders on British soil since Putin had come to power in 2001.

This score card, however, started to change on Wednesday 10 October 2018. Erdoğan's team planted a ground-laying leak with Reuters.

Turkish officials told the press agency's reporters that MoBeSe CC-TV showed that Khashoggi was wearing his Apple Watch and that the watch was at the heart of their forensic investigation.

'We have determined that it was on him when he walked into the consulate', the official told Reuters.

They were trying to find out whether it was connected to the phones Khashoggi had given Cengiz, and what was transmitted, the unnamed official leaked. 'Intelligence services, the prosecutor's office and a technology team are working on this. Turkey does not have the watch so we are trying to do it through connected devices.'

Reuters got this leak a day before the *Washington Post* published the its arresting scoop that Turkey had a recording of the assassination and had told the White House of it.

It is good to emphasise again that, before the optics started to change, the only memorable thing about MİT was that it had let a small army slip through its nets as opposed to, say, one or two Russian assassins.

Given the amount of CC-TV and customs data, MİT had identified the Saudi jets that were involved on the evening of 2 October, though evidently not quickly enough to be able to detain the Tiger Team members in terms of Erdoğan's 'all measures available' to MİT. By their own account, they were too late for the first one, and airport authorities had also cleared the second one for take-off at 10.46pm, never mind the departure of the four Saudi secret-service staff stationed at the consulate.

Even then MİT could still intercept the last two stragglers on Turkish soil – major-general Mustafa al-Madani and Saif al-Qahtani, but hadn't.

These two Saudis had first come through passport control at the private-jet terminal at 3.41am that day. But they only exited through passport control at 0.18am to board Turkish Airlines flight TK144 to Riyadh for scheduled take-off at 1.20am.

This gave MİT at least another two hours to detain these last two perpetrators while still on Turkish soil and prevent them from boarding; they could even have taken them off the plane. Turkey did leak information their stamp-time going through the security gate in the main Atatürk terminal. It was an unarguable fact that they, too, had left Turkey unhindered that evening.

But it wasn't clear whether this was because MİT failed to identify the two in time, or whether airport officials had at the very least searched their luggage or retained luggage scans as intelligence. Turkey's anonymous leaks were mainly dispersed through Turkish papers and that meant they were a one-way street: taken as read.

In any case, these failures were understandable. The process of matching visual and entry data was laborious and all that MİT had at 5.50pm to start with was a CC-TV grab of Khashoggi at the consulate's front door. They even had to show it to Hatice Cengiz to be certain this was the man they were after. It was like looking for a needle in a haystack.

At least Turkey had come within a hair's breadth of arresting the assassins – unlike Britain in the case of the 2018 Skripal attackers who flew home to Russia undetected and unbothered.

After the Washington Post's scoop, the only thing the media cared about was: how did Turkey obtain the recording and what did it say.

The explanation itself was leaked on Saturday the 13th of October. This was a poignant day as it was the day on which Khashoggi would have turned 60, at least so said Cengiz.

She tweeted in the morning, 'invited all his close friends to a restaurant on the detail TheBosporus to celebrate his birthday but detail WhereIsJamal'. She also published her oped piece in the *New York Times*.

However, back in Saudi Arabia, Dr Alaa Mahmoud Nasief (@anaseif), Khashoggi's divorced third wife countered what Cengiz said. An attractive woman with a traditional black *abaya* covering her hair, she was interviewed on al-Arabiya to tell her story.

Dr Nasief said, 'While Cengiz claims to be the fiancée of Jamal, I have not heard of that name beforehand and neither his family nor his son Abdullah, who was with him in Turkey for two weeks before his disappearance. If Cengiz was in Jamal's life, I would be the first to know, but she was never in his life.'

She was 'surprised' that Cengiz had his phones and expressed astonishment at how she could have access to his personal social media, enabling 'deletions and manipulation'.

She deftly covered over the tracks of the palace's motive for the attack. 'I did not know that Khashoggi moved from America to Turkey. He did not tell me that, and I do not know why'. She warned al-Arabiya's audience in Saudi Arabia that the important thing was 'that everyone has to keep silent'.

A Saudi TV pundit and writer for a Mecca newspaper, Faisal al-Shammari meanwhile tweeted on @Mr_Alshammeri pictures of Khashoggi's passport that showed a date of birth of 22 January 1958 and not 13 October 1958, as well as one of the Khashoggi family and of Khashoggi's divorced wife Dr Nasief with Khashoggi. By now, few took much notice of what Saudis were saying. But it was potentially a very strange situation that Cengiz to invited people to a birthday party of her fiancé that was early by three months. A few weeks later, evidence from an unexpected corner would support what @Mr_Alshammeri posted.

In a statement to the Saudi Press Agency on the same day, the Saudi interior minister still dismissed any involvement as 'outright lies'. But for the first time, he also acknowledged publically that the kingdom was being accused of killing one of its subjects.

Furthermore, a senior Saudi delegation of eleven men, led by the seventy-eight-year-old governor of Mecca, Prince Khalid bin Faisal, met Turkish delegates on that Saturday. Prince bin Faisal was to report back to his uncle, King Salman himself.

The scan of Jamal Khashoggi's passport leaked by Saudi officials.

This delegation was heavy with symbolism for those who understood the palace. Khashoggi's secret-service patron, Prince Turki bin Faisal, was Prince Khalid's half-brother, and according to some reports Prince Khalid himself was also a onetime patron of Khashoggi's. As we know the whole Faisal family had banded together, according to Maggie Salem Mitchell, to airlift Khashoggi to safety at the London embassy when he ran into trouble with Saudi's Wahhabi clerics in 2003.

It was AKP paper *Sabah* that led with its own audio scoop on the morning of Khashoggi's presumed birthday. Abdurrahman Şimşek, the head of its investigative team, explained the provenance of the watch recording in his article.

'Reliable sources' had leaked that Khashoggi had 'paired the smart watch on his arm with his iPhone' that he had left with Cengiz. From Khashoggi's wrist, the Apple Watch had recorded how he 'was interrogated, tortured, and then killed', and transmitted the recording to the iPhone and his i-Cloud. The Saudis realised all this, Turkish officials leaked to the paper, and they had tried to log into the i-Cloud account with a password and the Apple Watch by PIN but failed and instead had used Khashoggi's fingers, or at any rate 'fingerprints to log in and try to erase some files'.

'Saudi intelligence... managed to erase some files. However, it could not delete all of the files', *Sabah* dutifully reported on the leaked information it had been given.

It was sensational, like a scene from From Russia with Love with MBS's villains failing at their job.

But it was also entirely untrue.

Unlike *Sabah*, rather than slavishly copy the leak, Reuters had done its due diligence to verify whether there was any relevance in that line of investigation. In its piece of 10 October it reported that an Apple Watch can 'provide data such as location and heart rate'. But, even so, that it would depend 'on the model of watch, whether it was connected to the internet, and whether it is near enough an iPhone to synchronise.'

However, neither the Turkish investigators nor, indeed, *Sabah*'s investigative journalists had checked the Apple Watch facts with equal care to see whether it could make andthen transmit recordings.

Apple stated fingerprint access was not an Apple Watch feature (Saudi trolls jeered sarcastically that there must have been a 'Turkish update'). As for the connection, the third-generation phone visible on Khashoggi's wrist couldn't directly connect through Turkish cellular networks to an iPhone or its iCloud in any case. Cengiz herself was out of range for a bluetooth transfer of the audio file to the iPhone.

This left the consulate's wifi as the only alternative for the transmission, and the idea that Khashoggi, in self-imposed exile, would have logged in on the consular network before entering was unbelievable. He knew that he would have to hand his phones over to consulate security anyway if he brought them inside.

Not only had Turkey been caught out in a lie, MİT had shown itself to be less technologically savvy than the news reporters at Reuters. Used to just providing a story that would be copied at face value in Turkey, the organisation – despite having the word 'intelligence' in its name – wasn't expecting scrutiny. It hadn't really thought through whether they could be called out on what they said.

Observers of the Turkish media certainly recognised that the story fit a pattern where the Turkish government put out a convenient explanation that AKP supporters accept unconditionally but that doesn't check out with the facts. Carried away by their success (or, more or equally likely, unable to challenge internally what the powerful MİT laid down) Turkish officials had relied on the same cheer-leading from international media.

With the shoe now firmly on the other foot, Saudi-sponsored al-Arabiya howled, 'Another blatant inaccuracy.'

Sabah had badly relied on the expertise of its government sources (as had the Middle East Eye's Turkey correspondent, who had tweeted the story on without critical comment).

It made Abdurrahman Şimşek, *Sabah*'s head of investigations look very unimpressive. He 'got angry' and complained 'directly to government officials that Turkish newspapers were not getting information on the case', though he didn't complain about the Apple Watch story as such – for which he was responsible.

Instead, he was angry about the fact that Cengiz had been writing pieces for the US papers, whereas Turkish readers also wanted to hear from her.

Next, on Sunday 14 October, *Sabah* published the first-exclusive interview in Turkey with her.

The international media, nonetheless, was giving MİT and *Sabah* a pass on its lie.

It rather appreciated the fact that the Apple Watch story proved to be bogus. In a case of reverse psychology, it was seen as an acceptable rather than a dim ruse to cover up how Erdoğan's team had come in possession of a recording in breach of diplomatic law – even though it was doubtful Western papers would have let their own spooks get away with such a clumsy fantasy about the facts.

How an intelligence organisation that lacks a basic grasp of consumer technology could make exceptionally sophisticated recordings was a question left for what it was.

In a rare exception to their keenness to leak information about the Khashoggi case, Turkish officials leaked no more on the Apple Watch.

However, once the optics had changed and it was thought to have scored a triumph with the recordings, MİT did produce yet another artless lie about the audio a few months later.

Again *Sabah* was the conduit. *Diplomatik Vahşet* ('diplomatic brutality'), a book published on 28 December 2018 by *Sabah*'s three journalists covering the Khashoggi story for the paper, contained yet another boast that cannot have been true.

Based on the testimony of Turkish secret-service officials, the book revealed 'news' that MİT did after all have advance notice. A day before Cengiz's phone call to Aktay, it knew that something was afoot in the Saudi consulate. That is to say, MİT's spycraft was of such quality that they were there before Cengiz, a mere member of the public, made her well-placed call which mobilised Erdoğan to get them on the case.

The book said that MİT had traced the local Saudi secret service chief, al-Muzaini as he travelled with a couple of his staff to Belgrad Forest in a consular BMW on 1 October.

One of the authors, head of *Sabah* investigations Abdurrahman Şimşek, added in a book interview on publication that 'al-Muzaini was unaware that MİT was tracking him when he went to Istanbul's Belgrad Forest on October 1 with two other Saudi intelligence officers'.

'MİT had initially thought that their visit to the forest was a part of an espionage operation but they had later understood that it was actually conducted as a reconnaissance mission before the Khashoggi murder', Şimşek concluded.

But, if MİT habitually recorded audio inside the consulate, why did they not access all of their audio capability on Friday? It would be an easy way to find out what was being said inside about the espionage goals of al-Muzaini's forest visit and the trip to Yalova for such a clever organisation?

Was MİT only interested in shadowing people, but not in using everything at their disposal to find out what kind of nefarious espionage the Saudis were up to on Turkish soil? It was as if Five Eyes decided to shadow some suspect with manpower but go blind on the astonishing technology that made it so effective.

While it cast yet more doubt whether MİT was the originator of all the secret internal audio recordings, this was not only issue. Interesting in its own right, the question also raised whether Turkey had shared all it knew about Khashoggi death itself or was withholding forensic information for its own strategic reasons.

On 13 October Şimşek still wrote in *Sabah* that Khashoggi 'was interrogated, tortured'. But in later weeks Turkey would sanitise this horrifying and despicable prelude to the assassination, and tow instead a version which saw Khashoggi dying in a little over ten minutes – hardly enough to drink a cup of tea – after entering the consulate as a result of the fifty-nine year old being man-handled. The story was accepted without question by the *Sabah* journalists of *Diplomatik Vahşet*. It was also accepted by the UN delegation in its 2019 report as a consequence of its decision not to consider leaks to the press as facts worthy of investigation.

Whether there is further evidence to suggest that brigadier-general Mutreb and his five specialists inside the consulate, in fact, laid their hands on Khashoggi for a far longer time will be returned to later in the book.

XIV
Crucial Hours

⁂

Where, then, did the recording come from was now the big question and the subject of fevered guess work in the media. International speculation ranged from bugs placed in the consulate itself to a directional microphone focused on the building from outside – both technically within the realms of Turkey's capabilities, it was thought by pundits. Another possibility, being discussed in Turkey and elsewhere, was a variation on the snuff movie: some operatives of the hit-squad recorded the abduction on their own phones for trophy purposes and those recordings were either intercepted in real time or retrieved from at least one of the killers' phones. While not uncreative, it did beg the question why MİT would come up with the bungling Apple Watch tale instead of the plain truth?

Now that the watch explanation had been shot down, what did Turkish officials say on the record about the provenance of the recording in their possession?

One top official who was to address that question directly was Turkish defence minister Hulusi Akar when he spoke on 19 November at the Halifax International Security Forum. His words were not widely reported, except in a number of Turkish media. In a tenacious interview in English on the Khashoggi affair, Afghani-Australian BBC correspondent Yalda Hakim asked the minister point-blank, 'There are a lot of questions about the consulate being bugged. Is this common practise for Turkey?'

'There is no such thing as us bugging within the consulate. We do not disclose the origin of the audio recordings', Akar replied with a wan smile.

Akar's concession that Turkey wasn't the author of the recording was also consistent with the words of Ibrahim Kalin, Erdoğan's personal spokesman. He said on 3 October, 'according to the information that we have, this Saudi citizen is still in the Saudi Arabian consulate in Istanbul. We don't have any information to the contrary.'

If MİT had already heard everything there was to know, Kalin's words were just another Turkish Apple Watch story with hindsight – and the same, for that matter, Akar's words. The ponderous watch lie had the unintended consequence that it exposed the words of two of Turkey's highest officials as lies.

Nine days after telling the Apple Watch tale to *Sabah*, Turkish security officials volunteered to reporters of the *Wall Street Journal* on 22 October a new story about when they first heard the audio.

For the sake of clarity, it should be emphasised that the *Wall Street Journal* didn't know about al-Muzaini and so couldn't ask why MİT hadn't pulled up 'passive' audio when their suspicion was first raised the day before as discussed above: the al-Muzaini intel should have prompted calling on MİT 'passive' audio more than 24 hours before Erdoğan's three-line whip. MİT would have heard the Khashoggi-related chatter from Friday onwards, including the secret service bookings for fifteen Saudis at the two hotels by the consulate's secret service station. Simply put, the audio – if it indeed originated from MİT, as Turkey claimed – could have prevented the assassination.

'The recording was in MİT's possession as early as the evening of 2 October', the *Wall Street Journal* reported on what MİT was saying at this time. Leaked by a senior Turkish security office, it was at least consistent with the time-line given to Şimşek for his nonsense 13 October Apple-Watch news article.

He had reported that the recording 'was found by the security forces after his fiancée handed over the phone' on 2 October (setting aside the conflicting detail that Cengiz said in a Turkish interview that she did this the next day).

Yet this claim made to the *Wall Street Journal* was also problematic in view of what the Turkish officials later told the writers of *Diplomatik Vahşet* in December.

On 22 October, the MİT claimed to the *Journal* it had pulled up the audio for that day inside the consulate after 5.50pm when the consulate was closed. The senior official leaked to the paper that these were 'passive' recordings rather than a live feed.

Turkish officials also leaked to the *Wall Street Journal* that 'within hours they reached a sobering conclusion: Mr. Khashoggi never left the consulate'. This in its own way created a mystery with what they leaked two months later to the book authors.

If MİT had the recordings on the evening of 2 October – as they would repeat to the writers of *Diplomatik Vahşet* in December – this would have removed any doubt as to what had happened on the day. It would have been instantly evident that a serious crime had been committed on Khashoggi's person and that this was not merely a hostage situation in the consulate or a case of abduction.

Certainly, what was on it was so gruesome that its violent nature spoke volumes when CIA Director Gina Haspel and select other top-level investigators were later given, or rather allowed to listen to a clip of the recording.

Having the recording on 2 October made a mockery of Kalin's words spoken on behalf of President Erdoğan ('we don't have any information'). Hulusi Akar's words were also contradicted by MİT's story leaked to uncritical Turkish media.

At the end of December, Turkish officials would give another precise time detail about the audio to the journalists who wrote *Diplomatik Vahşet*. They boasted that 'sound analysts... solved MİT's question within two hours' (*Ses analistleri geriye doğru analizlerini yaptı ve iki saat içinde MİT olayi çözdü*), that is, no later than 7.50pm. It took CIA Director Gina Haspel, not an Arab speaker, seven minutes to understand that Khashoggi was being killed. But let's assume that the 'two hours' included retrieval logistics and not just listening.

Thus, according to the *Wall Street Journal–Diplomatik Vahşet* leaks, MİT knew all they needed to know from about 7.50pm on 2 October. This was around the time that MoBeSe CC-TV captured three Tiger Team men – Tubaigy, al-Hawsawi, and Khalid al-Otaibi – leaving the consul-general's residence in the consulate's Mercedes Vito Van with plates 34 CC 1865 for the private-jet terminal where the 'sitting duck' Gulfstream IV was waiting for them on the tarmac. It would still be another full two hours before the final four of the seven Saudis on this jet – brigadier-general Abahussein, major al-Arifi, al-Zahrani, and al-Bostani – had their passports scanned between 9.44 and 9.46pm while their luggage was X-rayed.

That meant there were up to two hours (three if one included the time the jet took off at 10.46pm) to brief Erdoğan on the gravity of the situation and to threaten Riyadh with exposure, even before a decision to detain the Saudi crew or delay their jet's departure was made. Turkish authorities had already leaked that calls to Saudi authorities remained unanswered on the evening of 2 October.

Did Erdoğan blink first? Despite solving the problem 'within two hours' according to MİT, not 'all measures' were taken, as Erdoğan had instructed. All that happened was that the 'sitting duck' jet, the luggage, and passengers were thoroughly searched for Khashoggi before the Gulfstream IV was cleared for 10.46pm take-off.

MİT's time-and-date information raised a legal question. The nature of what was on the recording made anyone inside the consulate at the time a prima facie murder suspect, not least the seven of the Tiger Team MİT tracked down via MoBeSe etc waiting in the Atatürk Airport's private-jet lounge for the second jet to leave.

If Turkey knew at 7.50pm murder had been committed, why did it not act within the boundaries set by international law?

It could have detained at the very least four of these seven Saudis on suspicion of murder. The Vienna Convention (VCCR) only prohibits entry to a designated diplomatic space without the mission head's permission. But by 9.45pm all remaining nine members of the Tiger Team had left the consul-general's residence anyway and seven were grouped together at Atatürk airport's Genel Havacilik lounge for private jets.

Callamard addressed this question in detail. The focus of her report was almost exclusively on the legal liabilities of the parties involved. With the benefit of expert legal advice, she squarely addressed whether diplomats could be arrested in this case under the Vienna Convention (VCCR).

'The VCCR's limits on interviewing and prosecuting consulate employees did not apply in this case. Most of those responsible had already left the country before Turkey was fully aware of the magnitude of the crime, but if they had remained, Turkey would have been able to arrest them, despite any immunity, for a 'grave crime' (VCCR, Art. 41). Turkey also was able to compel witness testimony, as that testimony relates to a murder, not consular functions (VCCR, Art. 44). The operatives travelling on ordinary passports could in any case not even hope to claim diplomatic immunity outside the consulate. (Her legal advisors also stated that under international law, the consul-general's residence was 'not protected' by the VCCR – nor were cars used by the consulate.)

Four of the private jet passengers – al-Bostani, al-Hawsawi, al-Zahrani and Khalid al-Otaibi – were travelling on regular passports. Only major al-Arifi travelled on a diplomatic passport, while professor Tubaigy, the forensic expert, and major-general Abahussein travelled on government passports, which also afford a certain diplomatic protection. Not all diplomatic immunity is the same, though. Only the highest-ranking diplomats have absolute immunity under the Vienna Convention.

In addition, Turkish authorities could have tracked down and detained the other two team members – al-Madani and Saif al-Qahtani – who left on the commercial flights well after midnight. These two, who brought up the rear of the Saudi operation, also flew on regular passports (though al-Madani may also have flown on a government passport given that he was a two-star general). Up to a total of six, or more than a third of the Tiger Team, could have been detained without a Vienna Convention conflict.

While the recording would have removed any doubt that a criminal foul had been committed, the MoBeSe evidence itself already showed that Khashoggi never left the building and that, apart from kidnapping, there were suspicious movements and large pieces of luggage being shunted around. With their president's *carte blanche*, what else did the Turk's need to delay the departure of the jet under the broad sweep of Turkish law, if not some of the operatives, pending further investigation?

Whatever the truth of the state of the Turkish investigation on 2 October, MİT was the organisation whose knowledge of what happened inside was undoubtedly the closest to what Maher Mutreb knew of the execution of his plans and yet it seemed incapable of passing on the facts without holes in it.

From Tuesday to Saturday evening, Ankara had accused Riyadh of holding Khashoggi hostage. During those days, Turkey's bargaining power would with two, let alone up to six or nine operatives, have been a sharp incentive for a rapid solution. Doubtless, Saudi Arabia's fobbing off of Ankara would have been different if Turkey held, for example, the man with the bone saw, professor lieutenant-colonel Tubaigy. But even holding six 'regular tourists' at Atatürk airport on suspicion of murder would have been a much stronger hand to play against Saudi Arabia and side-stepped the need for making the audio recording public. Why would any nation let a hostile 'Skripal team' slip through their fingers? Two months later, on 30 November, the Istanbul Crime Court would indeed issue warrants for the arrests of all fifteen members of the Tiger Team *in absentia*, and demand that Saudi Arabia extradite them. But on 2 October Turkey had most of them, right there and most of the evidence it was going to get, that is if the information MİT gave the media was accurate in the first place.

Did Turkey really know as much on that day as it said it did in December? What was the point of searching a plane and luggage for incriminating evidence if Turkish authorities were investigating a complaint of kidnapping and already knew the seven passengers were murder suspects? It seemed a good question to ask.

Abdurrahman Şimşek, head of *Sabah* investigations, in fact, was the one who had not only reported on the Apple Watch story but also on 10 October on Turkey's search of the second jet for *Sabah*. He wrote in that piece that it had been be done 'by eye' with the seven team members waiting in the lounge, and that the Gulfstream jet was cleared for take-off after 'it was seen [Khashoggi] was not among the passengers.' Either that October story was yet another Apple Watch story, or the December one. Was anyone in Turkey interested in finding out which was which?

In October, Turkish officials segued over the complication the audio story was creating.

The *Wall Street Journal* reported, 'it took security agencies time to identify Arabic voices on the recording, but noted its content and a detailed analysis were shared among investigators within two days.' Folded inside this time lag was the explanation why Turkey did nothing on 2 October. The 'two days' implied that by Thursday or Friday Turkey was in a position to act but not before. This was congruent with the moment when Turkish officials leaked the bombshell on Saturday that 'Mr Khashoggi has been killed at the consulate' and his death was 'premeditated' and also with the leaked secret meeting on Friday with Saudi diplomats in Ankara in the same piece. It also explained why none of the operatives got arrested despite the fact that MİT had caught seven of them and then released them. On this point, the source told the *Journal,* intelligence had also concluded they had 'missed chances' to detain members of the hit-squad.

While the *Wall Street Journal* leaks corresponded to the facts, then, they deepened the mystery surrounding the recording once MİT replaced its humble pie with self-congratulation through *Diplomatik Vahşet*. There the source claimed two months later that MİT grasped everything within 'two hours' on the same evening. MİT would hardly have merely 'noted' what was on the tape and done nothing for two days.

A few days later would explain why Turkey didn't act against the perpetrators in the Genel Havacilik departure hall. It would also mean that top officials Hulusi Akar and Ibrahim Kalin didn't tell stories that they knew to be untrue and which implicated President Erdoğan himself in factual misrepresentations. Yet the 'evening of 2 October' is the date MİT claimed for itself, like the Apple Watch story.

Why did the tail constantly wag the dog? Did Turkey's MİT obtain the recording 'as early as the evening of 2 October', or in actual fact later? It couldn't all be down to underwhelming journalism, and certainly not in the case of the *Wall Street Journal* with its staff trained in the persnickety style of US journalism. The chopping and changing in MİT's storyboard and the sequence of events as they unfolded in the world news did, however, make perfect sense if Turkey simply didn't have or make the recording itself. In any case, setting side by side its leaks, MİT was putting together quite a tribute of Apple Watches for itself.

***

While host nations try to listen in clandestinely to diplomatic missions, guest nations, particularly rich and technologically sophisticated ones, typically do everything they can to keep unwanted ears out of their buildings, and safe, sound-proof rooms.

Saudi Arabia with its thirty-two-year-old ruler, in particular, was not a notably unsophisticated country. There were reports in December 2019 that Khashoggi's WhatsApp messages were intercepted with advanced software. And if this didn't impress anyone, on 31 March 2019 even the messages of Amazon's billionaire owner Jeff Bezos, the richest man in the world, were hacked by Saudi Arabia. In the latter case it was to expose his marital infidelity which led to his $38bn divorce of his wife of twenty five years. The kingdom had a very skilled edge in digital warfare that could even put the engineers of Facebook in the US, owner of WhatsApp, to shame.

On the other hand, Turkey's handling of technology during the first alarm in the Khashoggi case seemed as leaden and mediocre as Ankara's later international manipulation of traditional media such as TV and newspapers was nimble.

In Saudi Arabia al-Qahtani's Center for Studies and Media Affairs (it had a black list of twenty people of which Khashoggi, who had just gone into self-exile, was one) was deeply embedded with MBS's Tiger Team. When the fifty-strong Tiger Team was formed in deep secrecy on MBS's appointment as crown prince, al-Qahtani also became a pivotal part of this operation, with his center providing the cyber, digital and technological expertise – the center had experience training up warriors with such skills well before the formation of the

Tiger Team.

Brigadier-general Maher Mutreb was also an early Saudi cyber expert apart from evidently being fluent in English. Wikileaks revealed on 19 October that Mutreb's had taken part in an advanced two-week spyware course in Riyadh in 2011, organised by Hacking Team, an Italian specialist firm. Speaking rarely and nicknamed 'glum face' by the training team because of his gloomy Lurch-like presence, he would 'come and go' and was in the group that received training in 'physical intelligence… so cameras, microphones'. Other Tiger Team members had been trained in the latest intelligence techniques in the US by leading companies owned by Cerberus Capital Management, NY, whose co-CEO was on Trump's Intelligence Advisory Board.

Both men first met when al-Qahtani invited Mutreb to become a member of another organisation he chaired, the Saudi Federation of Cyber Security, Programming, and Drones. US intelligence said that, thereafter, Mutreb was tapped in 2017 as assistant secretary-general for security at al-Qahtani's new Center for Studies and Media Affairs.

The Tiger Team brought at least one scrambler, apart from other comms. Undoubtedly the Saudi consulate itself also relied on more expensive and sophisticated technology than most nations to maintain secrecy. It certainly had many more high-tech protocols than merely dismissing or sequestering Turkish staff at key moments by way of removing unwanted ears and eyes.

Although the consulate was otherwise plain, it did have two large and one enormous white parabolic satellite dishes pointing to the sky on terrace-level at the back of the building. They were not visible from the street. Due to the sloping of Istanbul's hills, the terrace itself was the roof of a one-level basement extension at the back that opened up to a court with its own carport and the exit through which the six consular cars left without being seen by Hatice Cengiz waiting at the front of the building.

Nor was it very likely that the Tiger Team had opted for recklessness or a gamble on the occasion of their covert rendition on 2 October.

Whichever organisation pierced the electronic cloaking devices of the Saudi consulate and made clear recordings that day must have been exceptionally skilled in such intercepts.

There is one country that can undoubtedly match the Five Eyes Alliance's technological capability and manpower, or indeed that of Saudi Arabia's. If British and US intelligence knew about the attack beforehand, that country with very sensitive ears on the ground in Istanbul may well have known, too.

If one looks at the 2016 US elections, the UK Brexit Referendum, and democratic elections elsewhere in Europe, Russia's deployment of digital technology may, in fact, be superior in some ways to the Five Eyes, who often seem to be on the back foot: able to detect but not able to create a shield against interference. US Special Counsel Robert Mueller said Russia's US electoral interference was 'sweeping and systematic' in his report of 10 April 2019. Once unified behind one holistic communist ideology ('electrification and Soviets' according to Lenin), the country under Putin was gigabytes and cronies. Given Istanbul's abiding importance to Russia from Catherine the Great's first expansion to the Black Sea, it would not be a surprise if there were almost as much Russian-spyware cabling underneath its pavements as in Moscow. Furthermore, knowing what Saudi officials – the world's number 2 oil exporter ahead of number 3 Russia, and the world's largest arms buyer since the war in Yemen – were discussing in private was a key strategic interest.

In December, *Sabah* would proudly report in Turkish that Gina Haspel, director of the CIA (a Turkish speaker and one-time chief of station in Ankara), praised MİT chief Hakan Fidan for a success achieved only 'once or twice in the history of intelligence', as leaked to the authors of *Diplomatik Vahşet*. The point was a self-serving one – how quickly MİT had 'solved' the Khashoggi case, transmogrifying MİT's middling performance to one that the Turkish population could be proud of.

One of *Sabah*'s columnists observed on 18 October, Vladimir Putin 'patiently waits for Trump to make mistakes and employs diplomacy to exploit them. As a leader who knows the Western alliance's weaknesses, he never misses an opportunity... Washington has been withdrawing from its former sphere of influence, and the Russians replaced the US at a low cost.'

Even if the recording was a lucky break by Turkey all along – and not the gift of a nation like Russia looking to cause trouble and selling nuclear reactors and air-defence systems – it was once again a brick through the window of the US. Once again the Trump administration was in trouble abroad and at home as a result of the ramifications of the Khashoggi affair.

XV
'Rogue' Operators

On Monday evening, thirteen days after Jamal Khashoggi disappeared, Turkish criminal investigators were finally allowed to enter the Saudi consulate to collect evidence. The joint-group of Saudi and Turkish official investigators had at last signed off on the rules of engagement under a diplomatic protocol of temporary access to both the consulate and the consular residence.

Turkish investigators would be given access for six hours to the consulate and thirteen hours to the consul general's residence, and the consular fleet of cars had to be inspected in this time as well. Strictly speaking, the cars and residence were not covered by diplomatic immunity and did not require Riyadh's permission, but Turkey was afraid of Saudi 'retribution' UN rapporteur Callamard would later write. The palace only gave permission for 'swabbing'. No other forensic protocols were permitted.

The night before the inspection, King Salman had called President Erdoğan. The governor of Mecca Prince bin Faisal, who headed the king's Khashoggi delegation, had reported back to him from Turkey and allegedly said 'It is really difficult to get out of this one'.

While in Ankara, the prince had 'begged the president to save them', a Turkish source now leaked to the media. In return, the source further leaked, Erdoğan had demanded 'complete cooperation' from Riyadh. Turkey wanted to 'search the consulate and the consul-general's house, and interview the consul-general... and that the Saudis tell them where Khashoggi's body is buried', the news site Middle East Eye reported. They also wanted to inspect the twenty-two cars that had driven in and out of the consulate on 2 October.

Erdoğan had been direct to the king on the call. In return the king had thanked the president for not using the murder as an opportunity for exploitation.

That evening King Salman would instruct the Saudi prosecutor general Sheikh Saud al-Mojeb to start an internal investigation, issuing royal decree 5709. To CNN Turk, Riyadh leaked no more than twenty-four hours later through two sources that the prosecutor would discover that 'Khashoggi's death was the result of an interrogation that went wrong, one that was intended to lead to his abduction from Turkey.'

Hours before the Turkish investigators entered the consulate, a Saudi team of 'investigators' had done their preparatory job at the consulate on Monday. They were really a cleaning crew who had arrived to set about their work defiantly under the full glare of the TV cameras outside the consulate. Eight large bottles of floor-cleaning fluid along with other chemicals and six hundred bin liners were wheeled through the big silver-riveted gate adorned with a large gold relief of two swords and a palm tree – Saudi Arabia's national emblem.

Prince bin Faisal's delegation four days earlier had also included a chemist and a toxicologist – Ahmed al-Janobi and Khaled al-Zahrani. They hadn't returned to Riyadh with the prince, but stayed on to work secretly on removing all traces from the two buildings. The two highly-trained forensics experts would remain in Istanbul until the 20th, repairing every night to an elegant five-star hotel 20 minutes or so away from the consulate.

The Turkish team, including forensics specialists from the Istanbul anti-terror branch and crime-scene investigation, arrived in a motorcade of six cars at night. The Turkish prosecutor had entered the yellow-cream building earlier during the day with a policeman and the joint-team had gathered at a police station for a meeting that lasted almost two hours. The Saudi investigators entered the consulate an hour before the prosecutor arrived and remained inside until the Turkish search was concluded on Wednesday morning.

The chiaroscuro of night time and blindingly-bright halogen lights increased the dramatic impact of press photos from outside, with long shadows cast outside the building. The dark window frames with their finely crafted Islamic-patterned grills captured the Turkish forensic team executing tasks that required crouching on all fours as they were lit up like reality TV. Clad in white dust-free overalls, gasmasks, which some investigators even kept on outside, and wearing blue-and-white shoe protectors, blue gloves and vests that looked bullet proof, they went into the consulate under more stark halogen lighting. Meanwhile policemen in riot gear brandishing automatic rifles stood on either side of the consulate to protect and escort the team moving like a scientific pageant through the doors.

The Turkish investigators were carrying limited equipment after the Saudis had banned the use of Luminol, the chemical that reveals bloodstains even if they have been washed clean. Nonetheless, their kit consisted of large, dark, heavy-duty, professional-looking plastic cases that the team carried into the building. After a night-time search of up to nine hours, the Turks left with numerous uniform brown-paper bags and brown cardboard boxes and samples, including soil from outside the consulate.

President Erdoğan suggested in a press conference that his team found evidence of fresh coats of paint and 'toxic materials', but did not elaborate. One senior Turkish official leaked anonymously to the *Washington Post* that there had been apparent attempts to scrub the scene and repaint areas, commenting:

'People who have nothing to hide don't behave like this.' Another official said to Associated Press they had 'found evidence' that Khashoggi had been killed there, but didn't expand on what those words actually meant.

The two Saudi specialists had, in fact, done a meticulous job in scrubbing the building clean over more than a week while Riyadh had stalled the Turks. The forensic evidence Turkish investigators found that could even remotely support their murder case was modest. Turkish officials would leak three small forensic details of their investigation over the next half year. But Turkey never officially released the full findings of its inspection, nor would actual measurements or other scientific details ever be leaked or published.

Meanwhile the US continued to mediate. President Trump said that he had spoken to the infirm King Salman himself, who professed to having no knowledge about the missing journalist. Trump then speculated that 'rogue killers' may have been responsible for the murder, a repetition of the story Aktay had first introduced and then withdrawn. By now there had already been several Saudi leaks in the press that the palace was preparing to make a statement along those lines.

'Been hearing the ridiculous "rogue killers" theory was where the Saudis would go with this. Absolutely extraordinary they were able to enlist the president as their PR agent to float it,' retorted Chris Murphy, a Democrat senator.

The *New York Times* took up President Trump's theme. Information had been leaked by Saudi officials that the crown prince had either indeed approved the questioning of Jamal Khashoggi, or his extraordinary rendition back to Saudi Arabia. But a member of its intelligence services, who merely happened to be a friend of the crown prince, had been 'tragically incompetent'. He had been trying to prove himself during the operation, which led to the journalist's death. The shift in the Saudi position had come after the US finally threatened sanctions against the kingdom.

On Tuesday, Secretary of State Mike Pompeo flew out to meet with King Salman and have dinner with the crown prince, ostensibly to have talks over Jamal Khashoggi's disappearance. He said, 'They made a commitment they would show the entire world the result of their investigation. They also indicated they would get this done quickly'. On the same day, it was leaked that $100 million was transferred from the palace's coffers to the US treasury.

President Trump also spoke to MBS on the phone. He tweeted: 'Just spoke with the crown prince of Saudi Arabia who totally denied any knowledge of what took place in their Turkish consulate.' Trump defended Saudi Arabia from further criticism over the case, telling Associated Press that it was a case of 'you're guilty until proven innocent, I don't like that'.

Then, on Tuesday afternoon, as Turkish police started putting up barricades around his elegant residence, consul-general Mohammed al-Otaibi left for Riyadh after the UN asked for his immunity to be lifted. He had not left his home for days and all his appointments had been cancelled.

In the early hours of Wednesday 16 October, Khashoggi's younger son Abdullah tweeted a typed Arabic statement posted 'for immediate release', which the *Washington Post* picked up and published. It said: 'We, the children of journalist Jamal Khashoggi are following with growing concern the conflicting reports on his fate after we lost contact with him two weeks ago following his entry into the Saudi consulate in Istanbul.'

'The family is now trying to overcome the shock of the developments and gather all his children. Out of our moral and legal responsibility, we demand the immediate formation of an independent and neutral international committee to gather the facts into his disappearance and conflicting reports on his death.'

But the message also reaffirmed the family's belief in the Saudi government and the Khashoggi family name.

'Ultimately, the family calls on all sides to respect our privacy, particularly at this difficult time, and refrain from politicising his case and undermining his good reputation, which all people attest to.'

Inside the kingdom those who only received Saudi media and didn't have access to foreign media were now thoroughly confused by Riyadh's investigation and whether Jamal Khashoggi had been killed at the Istanbul consulate. His disappearance no longer seemed like fake-news agitation by nefarious foreigners.

President Erdoğan was to meet Mike Pompeo the same day as King Salman and Turkish authorities released a barrage of lurid leaks from the recording ahead of his arrival from Riyadh in Ankara. The Turkish publicity team first circulated that they had edited a 3-minute clip from the audio recording at their disposal – not unlike the first clip of CC-TV coverage – and given it to *Sabah*. At, least that is what was rumoured.

'Jamal Khashoggi's killing took 7 minutes', the Middle East Eye revealed at 7pm that night, before the first news leak appeared in a morning newspaper. Its source, who provided the scoop, the news site said, was an official who had listened to the 'whole recording' rather than the short 3-minute clip that was edited for *Sabah*.

'Horrendous screams were heard', the site revealed. 'Khashoggi was dragged from the consul-general's office at the Saudi consulate in Istanbul and onto the table of his study next door.'

'The consul[-general] himself was taken out of the room. There was no attempt to interrogate [Khashoggi]. They had come to kill him', the source leaked.

Khashoggi was then injected with a substance and the screaming stopped. While he was still breathing, it was suggested, professor Salah Tubaigy, the forensic expert on the team, started dismembering him in a third room set up for this purpose.

'When I do this job, I listen to music. You should do [that] too', he advised the team members in the consulate, the source had leaked to the website.

'Tubaigy began to cut Khashoggi's body up on a table in the study while he was still alive. The killing took 7 minutes,' the source also claimed.

Finally, the Middle East Eye said slightly outlandishly that it was reporting on what someone else was going to report, 'A three-minute version of the audio tape has been given to Turkish newspaper *Sabah*, but they have yet to release it.'

It is not that the Middle East Eye's scoop of the audio text was wrong, but curiously – if the paper had indeed been given an audio clip in the first place, which seems very unlikely – *Sabah* never published it or released it on its website, nor did any other paper. Yet any editor in the world would have given their right hand to be the first to publish that clip.

The reason was, likely, not so much that the false Apple-Watch story had compromised *Sabah*'s reputation for being believed, but rather that Ankara had no intention whatsoever of releasing any part of the recording directly to the public. It wanted to dangle the threat of full exposure over the palace in Riyadh. Certainly the subsequent theatrical smoke-and-mirror release of the audio into other hands confirmed this reluctance to share the facts.

The rumour that *Sabah* had a (non-existing as yet) three-minute audio clip had, meanwhile, done its job.

Sabah itself would merely report that day what other papers disclosed on the audio. It would take *Sabah*'s head of investigations Abdurrahman Şimşek, until December, when his book *Diplomatik Vahşet* came out, to publish more anonymous news leaks on the audio recording at the consulate in *Sabah*.

In the morning, more gruesome scoops tumbled across the media on Pompeo's arrival. 'Recordings reveal Khashoggi tortured then dismembered while still alive', ran *Yeni Şafak*'s headline on Wednesday morning, ahead of the world press, saying there were 'several recordings'.

'If you want to live, be quiet!' consul-general al-Otaibi had snarled at the US resident he had invited up for tea.

Jamal Khashoggi was 'tortured', the paper claimed. His fingers were 'cut off during the interrogation process before he was decapitated.'

'Shut up if you want to live when you return to (Saudi) Arabia', the team had shouted at the consul-general himself when he pleaded, 'Do this outside. You're going to get me into trouble'.

Later that day the Saudi press would report that consul-general al-Otaibi had been sacked by Riyadh. President Erdoğan would claim credit for this modest victory. In a landmark speech to the Turkish parliament he referred to the consul-general's dismissal and said that he had complained to both Prince bin Faisal and King Salman about the consul-general's refusal to allow entry to the consulate and consular residence to Turkish investigators.

To Qatar-based al-Jazeera Turkish officials leaked that 'the journalist was assaulted immediately after he entered the consulate.' This was based on an '11-minute recording' with three Arabic voices, in addition to Khashoggi's own voice, shortly after he entered the consulate.

Turkish investigators now leaked that they had tracked down a consular BMW (possibly carrying plates 34 CC 2665) to Belgrad Forest on the city's northern outskirts captured on CC-TV at 6.28pm on 1 October, the day before Khashoggi's assassination. The news that the investigation extended to areas outside of Turkey beyond Istanbul came only a few hours after 'Turkish crime-scene investigators finished a nine-hour overnight search of both the consul general's residence and a second search of the consulate itself', reported *Sabah*. This was the Belgrad Forest story the *Sabah* journalists who wrote *Diplomatik Vahşet* would revisit in December.

Turkey has taken 'open and transparent actions' in the Khashoggi case, Turkish interior minister Süleyman Soylu told the Anadolu press agency without merit. The press agency was under tight AKP control and just took the minister's word for it.

Turkish prosecutors also focused their attention on farmlands in Yalova Province about fifty miles from Istanbul on the other side of the Marmara Sea. A woman who lived there said that there had been more traffic than usual on the night of 2 October.

At the same time, Turkish authorities fed rumours about the complimentary question of the murder – where were the victim's body parts? The rumour from 'sources' circulated that Khashoggi's body had been dissolved in acid after he had been killed. An anonymous source close to the investigation told Sky News that the assumption was that a 'very fast-acting chemical' had been used.

Meanwhile, in the afternoon, Turkish investigators were allowed access to consul-general al-Otaibi's residence. They had so far been refused entry because the consul-general's family was still in residence. Floodlights and a drone were deployed to search the garden outside. Turkish authorities were prevented access to this potentially crucial part of the crime scene, however. Turkey's diplomatic delegates hadn't thought that far ahead and had not listed the outside of the property on the diplomatic search protocol they had thrashed out with Riyadh.

XVI
Last Words

Jamal Khashoggi then found a voice from beyond the grave. His last column, ostensibly submitted on the day he went missing, was finally published in the *Washington Post* on 18 October. It was only the second time that a piece of his was published in the printed edition. The first time was an op-ed piece on 23 May 2018 on Saudi arrests in relation to women's rights.

In a note with the column, Karen Attiah, his *Post*'s global-opinions editor, said the piece perfectly captured Khashoggi's commitment to freedom in the Arab world, 'a freedom he apparently gave his life for.' Although it wasn't the reason why Riyadh had had him assassinated, it was true in a broader sense that he wanted a return at the very least of the freedom that had existed in Saudi Arabia under King Abdullah.

The *Washington Post* had held off publishing it in the hope that Khashoggi was still alive and would return, but with talk of rogue Saudi operators and bone saws, intelligence services on all sides seemed to have confirmed Khashoggi's death.

'Now I have to accept: That is not going to happen,' she wrote. 'This is the last piece of his I will edit for the *Post*.'

In the article, headed 'What the Arab world needs most is free expression', Khashoggi described how the optimism of the Arab Spring in 2011 was quickly dashed and replaced by the Middle East's version of an Iron Curtain, imposed by domestic forces as they grappled for power. The rest of the world had done little as journalists were arrested and newspapers silenced, he observed.

'Instead, these actions may trigger condemnation quickly followed by silence', the column continued. 'As a result, Arab governments have been given free rein to continue silencing the media at an increasing rate....'

'The Arab world is facing its own version of an Iron Curtain, imposed not by external actors but through domestic forces vying for power. The Arab world needs a modern version of the old transnational media so citizens can be informed about global events. More important, we need to provide a platform for Arab voices....'

'We suffer from poverty, mismanagement and poor education,' he wrote. 'Through the creation of an independent international forum, isolated from the influence of nationalist governments spreading hate through propaganda, ordinary people in the Arab world would be able to address the structural problems their societies face.'

***

Before the weekend of 20-21 October more background data started circulating in the press on the hitherto unidentified members of the fifteen-strong assassination squad.

The leaks provided visual proof that connected the squad directly to MBS. Turkish officials leaked high-resolution pictures of the identity cards of the seven men on the second jet, saying the cards of the other eight members might be released another time. The *Washington Post* published all seven pictures with the faces pixilated in a piece by Kareem Fahim, who had written the first blog on Khashoggi's disappearance for the paper. Next day NBC, given the same IDs, published its follow-up scoop: the cards without pixilation.

The *Post* said it reviewed 'posts on social media, and emails, previous reports in local media and other material' of the men which showed links with Saudi security forces. Using Menom3ay, a caller-ID app popular in the Middle East, it found the telephone numbers of twelve of the fifteen men and called one of them, royal guard Mohammed al-Zahrani, whom *Sabah* had first identified together with professor Tubaigy. He denied being in Turkey at the time and calls to the other eleven members remained unanswered. The *Post* also, somehow, was given access to US travel records by US authorities and was able to establish that five of the fifteen Tiger Team members had travelled to the US at similar times as MBS, together with press photographs of the trips.

It became embarrassingly clear that almost all members were intimately connected with MBS's personal security and intelligence team and not just the Tiger Team. Among the operatives was Abdulaziz al-Hawsawi. A French colleague of his who had worked with the Saudi royal family told the *New York Times* that al-Hawsawi was a member of the security team that travelled with the crown prince.

Thaar al-Harbi was mentioned in Saudi media in 2017, when he was promoted to lieutenant in the Saudi royal guard, apparently for his bravery defending the crown prince's palace al-Salam in Jeddah during an attack on MBS by a Saudi man called Mansour al-Amri.

Then there was Mohammed al-Zahrani, who had answered his phone. A 2017 video by the Saudi-owned TV channel al-Ekhbariya published on YouTube showed a man wearing a royal-guard uniform and name tag with his name standing next to the Crown Prince. At one time, he had also been on the embassy staff in London according to a list given to the *Daily Telegraph*.

Middle East Eye also identified Badr al-Otaibi as an officer in the crown prince's entourage. He had helped with the preparations for the Ritz Carlton imprisonment and travelled with MBS to France in 2018, along with major Nayif al-Arifi, also a security and protection officer for the crown prince. On Saudi number-sharing app Menom3ay he identified himself as an 'employee of the crown prince's office'. A document seen by Middle East Eye also listed Mansour Abahussein as an officer for the crown prince. He was one of the oldest and most senior of the Saudi operatives, and a big heavy set man who was a brigadier-general – in November he would be identified indirectly as the leader of the Tiger Team rendition by the Saudi prosecutor.

Fahad al-Balawi was listed as a member of the royal guard by two users on Menom3ay, while seven Menom3ay users identified Saif al-Qahtani as an employee of the crown prince. Khalid al-Otaibi also identified himself as a member of the royal guard. He travelled to the United States at the same time as official visits by members of the Saudi royal family. Hit-squad member sergeant-major al-Sehri was identified as an air force officer from an online video, while the Facebook profile of Meshal al-Bostani said he was an air force lieutenant who lived in Jeddah and had studied at the University of Louisville, Kentucky. He died in a traffic accident at about this time and it immediately raised suspicions that he had been silenced by the Saudi regime in the crackdown on the team that had loyally executed the rendition.

Born in 1961 Mustafa al-Madani was by some way the oldest of the group. The UN team would be the first to reveal his high-rank as major general as late as 19 June 2019. No public information had been unearthed regarding Turki al-Sehri but he was thought to have links to the crown prince, too. The UN confirmed seven months later that the media research was correct. It also found that Badr al-Otaibi may have been another one of Khashoggi's intelligence colleagues under ambassador Prince Turki.

At least three of the suspects – lieutenant Thaar al-Harbi, major Waleed al-Sehri and Abdul al-Hawsawi – had been part of MBS's entourage when he made a three-day visit to London in March 2018, where he met the Queen and Prime Minister Theresa May. Al-Qahtani's subordinate, brigadier-general Maher Mutreb, was also seen emerging from a car in Downing Street during the visit.

In total the UN report would link at least eight operatives directly to MBS and find that there were at least seven commissioned officers on the team ranging from a rank of lieutenant to a two-star general.

Despite the mounting weight of circumstantial evidence, Saudi Arabia denied MBS ordered the killing or had involvement with it.

If it wasn't MBS, who, then, was going to be the fall guy for him? The prime suspect emerged as a two-star general 'new' to intelligence work as a Saudi 'source' had already predicted days before. According to the *Washington Post*, this was major-general Ahmed al-Asiri, the boss of the Saudi-Istanbul secret-service chief al-Muzaini. 'The Tiger from the South', the two-star general who had given the *Firqat el-Nemr* or Tiger Team its name, was now portrayed as someone who was unable to listen.

The general was deputy head of the Saudi general intelligence directorate and one of the crown prince's right-hand men after MBS was made defence minister when his father came to power as king in January 2015. A graduate of Sandhurst, West Point in the US, and St Cyr Academy in France, al-Asiri was a career airforce officer who came to prominence as spokesman for the Saudi-led coalition fighting in Yemen that had been unleashed by the crown prince as one of his first acts as Saudi defence minister. In March 2017, al-Asiri was filmed sticking his middle finger up at protesters in London which did not damage his standing with the crown prince.

He had no formal training in intelligence it was leaked by way of explanation. Yet he won the Crown Prince's permission to interrogate Khashoggi on suspicion that he had become part of the Muslim Brotherhood, a crime in Saudi Arabia. Riyadh also wanted to pressure Khashoggi as they reckoned he had taken money from Qatar, an assumption no doubt fed by his closeness to Maggie Salem Mitchell of the Qatar Foundation International, who had certainly paid for translation and research help with his *Post* pieces. According to the *Daily Beast*, 'the over-eager general exceeded bin Salman's intentions. He improvised an extraordinary rendition to send Khashoggi from Turkey back to Saudi Arabia – and botched it, killing him. Then he lied to his Saudi superiors about what happened.'

How plausible were these new rumours leaked by anonymous Saudi 'sources'? 'It's not going to wash,' said Bruce Riedel, a former CIA official and the Gulf expert at the Brookings Institution. 'It's ludicrous in the extreme. Saudi Arabia doesn't work that way. They don't do freelance operations.'

'If this is a rogue operation, the rogue is MBS,' said Barbara Bodine, a retired US ambassador to Yemen.

XVII
Uncomfortable Truths

At 12pm on Friday 19 October, Saudi Arabia officially admitted that Khashoggi was dead. Khashoggi had, Riyadh claimed, died in a fight in the Istanbul consulate. But it had been an accident. In a statement on state TV the country's prosecutor said that the fifteen-man squad confronted the former courtier when he entered the consulate and a brawl broke out. In another evening call with Erdoğan, King Salman had already given the president advance warning of this announcement.

The Saudi statement read: 'In implementation to the directives of the leadership of the need to clearly know the truth and declare it transparently whatever, the preliminary investigations conducted by the Public Prosecution showed that the suspects had travelled to Istanbul to meet with the citizen Jamal Khashoggi as there were indications of the possibility of his returning back to the country.'

What the phrase 'indications of the possibility of his returning' meant according to the palace was not easy to understand, as Khashoggi had been vocal, when asked by al-Qahtani on many occasions over two years, that he had no intention of moving back to Saudi Arabia and instead intended to get married in Turkey that week and had applied for US citizenship.

In a reference to Khashoggi's first 11 minutes at the consulate, the prosecutor's statement said: 'The results of the preliminary investigations also revealed that the discussions that took place with the citizen Jamal Khashoggi during his presence in the consulate of the kingdom in Istanbul by the suspects did not go as required and developed in a negative way, this led to a fight and a quarrel between some of them and the citizen Jamal Khashoggi, yet the brawl aggravated to lead to his death and their attempt to conceal and cover what happened.'

The prosecutor said that eighteen people had been arrested in connection with his death: all fifteen men in the hit-squad along with two consular staff and a driver, pending investigations. Saudi Arabia said the eighteen would be tried in Saudi courts. Saudi Arabia now conceded they were Saudi soldiers and intelligence operatives. Nonetheless, no individual names were given. And since the kingdom is hermetically sealed to the free press, there was no way of checking whether anyone had actually been arrested.

Showing that they were taking Pompeo's words 'get this done quickly' at face value, it was also revealed that the death penalty would be sought by the Saudi prosecutor general against five of the eighteen in an exceptionally rapid development of the criminal case's investigation. Saudi Arabia had still not been given Turkey's recordings, but Sheikh al-Mojeb presumably had access to any visual and audio evidence that the Tiger Team had made during their mission.

Furthermore, two further intelligence officials were also sacked from their high-level jobs, apart from major-general Ahmed al-Asiri, the deputy intelligence chief, and Saud al-Qahtani. Al-Qahtani, viewed as Prince Mohammed's enforcer, had thus far been considered untouchable by many Saudis. During the Ritz-Carlton shake-down, his secret files containing years of wiretaps of the high-flying Saudi guests were no doubt useful in convincing them to part with their money rather than face disgrace at the hands of Sheikh al-Mojab in court. His demotion was a big prize for Erdoğan.

When the message came through on Twitter, Hatice Cengiz dropped the phone she was holding while talking to one of Khashoggi's friends. She had woken up to morning prayer at 5.30am and stayed inside all day to follow the news. She had relied heavily on her father during this lonely and confusing time for her. But for the first time the truth hit home. 'That's when I felt he was dead', she said.

Information was now leaked by Turkish sources that a Skype call from Saudi Arabia to the consulate in Istanbul was made on 2 October after Khashoggi entered the building. During that call MBS adviser Saud al-Qahtani had begun to hurl insults and profanities at Khashoggi. According to the Turkish official, Khashoggi answered al-Qahtani's insults with his own. 'Bring me the head of the dog,' al-Qahtani thereupon told his men – suggesting that the Turkish leak meant to incriminate al-Qahtani as the one who gave the assassination order. No audio was released to make the leak 'open and transparent', however.

Critics of Saudi Arabia completed the link back to MBS. They pointed to several tweets by al-Qahtani as evidence that the crown prince was fully aware of the orders his aide was executing. In one 2017 tweet, al-Qahtani said: 'Do you think I make decisions without guidance? I am an employee and a faithful executor of the orders of my lord the king and my lord the faithful crown prince.'

On the same day, he apparently warned a Saudi dissident living in London that his 'assassination file has been reopened'. Even after being sacked, al-Qahtani tweeted: 'I express my gratitude to the king and the crown prince for the great confidence they have given me and for providing me with the great opportunity to serve my nation over the past years.' He added: 'I will always be a loyal servant of my country.'

King Salman now ordered MBS to head a committee to restructure the intelligence services within thirty days. The decree confirmed that the crown prince was not to blame as far as the king was concerned.

'The kingdom has taken the necessary procedures to find out the truth,' the Saudi state news agency said, adding that the country's leadership had stressed 'the importance of knowing the truth clearly and announcing it transparently, whatever it is'.

However, from exile in Germany, Prince Khalid bin Farhan insisted on German TV that King Salman instead should abdicate in favour of his Sudairi brother in London-exile, Prince Ahmed. He accused the king of wanting to hog the royal succession with his own bloodline and deplored a future where 'your offspring monopolises the throne'. Prince Ahmed, he told the Saudi king via DW TV is 'highly ethical'.

Prince Ahmed himself avoided the media spotlight. But there was one choice piece of Youtube footage of him. Noisily heckled on the Yemen war outside his £50 million London home on 5 September 2018, Prince Ahmed had engaged with the protestors and politely asked his Pakistani interlocutors not to lump the whole al-Saud family with those who ran it currently.

King Salman was the opposite of his brother, in the opinion of Prince bin Farhan, and indistinguishable from MBS. He is a 'tyrant ruler who uses violence because he lacks political experience... When he became king, he applied a similar method to the one he used to follow when he was the governor of Riyadh Province.'

There was no doubt in bin Farhan's mind that 'the killers would have received a direct authorisation from the head of state'. But as Salman was merely a 'facade' 'the order must have been executed by crown prince Mohammed bin Salman.'

Former MI6 mandarin Sir John Sawers told the BBC more nebulously: 'All the evidence points to it being ordered and carried out by people close to Mohammed bin Salman.'

But, pointing a finger at the US, Sir John believed that MBS thought he had a 'licence' from Donald Trump, who frequently condemned journalists as the 'enemy of the people', even praising Republican Congressman Greg Gianforte for body-slamming *Guardian* reporter Ben Jacobs, saying 'he's my kind of guy'.

'I don't think [MBS] would have done this if he hadn't thought he had licence from the US administration to frankly behave as he wished to do so,' said Sir John. 'I think President Trump and his ministerial team are waking up to just how dangerous it is to have people acting with a sense that they have impunity in their relationship with the United States.'

The former spy chief also judged that 'there has been such tension between Turkey and Saudi Arabia over the last ten years or so they would have been monitoring very carefully what goes on inside Saudi offices.'

He went on to speculate that Turkey was listening in to the assassination as it unfolded. 'They could well have had the consulate general bugged in some way or there may have been other devices carried by the squad which carried out the assassination which they were able to intercept.'

It was not easy to see how, even in October, Sir John's words were congruent with the known facts. On his own watch at MI6, from 2009 to 2014, British intelligence had not been able to prevent six Russian assassinations on British soil and Sir John's words flattered the capability of Turkish intelligence with being far more competent. Yet Turkey's only advantage was its live MoBeSe system. London had the third largest CC-TV coverage in the world, but it was operated by security-obsessed citizens rather than the British state. Britain, however, had the state of the art capability of GCHQ. What Sir John's words did do was draw attention away from the fact that Five Eyes knew in advance of the attack on Khashoggi and that MİT didn't – even by their own admission.

Another 'senior' British security source's speculation sought anonymously to impute even more tremendous powers of foresight to MİT: 'Turkey launched a large-scale surveillance operation. Many in the intelligence community believe the consul was bugged, and this Saudi team was followed.' Turkey, the 'source' suggested, had been taken by surprise.

'Turkey was expecting a rendition attempt, which they could interdict, rescuing Khashoggi. Instead, they witnessed a murder,' the 'source' said without advancing plausible evidence. 'The uncomfortable truth may emerge one day that the hit team was listened to live as they killed Khashoggi, but [Turkey] was powerless to do anything about it.'

Leaving aside that no one had ever claimed there was audio inside the consul's residence, it is not easy to see how this claim could be true either. It assumed that MİT officials knew everything there was to know even before 1.13pm – after all, they 'witnessed' the murder – when Khashoggi entered the consulate and, therefore, that they had already decided not to do anything. Somehow it was Hatice Cengiz's calls, inconveniently standing outside, that forced MİT to change that decision not to intervene.

If Turkey had already decided not to do anything about Khashoggi while they heard the assassination taking place, the official investigation would have started the next day. The Turks could have played exactly the same game of hide and seek with the evidence and forced Riyadh's hand. In addition, Turkey wouldn't look inept in having caught some of the perpetrators and yet setting them free anyway.

If it was an MİT internal decision not to act that had been overruled by Erdoğan at 5.50pm, initiated by Hatice's-Turan's-Yasin Aktay's calls, the facts merely indicated temporary indecisiveness. The people who set MİT policies in Ankara evidently reached the same decision a few hours later to stay out of it by allowing the final Gulfstream IV to take-off, confirming the decision their Istanbul inferiors had already reached while executing Ankara's policies before the president got in touch. Ordinary criminal investigators in Istanbul did get the audio recording only two days later, as leaked to the *Wall Street Journal*. But in a diplomatic case with the president involved, Istanbul officials would not likely call the shots.

Saudi officials now leaked anonymously that the kingdom had a generic catch-all order on its books – presumably issued by MBS himself as crown prince – for Saudi dissidents to return home. The overly-keen major-general al-Asiri, as the leaked unofficial story went, had wanted to impress MBS and acted on autopilot under this order to plan an operation to capture Khashoggi in Turkey.

'There were no orders for them to kill him or even specifically kidnap him,' a Saudi official said. 'Crown Prince Mohammed had no knowledge of this specific operation and certainly did not order a kidnapping or murder of anybody. He will have been aware of the general instruction to tell people to come back.'

Yet on the record during his Bloomberg interview on 3 October when asked whether Khashoggi was 'facing charges' the crown prince had not mentioned this 'order' and that it applied to his friend Jamal. Presumably this was because – if indeed such a palace directive existed – the six Bloomberg journalists might well have understood the word 'order to return' to mean that there was a royal charge against the exile after all. In the first few days, the palace wanted to present Khashoggi and MBS as friends to avoid any suggestion that they were instead after him.

XVIII
Bone Saw

As Erdoğan's demand to the king for interviewing consul-general al-Otaibi and for Khashoggi's remains had not been met, there were renewed calls by Turkey for the Saudis to hand over the body. Turkey in turn refused to hand over its recordings and evidence to the kingdom until such time.

Meanwhile, the official Saudi investigators said it had found that Khashoggi's remains had been carried out of the building by the team of fifteen 'rogue' operatives. They had been handed over to a Turkish 'local collaborator' to dispose of. Riyadh didn't know where it was, so the story ran. But when pressed to disclose the name of the Turkish 'collaborator', Saudi prosecutor general Sheikh al-Mojeb declined to provide details to his Turkish counterparts.

After the admission of Khashoggi's death on Saturday, official Saudi sources started anonymously leaking further details to the media. Among other things, it was explained that the government had wanted to convince Khashoggi to return to the kingdom from voluntary exile in America as part of a campaign to prevent Saudi dissidents from being recruited by the country's enemies. This was, doubtless, the truth.

Major-general Ahmed al-Asiri had put together the fifteen-member team from the intelligence and security forces to go to Istanbul, meet Khashoggi at the consulate and try to convince him to return to Saudi Arabia.

The anonymous 'sources' also came up with more detail on how the *deus-ex-machina* regulation on dissidents supposedly worked under the Saudi rule of law.

'There is a standing order to negotiate the return of dissidents peacefully, which gives [the Saudi secret service] the authority to act without going back to the leadership' the official said. 'Al-Asiri is the one who formed the team and asked for an employee who worked with al-Qahtani and who knew Khashoggi from the time they both worked at the embassy in London.' This employee was brigadier-general Maher Mutreb.

The unnamed official said al-Qahtani had sent one of his subordinates to conduct the negotiations. According to the plan, the team would hold Khashoggi for some time in a safe house outside Istanbul, but would release him if he ultimately refused to return to Saudi Arabia. (If that was plan A, why though did you need a forensic pathologist on your team?)

The official had so much detail, it almost seemed as if he was reading from a blueprint.

Things went wrong from the start as the team overstepped al-Asiri's and al-Qahtani's orders and quickly employed violence, the anonymous Saudi official said while leaking Riyadh's new story. Khashoggi was ushered into the consul general's office where Maher Mutreb, consul-general al-Otaibi and another man were waiting for him. Mutreb spoke to Khashoggi about returning to Saudi Arabia. Khashoggi refused and told Mutreb that someone was waiting outside for him and would contact the Turkish authorities if he did not reappear within an hour.

According to the Saudi official, Khashoggi told Mutreb he was violating diplomatic law and said, 'What are you going to do with me? Do you intend to kidnap me?'

Mutreb replied, 'Yes, we will drug you and kidnap you.'

The official also observed that the words of the one-star general were an attempt at intimidation that, regrettably, violated the mission's peaceful objective.

When Khashoggi raised his voice, the team of Saudi officers panicked. They tried to restrain him, placing him in a chokehold and covering his mouth, the official said.

'They tried to prevent him from shouting but he died,' the government account went on. 'The intention was not to kill him.'

Asked if the team had smothered Khashoggi, the anonymous official subtly shifted the cause of death away from the team: 'If you put someone of Jamal's age in this position, he would probably die.' It was accidental suffocation as a result of age and ill health according to the Saudi investigation.

Saudi investigators also did not think that the special-ops Tiger-Team had dismembered Khashoggi, nor had they tortured him in their opinion, it was leaked.

After Riyadh's public admission on 19 October that Khashoggi had been killed at the consulate, Turkish authorities would, in tandem, both stop deploying the words 'torture' and 'interrogation' in their leaks and deny the existence of facts that indicated a slow and painful death that was meant to extract information from Khashoggi that could be used against other Saudis.

This watershed was remarkable. Before the 19th, Turkish-government contacts at newspapers had painted a garish Pulp Fiction murder story on the basis of official leaks. After this date, the new leaks that characterised the Saudi operation in the Turkish press – and therefore the rest of the world as only Turkey possessed evidence of events at the Turkish consulate – became less twisted and more business-like.

By the time the UN inquiry into Jamal Khashoggi started in January 2019, the two words had disappeared entirely from the news narrative. In line with this new picture, nine months later to the day, the June UN report into Khashoggi's killing would label it as an 'execution' and dig no deeper. That word was an accurate description of the sum total of leaks after the watershed, though not of those before.

Estimates of how quickly Khashoggi was killed after entering the consulate started to shorten to between 7 and 11 minutes and previous story lines were sanitised.

It is not easy to escape the conclusion that through bare-knuckle mediation Trump administration officials got Ankara to remove the most stinging facts from its assault on Riyadh in exchange for a public admission of responsibility that was palatable to the palace and usable for Saudi home-media consumption.

In an attempt to cover up what they had done in a panic, so the Saudi leaks went, the Tiger-Team had rolled up the whole of Khashoggi's body – intact and Agatha-Christie-style – in a consular rug. When queried, the anonymous Saudi officer could not give the nationality of the local man. After the rug-rolling and disposal, forensic expert professor Salah Tubaigy tried to remove any trace of the incident inside the consulate. Here, the Saudi story was very different from the Turkish version. And it was one red line over which Saudi Arabia would continue to publically rebuff Turkey.

The intactness of the body was an ideological point. Even the mutilation of non-Muslim enemies is repulsive to the orthodoxy of Wahhabi Islam. Even so, the strict Wahhabist interpretation of sharia law prevalent in Saudi Arabia does not label legal punishments – such as beheading or the cutting off of extremities – as mutilation. Instead such penalties are thought to be sacrificial and therefore not a breach of religious practise.

It was not for nothing that the Tiger Team's secret code-name for Khashoggi was 'sacrificial animal', a term used by Maher Mutreb while waiting for Khashoggi and by pathologist Tubaigy when talking to other team members (UN report detail 91). The story of the Tiger-Team operation could either be 'rogue' yet respectful of Khashoggi's body, or legally ordered under Saudi law by the palace ('sacrificial' with permissible mutilation by a pathologist brought along for this reason, say), but not be both at the same time. For obvious reasons of consistency with what MBS had said publicly on the matter, Riyadh's narrative was the former.

The Saudis also leaked that the team-gone-rogue subsequently wrote a false report for their superiors, saying they had allowed Khashoggi to leave once he warned them that Turkish authorities might get involved, and he had promptly left the country before they were discovered. This false report was cited as the reason for the dramatic changes in the official Saudi version. The team and three other local employees had been arrested and were under investigation.

Saudi foreign minister Adel al-Jubeir expressed his condolences to the Khashoggi family, saying his death was a 'huge and grave mistake' and promised 'to punish those who are responsible for this murder'.

He told Fox News: 'This operation was a rogue operation, this was an operation where individuals ended up exceeding the authorities and responsibilities they had. They made a mistake when they killed Jamal Khashoggi in the consulate and they have tried to cover up for it. That is unacceptable in any government. We are determined to uncover every stone. We are determined to find out all the facts. And we are determined to punish those who are responsible for this murder. Even the senior leadership of the intelligence service was not aware of this.'

He described the media outcry over the death of Khashoggi as 'hysterical', which flagged that Riyadh had slightly moved on from the word 'disgusting' used by consul-general al-Otaibi and KBS.

The crown prince himself called Khashoggi's oldest son Salah to express his condolences as a sign of respect. Together King Salman and MBS later received Salah and Khashoggi's brother Sahel at his palace.

Cengiz meanwhile complained that the crown prince never sent his condolences to her.

'This incident, this assassination, took place inside a Saudi diplomatic mission,' she said. 'In such circumstances, the Saudi Arabian authorities are responsible.' There were fears for her safety – although it was not clear from whom – and the Turkish authorities gave her twenty-four-hour police protection.

MBS shares his condolences with Salah Khashoggi, 24 October.

Only Egypt's president Abdel el-Sisi backed the new Saudi story. With the aid of Saudi Arabia, the el-Sisi regime had overthrown the rule of Mohamed Morsi, the Muslim Brotherhood president elected after the Arab Spring. The Brotherhood was once again illegal in Egypt after Morsi's failed attempt to replace the Mubarak regime with an Islamist-style regime like Iran. El-Sisi was in effect the new Mubarak.

Few other nations found the new Saudi version of events credible, however.

Even Donald Trump said he struggled with the Saudis' account, while the UK, France and Germany issued a joint statement saying there was 'an urgent need for clarification' on what happened inside the Istanbul consulate that day.

It was the image of the bone saw that militated most against the Saudi story. 'You don't bring a bone saw to an accidental fist fight,' said Ben Sasse, a Republican congressman from Nebraska. 'The Saudis have said a whole bunch of crap that's not right, accurate, or true.'

Democrat Senator Jack Reed agreed across the aisles. 'This appears to have been a deliberate, planned act followed by a cover-up,' he said. 'You don't bring fifteen men and a bone saw to a fistfight with a sixty-year-old.'

Unsurprisingly, Turkish prosecutors did not accept the Saudi story either. 'We have clear evidence that what happened in the consulate was planned in advance,' they said. But they didn't disclose that 'clear evidence'.

The Saudis had given the Turkish government details of the eighteen suspects, and they had also interviewed twenty-five employees of the consulate in Istanbul. It was speculated that the hit-squad would simply be beheaded by the Saudis to prevent them from talking. Turkey was seeking the extradition of the men, but Saudi Arabia's justice minister and chairman of its higher judicial council, Waleed al-Samaani, said that those responsible for Khashoggi's death would be tried inside the kingdom.

Agnes Callamard, UN special rapporteur on extrajudicial, summary or arbitrary executions, agreed with Turkey and said the Saudi explanation was 'not plausible'. 'No government should accept it, or the pretence at investigation,' she said.

Protesting outside the Saudi consulate, Turan Kişlakçi, the head of the Turkish-Arab Journalists' Association summarised all questions that remained unanswered with regards to the 'rogue' operation.

'Did they kidnap him? Where did they take him? How did they do this? These questions don't matter,' he said. 'There's only one thing that matters right now. Give Khashoggi back to us. Give him back so that we can raise his funeral. Let the whole world watch Jamal Khashoggi's farewell.'

Erdoğan and Trump spoke comprehensively about the case on Sunday 21 October, and President Erdoğan promised 'to enlighten all aspects.'

***

Anything was news by now. Next Monday morning at 8am, 22 October, Turkish state broadcaster TRT aired a new leaked surveillance video showing what Turkish security officials described as suspicious movement in a car park in Istanbul's Sultangazi neighbourhood. This included the image of a man moving a bag from one vehicle to another. It suggested that Saudi consular workers were still trying to get rid of evidence of the crime on the orders of Riyadh.

Turkish crime-scene investigators went to the car park and found a black 2011 Mercedes E-series sedan with plates 34 CC 1736 covered in dust belonging to the Saudi consulate. The man had parked a grey BMW with consular license plates 34 CC 2665 in front. This appeared to be the same car the consulate's secret-service chief al-Muzaini had driven to Belgrad Forest on 1 October. The man was seen moving three bags, two quite large, between them and leaving the car park on 18 October. He was a regular user, identified as attaché Mohammed O. Another consular Mercedes was also parked in the parking garage.

'We know him as he has been using our parking lot sometimes. However, normally it's his Turkish driver. But on October 7, the attaché was driving it himself', one of the employees told *Hürriyet*.

He said he helped him and had joked 'Khashoggi's body is not inside the suitcases, is it?' and 'He laughed and answered no'.

A mask had fallen out of one of the bags and 'The attaché took it and put it in a trash bin' and 'I took the mask and showed it to a doctor. He told me that it was a mask that is used by those who work with heavy chemicals'. Scared the employee had thrown it away.

After investigators got a waiver to inspect the car they found two suitcases that contained clothes. A kettle and an iPhone box were visible on the backseat. Much media speculation surrounded the pictures and whether any or all belonged to Khashoggi, although it was unlikely he had brought a kettle into the consulate and 18 October was more than two weeks after the fact.

Really, the only vehicle of interest to anyone paying attention was the Mercedes Vito minivan with plates 34 CC 1865 featured in the very first CC-TV clip leaked to the media. It was the one that left the consulate at around 3pm for the consul's residence and carried the bags that 'held the remains of Khashoggi's dismembered corpse.' The forensics team spent three hours on the minivan with special chemicals and Luminol and found various DNA samples.

The investigations of all the consulate's vehicles evidently didn't lead to forensic discoveries either. But they, too, at least had the result of being widely covered as news on the case in media around the world.

XIX
'Crap'

൞

Then CNN Turk reported on another great leak whose visuals became iconic and a body blow to the new Saudi story as told by the Saudi prosecutor. On Monday 22 October, the broadcaster revealed new details about the oldest member of the Tiger Team, the fifty-seven-year-old Mustafa al-Madani, a very senior employee of Saudi's central intelligence agency.

The short, evocative, leaked clip showed al-Madani entering the consulate two hours before Khashoggi at 11.03am with two equally casually-clad team members, one of whom – Saif al Qahtani – shook the hands of the official in a dark-suit who is ushering them inside. The fifty-seven-year-old al-Madani was of a similar height and build as Jamal. The leak made the point he had been carefully picked and brought along as a body double as an act of premeditation by the Riyadh organisers of the rendition, though – unlike Khashoggi – al-Madani did not have a beard or glasses coming into the building.

The CC-TV footage leaked by the Turkish authorities showed al-Madani wearing a fake beard when he left the consulate by its back door at 2.52pm, while Hatice Cengiz was waiting out front near the roadblock. He was then also wearing Jamal Khashoggi's black jacket and glasses and had swapped his loud blue-and-white checked shirt and dark blue trousers for Khashoggi's light-grey shirt and grey trousers.

MoBeSe CC-TV images showing three similarities as well as the different shoes worn by al-Madani.

'Khashoggi's clothes were probably still warm when al-Madani put them on,' a senior Turkish official speculated.

However, when al-Madani emerged from the consulate he was still wearing the same pair of dark trainers, with a white stripe around the sole, he had on when he entered the building. Khashoggi, instead, had been wearing dark brogues. And while al-Madani had a full head of hair, Khashoggi was balding. CC-TV showed al-Madani was accompanied by a man wearing a hoodie and a hooped shirt, and was carrying a plastic bag believed to contain the clothes al-Madani had worn when he entered the consulate. They hailed a taxi.

Half-an-hour later al-Madani was captured at 4.06pm on CC-TV six miles away at Istanbul's famous Blue Mosque in the Sultanahmet district. About half-an-hour after that, al-Madani and his accomplice entered a public toilet, emerging again at 4.22pm. Al-Madani was now once-again dressed in the clothes he wore when he entered the consulate, while the plastic bag his accomplice was carrying was thought to contain Khashoggi's outfit.

The two then had dinner in the Mesale restaurant near the Blue Mosque, seemingly unperturbed by the events of the day. Then they took a taxi towards their hotel at 4.29pm and threw the bag into a large bin nearby. They were later seen back at the hotel laughing and smiling at 6.09pm, checking out four hours later at 10.25pm from the Mövenpick Hotel, which was the end of the short news clip. They could easily have flown back on either jet, but they didn't.

As we know, al-Madani and his associate were to leave Turkey unhindered on a commercial flight to Riyadh, going through customs at 18 minutes past midnight to catch their flight to Riyadh taking off at 1.25am (likely Turkish Airline flight TK 144). They had arrived on the first private jet 24 hours earlier, and were the last two operatives to leave Istanbul after midnight unhindered despite MİT's investigations that evening.

Turkish officials leaked to the *Wall Street Journal* that it hadn't taken them long to identify Khashoggi's imposter and his route through Istanbul. The impersonation was so self-evidently fake. If al-Madani had been quickly unmasked from MoBeSe footage alone, and they also had the audio, why hadn't they detained him in the 6 or 7 hours at their disposal? They had 2 extra hours after they had let the 'sitting duck' jet go and all they had to do was wait until he checked in. As mentioned, earlier, as to this point the source gave the *Journal* MİT's humble pie that there had been 'missed chances' to detain members of the hit-squad.

'It does give us a better understanding… why exactly the Saudis were sort of brazenly peddling this lie for the first several days if not the first week that Khashoggi had left the consulate unharmed. It may have been that they were waiting for the Turks to reveal surveillance footage', a CNN commentator in the US speculated.

More footage was leaked from the MoBeSe footage bank. Two men in suits standing around a burning oil drum in the consulate's back yard were throwing in sheaves of papers. 'This is how the Saudis destroyed the evidence in the consular garden one day later', Turkish TV station Haber TV headlined. The footage had been gathered by a drone on 3 October by Turkish security forces. The fire continued that day until night time, another clip given to Sabah TV showed. It didn't add much without knowing what they were burning, but it made Riyadh seem shifty.

Jamal Khashoggi had written a number of articles critical of Saudi Arabia for the Middle East Eye news site, but not under his own name as he feared for Saudi retribution. The kingdom suspected the London-based website of being a Qatari-funded organisation supportive of the Muslim Brotherhood. The Middle East Eye now had a scoop and revealed that Khashoggi's assassins were almost all members of the *Firqat el-Nemr*, or Tiger Squad, the Saudi team of around fifty highly-skilled intelligence and military operatives formed under the supervision of MBS upon becoming crown prince.

This volley of new Turkish MoBeSe footage was carefully timed by Turkey to undermine Saudi's public atonement. It broke on the day that Khashoggi's brother Sahel and oldest son Salah met King Salman and the crown prince at the royal palace. In a tweet, the Saudi foreign ministry shared a photograph of the four men shaking hands with the caption: 'King Salman receives Sahel bin Ahmed Khashoggi and Salah bin Jamal Khashoggi in the presence of the crown prince and share their deepest condolences and sympathy to the family of Jamal Khashoggi, may God rest his soul.'

However, according to the *Guardian* the meeting of the sons was electric: 'They stared straight at each other, seemingly locked in the moment: the bereaved, Salah Khashoggi, had eyes of cold sorrow while the man offering condolences, Mohammed bin Salman, gazed back at him with steely focus.'

Earlier, King Salman had shaken Khashoggi's brother Jahel's hand, and pointed and stabbed his index finger at him while talking. The royals and Khashoggi's Salah were wearing the patriotic Saudi red-blocked *ghutra* held by a black *igal* on their heads while Khashoggi's brother Jahel had a white one, indicating purity. All wore white long-sleeved *thaub* robes, but the two royals also wore their magnificent flowing black royal *bishts* of transparent wool with an elaborate gold-threaded *zari* trim. The elderly king barely looked at Salah, who respectfully listened and edged aside as the most powerful royal in the kingdom moved away leaning on his cane.

The meeting took place in the gilded and salmon-marbled offices of the crown prince. Salah Khashoggi did not speak as the two-year-younger MBS clutched his hands. But clearly relations, though stiff, had been satisfactory to both sides. The ban on Salah, who holds joint US-Saudi citizenship, against leaving Saudi Arabia was lifted. He flew to Washington two days later to be with his siblings. His two sisters happened to be staying with Maggie Salem Mitchell in

Washington, DC, when their father was assassinated.

On the same day, a rumour was released by two sources talking to Sky News that the victim's body parts had been found in a twelve-metre well in the garden of the Saudi consul general's residence. Not only had the body been dismembered, but Jamal Khashoggi's face had been disfigured and the fingers were missing. As Turkish investigators had complained about the fact that Saudi Arabia would not change the diplomatic protocol and permit investigators to search the garden or its two wells, it was not clear how Sky News thought Turkish authorities could have made such a discovery for which physical access was a requirement.

Another source leaked to the Middle East Eye news site that the victim's fingers had been flown back to Saudi Arabia to be presented to the crown prince as proof of the mission's success. The story about the fingers repeated what had been said during the first days. What was new was that the source also leaked that Khashoggi had been injected with morphine.

Meanwhile President Erdoğan stoked the fire once again personally in a keynote address to the Turkish parliament on Tuesday 23 October, three weeks after the assassination. It was Turkey's first public account by a named, as opposed to anonymous, top official directly in charge of Turkey's murder investigations and significant for that reason alone. His entire narrative, however, was either based on Saudi Arabia's concession of 19 October that Khashoggi was killed at the consulate or merely confirmed what could be deduced from evidence outside the consulate or the access given by Turkey's investigators to the diplomatic buildings.

Erdoğan reiterated that the hard drive of the consulate's CC-TV system had been removed. Turkish officials had already anonymously leaked this information, but Erdoğan confirmed it officially and revealed that it had been done just before the murder, showing Saudi premeditation of the Khashoggi Operation.

'We have strong signs that the murder was the product of a planned operation,' he told Turkish MPs. 'This is a political killing.'

Erdoğan also insisted that the eighteen suspects be tried in Turkish courts. However, that would not be enough.

'Leaving some security and intelligence forces holding the bag will not satisfy us or the international community,' Erdoğan said in his speech, while he claimed to speak for the world.

'Saudi Arabia has taken an important step by admitting the murder. As of now we expect of them to openly bring to light those responsible – from the person who gave the order to those who carried it out – and to bring them to justice.'

He also promised that Turkey would reveal the 'naked truth' about Jamal Khashoggi's death. In fact, from 19 October Turkey would steadily obstruct the process of truth-seeking where it could.

'All evidence gathered shows that Jamal Khashoggi was the victim of a savage murder,' he said. 'To cover up such brutality would hurt human conscience.' His speech slyly assumed the moral high ground. Yet the Turkish leader had not given his moral support in, for example, the case of nerve-agent poisoning in Salisbury that had led to the death of Dawn Sturgess and incapacitation of Sergei Skripal by novichok, Russia's top-secret chemical weapon.

President Erdoğan was again careful not to mention MBS by name or rank in his speech. But, Abdulkadir Selvi, whose *Hürriyet* (another newspaper beholden to the Turkish government, owned by the Demirören conglomerate) columns were studied for indications of Erdoğan's thinking, had no such qualms. He wrote, 'We cannot close this file until the crown prince is brought to account and removed from his post.'

Selvi also offered a new salacious leak of information – the victim had not only been cut into fifteen pieces, he had been strangled slowly.

As Erdoğan said the body had not been found, speculation continued with leaks saying that it had been dissolved in acid, possibly in the consul-general's garage. Family and friends in Saudi Arabia were still asking for its return so Khashoggi could be buried properly and they could mourn.

Sources told the Middle East Eye that Crown Prince Mohammed's intelligence officer Maher Mutreb, was thought to have taken part of the journalist's body out of Turkey in a large bag. When he left on the private jet the day of the murder, it was suggested, his bags were not checked before the plane left Atatürk Airport.

It was also revealed that Mutreb placed seven calls to the mobile phone of Bader al-Asaker, manager of the crown prince's private office on the day of the murder, four times after the murder itself. There was no precise tabulation of this data however, as when the names and airport entry times of the fifteen operatives were first revealed. That release was, in fact, the first and last time such factual information was provided by Turkey alongside a leak in order to back it up. Hungry for new things to say, the media no longer insisted on such evidence.

Donald Trump called the Saudi story 'the worst cover-up ever' and his administration put penalties on the conspirators. Among those sanctioned were Maher Mutreb and his team, but also Saud al-Qahtani, and consul-general al-Otaibi.

MBS, however, was not named. Congress did not agree. 'We are putting all our weight behind the Global Magnitsky request,' said a senior Senate aide. 'We do not want to sanction the low-hanging fruit, we want to go as high as possible.'

The UK's Prime Minister Theresa May followed President Trump's lead and announced that the Saudi officials suspected of being part of the plot to murder Khashoggi would be barred from entering Britain. Again there was no mention of the crown prince whom she had recently met as an honoured guest.

It was, in any case, not a very daring move by the US or the UK as the men had all been arrested in Saudi Arabia and, if not, would unlikely be allowed to leave the kingdom anytime soon.

It seemed that, privately, Saudi media were not buying the government's account of Khashoggi's death either – though they couldn't cross red lines and make any of their reservations public within the kingdom, or go on the record by name.

'People around me are feeling frustrated by this justification of it. They understand and know that everything, no matter how small, is ordered by the government. They don't buy it,' said one television journalist who worked for a pro-government station. He had worked alongside Khashoggi when he was a prominent media figure in Riyadh and still in favour with the regime.

Although the journalist had to peddle the official line on air to stay within the palace's red lines, he said, from his knowledge of the crown prince, 'there is no way he would not have known'.

XX
'Pre-meditated'

∽

The poorly attended Future Investment Initiative conference – Davos in the desert – kicked off on Tuesday 23 October in Riyadh with many of the key participants missing, even MBS was absent from the opening session that morning.

He did turn up in the afternoon though. Bankers, corporate executives and Saudis stood as one to applaud in the ornate conference room when he finally arrived. But the applause was subdued compared to the thunderous ovation he had received at the Future Investment Initiative a year ago. Crown Prince bin Salman spent only 15 minutes at the event and left without giving his planned speech.

On the second day, he spoke to a packed auditorium, smoothly calling the murder of Jamal Khashoggi a 'heinous crime which cannot be justified' and vowing to bring the perpetrators to justice. It was the first time he spoke publicly about Khashoggi after the Bloomberg interview on the day after Jamal Khashoggi had been dismembered by his palace's officials. Crown Prince Mohammed called the death of the *Washington Post* blogger 'very painful for both the Saudi people and the world'. In an echo of the Bloomberg interview, he claimed that the barbaric assassination was being exploited with malice by some to drive a wedge between Saudi Arabia and Turkey.

'I want to send them a message: They will not be able to do that as long as there is a king called King Salman bin Abdulaziz and a crown prince called Mohammed bin Salman in Saudi Arabia, and a president in Turkey called Erdoğan,' he said. 'Justice will be seen in the end.'

He could invoke the president's name because earlier on MBS had had his first telephone call with Erdoğan since the Khashoggi affair erupted. Tight-lipped, press agencies of both countries merely said the two leaders had agreed on 'joint efforts'.

While MBS said the two countries would work together to bring all the perpetrators to court, he did not address accusations that he ordered the assassination.

'He's not going to address the humongous elephant in the room, I bet,' one conference attendee, *Financial Times* Middle East correspondent Heba Saleh, had speculated before the crown prince gave his speech. Stunned silence met the first mention of Khashoggi's name, and a palpable relief followed. MBS's remarks received a short burst of applause, though the atmosphere remained strained.

Alongside MBS on the stage was the Lebanese prime minister. A year earlier, Saud al-Qahtani had led the Saudi interrogation of Saad al-Hariri during a longer stay than planned in Riyadh about the growing Iranian influence in Lebanon. The upshot was al-Hariri's announcement on TV from Riyadh that he intended to resign. The man now seated next to MBS was – the same Saad al-Hariri, once again prime minister of Lebanon.

The crown prince joked that al-Hariri would only be staying in the kingdom for two days this time – 'so I hope you don't spread rumours that he was kidnapped,' he told the audience.

Al-Hariri laughed nervously at this joke at his expense and applauded. He had come back in favour after a leading Lebanese talk-show host was summoned to appear before al-Hariri in Beirut. The comedian had made a Yemen/Qatar joke at the expense of the crown prince on TV. Associated Press reported that 'reacting to a clip on a rival network advising bin Salman to swear off fast food for his health, [the talk-show host] suggested he should swear off fast arrests, fast politics… fast military strikes, instead.'

Some delegates did not join the *folie à deux* and did little to hide their disdain – anonymously – for both the crime and the subsequent attempts to cover it up.

'These idiots have taken us back to the Stone Age,' said one. 'How do I defend this country to anyone anymore? The stupidity here is unparalleled.'

Others said the attempt to distance bin Salman from the slaying and blame it on his closest personal staff was doomed, but that they were forced to go along with it.

'It suits many of us to believe this, because the alternative is just too impossible,' said a Saudi businessman. 'But anyone who has lived here understands the fiction. And his friends outside cannot be expected to look away like us.'

Another said: 'This is very complicated. It is painful for the family and for the people. It is best to live in denial here.'

Abroad the crown prince's condemnation of the murder of Khashoggi was also seen as disingenuous.

As mentioned above, it was leaked on Wednesday 24 October by a US official that, in the days following the assassination MBS had told top White House officials that Khashoggi was a member of the banned (in Saudi Arabia) Muslim Brotherhood and a dangerous Islamist. The top officials he had spoken to were Jared Kushner and US national security advisor John Bolton. Unlike Tillerson, Bolton subscribed to the MBS/el-Sisi/Trump triangle that the Brotherhood was a terrorist rather than an embryonic political organisation.

'It will be harder under MBS to have the same degree of confidence we can work with Saudi Arabia in light of the brutal murder of Khashoggi,' said a former top western intelligence official.

The cryptic comment seemed to suggest there had been a level of cooperation or, at any rate, sharing of information between the US and their close Saudi ally under Donald Trump on Jamal Khashoggi's extraordinary rendition; and that cooperation on another rendition would be less likely because Saudi Arabia couldn't be relied on to keep the lid on things. Was it this that Putin had in fact referred to when he had accused the US of 'a certain responsibility' for the Khashoggi assassination?

***

On 25 October, Saudi Arabia changed its explanation of Khashoggi's death yet again. Now, the killing had no longer happened accidentally during a fistfight with rogue operatives.

Officials finally confirmed, that, yes, the fatal rendition had been planned all along. The Saudi prosecutor general Sheikh Saud al-Mojeb issued a statement on state television, saying: 'Information from the Turkish side affirms that the suspects in Khashoggi's case pre-meditated their crime.'

The Saudi announcement came hours after CIA director Gina Haspel, while on a fact-finding trip to Turkey, had listened to excerpts from the audio recording. While Riyadh might be sanguine ('we'll see'), the US seemed to worry that the domino stones would fall once the audio was in the public domain in the West.

Riyadh blinked first. 'The public prosecution continues its investigations with the accused in the light of what it has received and the results of its investigations,' the sheikh said.

Turkey kept up the pressure on Saudi Arabia by making public instead the information it had possessed for weeks on the two members of the Saudi delegation led by Prince bin Faisal who had been sent to clean up the crime scene. Unlike the consulate, again it didn't make the sheikh's investigation look squeaky clean.

'We believe that the two individuals came to Turkey for the sole purpose of covering up evidence of Jamal Khashoggi's murder before the Turkish police were allowed to search the premises,' an anonymous senior Turkish official leaked to the *Independent*. 'The fact that a clean-up team was dispatched from Saudi Arabia nine days after the murder suggests that Khashoggi's slaying was within the knowledge of top Saudi officials.'

After assiduously staying out of the media on Riyadh's orders, Khashoggi's two sons now suddenly took the spotlight on CNN to talk about their father in Washington DC. Khashoggi's oldest son Salah would later return to his family in Jeddah.

Seated next to each other they described their father as 'courageous, generous and very brave'. Thirty-five-year-old Salah told CNN: 'We just need to make sure that he rests in peace. Until now, I still can't believe that he's dead. It's not sinking in with me emotionally. It's not a normal situation, it's not a normal death at all. All what we want right now is to bury him in Al-Baqi [cemetery] in Medina with the rest of his family. I talked about that with the Saudi authorities and I just hope that it happens soon. It's an Islamic tradition. It's a basic humanitarian issue.'

Thirty-three-year-old Abdullah added: 'I really hope that whatever happened wasn't painful for him, or it was quick. Or he had a peaceful death.'

Asked how his father should be remembered, Salah said: 'As a moderate man who has common values with everyone... a man who loved his country, who believed so much in it and its potential. Khashoggi was never a dissident. He believed in the monarchy, that it is the thing that is keeping the country together. And he believed in the transformation that it is going through.'

The brothers also said their father was 'like a rock-'n'-roll star' when they were out with him in Saudi Arabia because of his career as a celebrated writer.

Their affection for their father showed the private and emotional side behind the news tragedy. Salah's words on his father's belief in the monarchy and its direction at the same time propped up the Saudi royal palace's latest version of events that deep-state secret-service officials had gone rogue.

There was another change in the Saudi choreography. Abdullah now confirmed he knew Hatice Cengiz, contradicting the words of his older brother – seated next to him – in the first week to al-Arabiya about how he had never heard of her. In fact, he knew her well. Abdullah said his father's Turkish fiancée was making Khashoggi happy. He was the last of Khashoggi's four children to see him alive on 10 September. He said: 'We hung out in Istanbul. We had fun. I was really lucky to have a last moment with him. I feel very grateful.'

Salah also spoke. 'The king has stressed that everybody involved will be brought to justice. And I have faith in that. This will happen. Otherwise Saudi Arabia wouldn't have started an internal investigation,' he said this time.

Khashoggi's two daughters, Noha and Razan, paid tribute to their father in the *Washington Post*, vowing that 'his light will never fade'. They called him 'Baba – a loving man with a big heart' and chimed in with their brothers.

'In truth, Dad was no dissident. If being a writer was ingrained in his identity, being a Saudi was part of that same grain,' they wrote, emphasising his passionate love of his homeland. 'It was vitally important to him to speak up, to share his opinions, to have candid discussions. And writing was not just a job; it was a compulsion. It was ingrained into the core of his identity, and it truly kept him alive.'

They recalled their childhood, when he would allow them to rifle through his paper-stuffed office.

'We loved it when he took us every weekend to the bookstore,' they wrote. 'We loved looking through his passport, deciphering new locations from pages covered with exit and entry stamps.... As children, we also knew our father as a traveller. His work took him everywhere, but he always returned to us with gifts and fascinating stories. We would stay up nights wondering where he was and what he was doing, trusting that no matter how long he was gone, we would see him again, wide-armed, waiting for a hug. As bittersweet as it was, we knew from a young age that Dad's work meant that his reach extended far beyond our family, that he was an important man whose words had an effect on people over a great distance.'

They recalled visiting him in Virginia during Ramadan (15 May – 14 June) in 2018. 'Dad... told us about the day he left Saudi Arabia, standing outside his doorstep, wondering if he would ever return. For while Dad had created a new life for himself in the United States, he grieved for the home he had left. Throughout all his trials and travels, he never abandoned hope for his country.'

They returned to his home in Virginia after his death. 'The hardest part was seeing his empty chair,' they said. 'His absence was deafening. We could see him sitting there, glasses on his forehead, reading or typing away. As we looked at his belongings, we knew he had chosen to write so tirelessly in the hopes that when he did return to the kingdom, it might be a better place for him and all Saudis. This is no eulogy, for that would confer a state of closure. Rather, this is a promise that his light will never fade.'

XXI
Theatre

❧

Anonymous Turkish investigators leaked to *Yeni Şafak* on Sunday 26 October they believed Khashoggi's remains were still in Istanbul and they had stopped searching elsewhere. The anonymous officials speculated that Hatice Cengiz's call to the consulate, sometime after public hours had ended at 3.30pm, had panicked the Tiger Team and forced a change of plan and a decision to hide the remains of the body in the garden well of the consul-general's residence. The original plan, Turkish investigators thought, had been to bury the body in Belgrad Forest.

The team had by now gone through 3,500 hours of MoBeSe footage from one hundred and thirty seven cameras placed in seventy two locations. After finally receiving Saudi permission to enter, they had searched the consulate, the twenty two cars going in and out, and the consul-general's residence. They had meanwhile been allowed to take water samples only of the residence's twelve-metre-deep garden well covered with a slab of marble. Prosecutors demanded that it be drained for inspection, but Saudi Arabia refused to give any further access citing the fact Turkey had not included the garden in the protocol for access to the kingdom's diplomatic property in Istanbul.

The reason for this public summary in Turkey's newspapers became clear on the Sunday night of 28 October.

Arriving for a three day fact-finding tour, clad in flowing white robes, a black *bisht* of transparent wool with ornate gold-threaded *zari* trim, and driven around in a top-of-the-range black Mercedes, looking from underneath the same style white *ghutra* head-covering as Khashoggi's brother that indicated purity, the Saudi prosecutor general, Sheikh al-Mojeb, met with his counterpart in Istanbul Irfan Fidan and visited the consulate and the offices of MİT. He requested the handover of all evidence, audio, images as well as testimony in the possession of Turkey. He was also very interested in a virtual copy of all the data on Khashoggi's iPhones even though MİT's technology experts had failed to crack their encryption – an indirect public confession of MİT's incompetence regarding the iCloud/Apple Watch download story.

To *Hürriyet* Turkish prosecutors leaked testily, 'We did not get the impression that they were keen on genuinely cooperating with the investigation'. To Middle East Eye, it was furthermore leaked that public prosecutor Fidan had felt 'humiliated' by the sheikh. It was noted that the Saudi prosecutor general was seen laughing and joking publically on camera in front of his hotel, the Swisshotel. This hotel – once, but no longer, Istanbul's top hotel since the arrival of a slew of more exclusive hotels in the economic upsurge following Erdoğan's rise to power in 2003 – had famously been stormed by Chechen Islamist terrorists in 2001 who rained bullets through its yawning marbled lobby and vast window overlooking the Bosphorus and took some 600 guests and staff hostage. The terrorists had killed no one on that occasion, though the Saudi government employees of course had done so.

Since al-Mojab did not provide the location of the body or the name of the collaborator, the Turkish team leaked that they declined to cooperate with his requests. Nonetheless, Erdoğan would confirm later that some audio from the consulate was played to the Saudi prosecutors, including the Skype calls by Saud al-Qahtani. One of the Saudis present said it was 'truly atrocious'.

The day after the Saudi prosecutor general left Istanbul, Erdoğan wrote in a *Washington Post* op-ed piece that Sheikh al-Mojab 'refused to answer simple questions' until his third day when he extended an invitation *in lieu* of answers to Turkish investigators to come to Riyadh. They could then interview suspects themselves. Erdoğan said it felt like a 'desperate and deliberate stalling tactic'. He added, 'We know that the order to kill Khashoggi came from the highest levels of the Saudi government'. Now that it was clear that the audio recording was real, Erdoğan threw down the gauntlet once more by implying their voices, or at least names, were on the recordings in Turkey's possession.

Istanbul chief prosecutor Irfan Fidan now issued his own statement, presenting for the first time his conclusions about the investigation into the assassination in a very brief statement. It was the second statement by a named official after the president's address in parliament.

'Jamal Khashoggi was strangled to death immediately after entering the consulate... The victim's body was dismembered and destroyed... in line with advance plans.'

This statement nailed Turkey's colours to the mast and circumscribed the crime. It was now the official version based on forensics from which Turkey couldn't really shift position without looking unreliable. Fidan also noted that al-Mojeb had again refrained from saying anything about the supposed Turkish 'local collaborator'.

Less officially, Yasin Aktay commented in *Hürriyet* for the first time the detail that the point of the dismemberment of the victim was to make dissolving the body 'easier'. The top politician didn't offer any evidence of this latest hunch, however.

The official Saudi response to Turkey's anger was finely parsed. It simply made the point that the trial would proceed without Turkish evidence being taken into consideration.

When criminal proceedings started against eleven of the accused on Thursday 3 January, the Saudi Press Agency would note that the prosecutors had sent four letters to their Turkish counterparts (two on 12 December, one on 17 October, another on 31 October). These letters had requested 'any evidence connected to this case'. The release stated, Sheikh al-Mojeb was 'still waiting [for] their response'. Riyadh was implying that fair justice was being done and that Turkey should either put up or shut up.

This suited Turkey just fine. While it had issued an arrest warrant *in absentia* for twenty one Saudis, handing over to someone else the criminal evidence they had gathered against the twenty one would also mean losing control of shaping the facts as it suited them.

Amnesty International called Turkey's bluff. 'What we have are two so-called investigations', commented its UN delegation's head Sherine Tadros drily to *Business Insider* on 2 November.

Turkey's conduct had been 'highly suspect' and 'highly politicised'. While Erdoğan would claim a few days later on 2 November in his *Washington Post* op-ed that 'Turkey has moved heaven and earth to shed light on all aspects of this case', Amnesty International's UN delegate instead noted the opposite in that Turkey's leaks to papers at times contradicted Turkish official statements.

It was polite of her not to reference that Erdoğan was the world's leading jailer of journalists by a long chalk.

On 15 November Turkish foreign minister Mevlüt Çavuşoğlu would call an international investigation 'a must'. The UN had, in fact, expressed interest in this on a number of occasions. But its officials could not act without a formal request from the Turkish government itself. When Çavuşoğlu met UN Secretary-General Antonio Guterres on 20 November, no request was made. Turkey couldn't care less.

Such a probe would 'set a precedent for future inquiries' into its own journalists, which explained Turkey's procrastination, said Amnesty International's Tadros. What was really needed now, she said, was not Turkey's dubious and opportunistic approach but a 'credible' and 'transparent' investigation into Jamal Khashoggi's death.

Nor – in a rare moment of diplomatic dissonance – was the French foreign minister, Jean-Yves le Drian, very impressed with Erdoğan. Like Amnesty International he accused the Turkish president on France 2 of playing 'a political game'. His ministry later wheeled his words back a notch, noting more diplomatically that their minister had meant there was 'an absence of the "full truth"'.

***

Borzou Daraghi, international correspondent of the *Independent*, now published probably the most disturbing piece of news in the middle of a 4000-word panoramic article in the news site's Long Read section on 30 October.

It had been passed on to him by sources who 'in the past provided accurate information about the Khashoggi case'. Separate from one another they had been informed respectively by a Saudi and a Turkish expert with first-hand knowledge of their country's forensic evidence that Khashoggi had been brutally tortured and beaten and interrogated.

This was a claim that went beyond what was publicly conceded by Turkey and Saudi Arabia. If it was true, the Tiger Team would have interrogated Khashoggi about any evidence he had kept on the time he had worked with Prince Turki in the aftermath of 9/11, what he had been planning for the future, and about Saudi and Arab activists he knew.

The Turkish source told Daraghi the ordeal had lasted for an hour whereas the Arab source had been given to understand it went on for two hours. Neither the details of the interrogation nor its duration was picked up by other media, even though the words 'tortured' and 'interrogated' had been regularly used in the leaks by Turkish officials since 7 October. Notably, in Turkish officials first-ever anonymous leak (to Middle East Eye) of what had been recorded they said, 'you can hear how he was interrogated, tortured... beaten'.

Daraghi's news filled in for the first time what had happened from the moment Khashoggi arrived at 1.15pm to the moment the consular cars left at 3.08pm. So far, Turkish leaks had covered at most 11 minutes.

No further Turkish leaks that corroborated Daraghi's account would appear thereafter. As mentioned, Turkish officials had already stopped using 'interrogated', 'torture' and 'beating' in their leaks after 19 October.

Irfan Fidan, the Istanbul lead prosecutor, had also just stated officially that Khashoggi had been 'strangled to death immediately after entering the consulate' and anything contradictory would undermine the credit Turkey had built up in salving 'hurt human conscience', in the words of Erdoğan to his parliament on 22 October.

Despite leaked protestations of being 'humiliated', the Istanbul prosecutor Fidan's statement concurred exactly on this point with the conclusions of Saudi prosecutor general Sheikh al-Mojeb. Looking back, the highpoint of the Khashoggi Affair had passed. The interrogation/torture question never returned to the news cycle after this date.

Back in Saudi Arabia, the crown prince was shoring up his support among the ruling al-Saud family by finally releasing from custody Prince Khaled bin Talal, King Salman's nephew, leading to speculation that other high-profile detainees would also be freed. Prince Khaled was the brother of billionaire investor Prince Alwaleed bin Talal, Khashoggi's sponsor who had been detained at the Ritz-Carlton anti-corruption shakedown, and had criticised MBS's reforms and the mass Ritz-Carlton detentions.

Khaled and Alwaleed's father was the king's half-brother Prince Talal, or the 'red prince', nick-named after his liberal beliefs. After Khashoggi's assassination, the talkative financier Prince Alwaleed dispensed effusive praise for Saudi Arabia's crown prince during a television interview, though he looked 'visibly uncomfortable', the *Financial Times* said. His brother, Prince Khaled, had by then been held for some eleven months with dissidents and activists in al-Hayer prison, south of the capital, without charge and without his family knowing where he was held.

Prince Khaled's belated release on 3 November came days after the return from self-imposed exile in London of seventy-three-year-old Prince Ahmed, the king's younger brother of their mother Sudairi, ibn Saud's fourteenth wife.

The release of Prince Alwaleed's brother was thought to have been a condition for Ahmed's return. Another condition was the guarantee for Prince Ahmed's own safety by the US and the UK. Though removed from succession in 2012, he was rumoured to be still *papabile* and being held in reserve as a possible replacement for MBS as crown prince by the other princes.

In a further attempt to limit the fallout from Khashoggi's murder, King Salman embarked on a week-long tour of Saudi Arabia, his first domestic tour since ascending the throne in 2015.

The crown prince claimed that only eight people were still being detained from the Ritz-Carlton shake-down, but the *Washington Post* put the figure closer to forty five. Despite MBS's claim, oppression was not easing. New regulations were introduced to control the media. They were, it was decreed by the government, intended to protect public order, strengthen national unity, preserve the social fabric, and preserve values and virtues. Women working in media also had to comply with strict Islamic dress codes.

MBS wants just 'one voice', said Yahya Assiri, a former Saudi airforce officer and UK-based activist. 'In the past there could be some criticism with red lines for the media, but now there's just one line, one voice, repeating MBS and that's it,' he said.

Notwithstanding the rumour of government torture of some of MBS's 2017–2018 non-royal guests at the Riyadh Ritz-Carlton, its hotel staff was named 'Hotel Team of the Year' and its general manager 'Highly Commended' at the 2018 Hotelier Middle East Awards held in Dubai.

The royal palace itself was seeking to recruit yet more London- and US-based public relations agencies to rehabilitate its shattered international image with huge fees.

Prince Khaled would be rearrested on unspecified charges days after his influential father died on 22 December.

XXII
The Recording

୬

Turkey still wanted Saudi Arabia to admit Khashoggi's death had been an assassination planned in Riyadh and not an operational accident. On 10 November President Erdoğan officially acknowledged the existence of the audio inside the consulate by confirming a clip had been released to the secret services of the US, UK, Germany, France and Saudi Arabia.

Like a cluster-bomb, it renewed global coverage with a vengeance. The story writers of Homeland couldn't have improved on Turkey's dramatic timing. By handing over the recordings (or rather, edited excerpted copies) to spooks, Turkey ensured that the recording retained its mystique while creating further news headlines. At the same time, the intelligence recipients would now be expected to give an official response to what they had been given.

President Erdoğan said: 'We played them to all who wanted them including the Saudis, the US, France, Canada, Germany, Britain. The recordings are really appalling. Indeed when the Saudi intelligence officer listened to the recordings he was so shocked he said: "This one must have taken heroin, only someone who takes heroin would do this".' The Saudi's implication that Tubaigy ('this one') had taken heroin suited their latest choreography that the Tiger Team had gone off-*piste* in a Manson-style murder. It underlined the Aktay/Trump 'gone rogue' story on which all the governments involved seemed to have settled finally.

He also called on Saudi Arabia to identify the actual killer from among the fifteen-man team who had arrived in Istanbul before the murder.

'There's no need to distort this issue, they know for certain that the killer, or the killers, is among these fifteen people,' he said.

In an interesting insight into his own hands-on approach to extracting facts from people, President Erdoğan furthermore suggested, 'Saudi Arabia's government can disclose this by making these fifteen people talk.'

Inevitably more detail of the assassination was leaked. *Sabah*, said on 12 November that Khashoggi's words at the beginning of his death were: 'I'm suffocating... Take this bag off my head, I have asthma' (but the paper made no mention of having the actual tape).

Donald Trump confirmed that the US had the tape, but expressed little interest in listening to it.

'We have the tape, I don't want to hear the tape. There's no reason for me to hear the tape,' he said. 'Because it's a suffering tape, it's a terrible tape. I've been fully briefed on it, there's no reason for me to hear it. I was told I really shouldn't. It was very violent, very vicious and terrible.'

Others did listen to the recording and once again its contents began to leak. It was said that, soon after Khashoggi entered the consulate, he could be heard saying at the beginning of the altercation: 'Let go of my arm. Who do you think you are? Why are you doing this?'

'It was premeditated murder,' Turkey's foreign minister Mevlüt Çavuşoğlu helpfully told Germany's *Sueddeutsche Zeitung* newspaper. Germany, was the first country to sanction Saudi Arabia over Khashoggi, suspending arms sales to the kingdom on 22 October (only The Netherlands, Finland and Denmark would follow suit).

'It can be heard how the forensics expert instructs the others they should listen to music while he cuts up the body. One notices how he enjoys it. He likes to cut up people. It is disgusting.'

He added that the Saudi crown prince 'said he wanted the journalist silenced' and confirmed that Khashoggi was dead within 7 minutes. Though he did not mention the three-hundred-and-eighty-four Turkish journalists in gaol or under criminal investigation his government sought to silence. Nor was he asked about them.

While the Saudis had conceded there were 'advance plans' for Khashoggi's dismemberment given the bone-saw, President Erdoğan impressed again on everyone that the order had come from the top level of Saudi authorities. Erdoğan's speech hadn't even acknowledged the recordings, despite the leaks by Turkish officials.

Then, on 13 November, Erdoğan for the first time criticised MBS directly: 'The crown prince says "I will clarify the matter, I will do what is necessary". We are waiting patiently', and, 'It must be revealed who gave them the order to murder.'

He added incredulously that Riyadh had offered to send identikit photos of the putative local 'collaborators' who had taken away Khashoggi's body in a rug. 'Why identikit pictures? The Saudis know the names,' he told the *Sueddeutsche Zeitung*.

Other countries kept the pressure up, too, for more to give. Secretary of State Mike Pompeo phoned MBS to tell him that the US would 'hold all of those involved in the killing of Jamal Khashoggi accountable, and that Saudi Arabia must do the same', while British Foreign Secretary Jeremy Hunt brought the matter up with King Salman during a visit to Saudi Arabia.

The *New York Times* was given its own leak and reported on 12 November that shortly after the assassination a member of the special ops team said, in a hacked phone call to his superior: 'The deed is done, tell your boss.' The words were uttered by brigadier-general Maher Mutreb. The source added that American intelligence officials believed 'your boss' ('yours' transliterated from the Arabic) was Crown Prince Mohammed bin Salman. At least three outside calls were placed by

Mutreb and during the last one he had said this, speaking calmly.

Sabah published on 13 November four X-ray scans of some of the Tiger Team's luggage. Turkish officials had the scans for more than a month but the images now told their own stark story in a fresh jacket. Visible in the grainy orange pictures were the outlines in blue of walkie-talkies, a signal jammer, scalpel blades, staple guns, long scissors and syringes. Also visible were, the paper said, electro-shock devices, though *Sabah* didn't speculate why they had been brought along. The bags themselves were not opened due to diplomatic immunity, the paper said. As was now the case with the Turkish leaks of visual material, it was not exactly stated whether it was luggage loaded on the first or the second jet, what the date stamps were and so on.

One paper showed a leaked CC-TV grab of major-general Abahussein in his white *thaub* with a red-white blocked *ghutra* arriving at Atatürk Airport on the afternoon of 1 October in tow with al-Hawsawi in a blue T-shirt and baseball cap pushing two large rolling suitcases. The four X-rays pictures were linked by arrows to the four pieces of luggage they were rolling in total, suggesting that the scans may not have dated to 2 October but to the day before when they arrived and were made at the commercial terminal where they entered, rather than at the Genel Havacilik private-jet lounge.

Most papers, including *Sabah*, implied, however, that the four suitcases belonged to Khashoggi's former colleague Maher Mutreb as he went through Genel Havacilik's airport security 5 minutes before MİT opened its investigation.

Yet this in itself contradicted what an anonymous official had leaked weeks before to Middle East Eye about how Mutreb's bags had not been checked, and that he might have taken body parts back to Riyadh. That leak, at the time, precluded news-cycle questions why MİT had not arrested the operatives on the second jet after it had identified the tools used for the assassination which they supposedly knew about all along. (All the detail matters in weighing whether the team indeed shipped instruments of torture in and out of the country, even if Turkish officials later made a U-turn and denied this was the case to the UN delegation.)

In Riyadh, Saudi deputy prosecutor Shalaan al-Shalaan revealed on 15 November that by now twenty one 'conspirators' were in custody – although it was not possible to verify what this meant exactly, given the prohibition of a free press in Saudi Arabia. Eleven of the people in custody were indicted, with the death penalty being demanded for five of them, while investigations continued into the remaining ten. The death-penalty five were negotiation-team leader Mutreb, Tubaigy, al-Balawi, Waleed and Turki al-Sehri. Four others were indicted under lesser criminal charges and included al-Madani, Saif al-Qahtani, and al-Zahrani. The operatives who had gone to the consulate-general's residence were not charged, except for major-general Abahussein, who was in over-all command of the operation. Of the Istanbul consulate staff only attaché al-Musleh was indicted, but not al-Muzaini. From Riyadh, only major-general al-Asiri was charged (UN detail 192, Table D).

The Saudi deputy prosecutor gave a rare press statement to set out in person in seventeen bullet points what Saudi Arabia agreed had happened. Although, al-Shalaan didn't mention names, he did mention the official functions of the perpetrators.

Saudi Arabia conceded that the killers had set their plans in motion on 29 September, three days before Khashoggi was murdered and the day after he had first visited the kingdom's consulate in Istanbul. The deputy chief of Saudi Arabia's intelligence, major-general Ahmed al-Asiri, issued the order to repatriate Jamal. But the head of 'the negotiating team', brigadier-general Mutreb, was in fact the one who had issued the order for his killing while in Istanbul.

The team had consisted of 'three groups (negotiations/ intelligence/ logistics) to persuade and return the victim' and Mutreb had been assigned as leader of the negotiation team, 'because of his previous relationship with the victim' when they were both working at the London embassy. As to the body, the leader of the three groups major-general Abahussein, 'contacted a collaborator in Turkey to secure a safe location in case force had to be used [to] return the victim'.

'After surveying the consulate, the head of the negotiation team [Maher Mutreb] concluded that it would not be possible to transfer the victim by force to the safe location in case the negotiations with him to return failed', the prosecutor told the press. 'The head of the negotiation team decided to murder the victim if the negotiations failed.'

'The crime was carried out after a physical altercation with the victim where he was forcibly restrained and injected with a large amount of a drug resulting in an overdose that led to his death'.

Riyadh accepted that Jamal Khashoggi had been assassinated by royal officials. The conditional decision, they now said, had been made by Mutreb on the day to kill him with an overdose.

'Those who ordered and carried out the murder, totalling (five) individuals', the Saudi press statement added, 'have confessed to the murder.'

Unfortunately, the whereabouts of the body were unknown, because there was the mystery 'local collaborator' who received the body from one of the team. That team member, however, did give a description which was the basis for a 'composite sketch.'

Prosecutor al-Shalaan went on to insulate MBS from criticism by providing other reasons to show it was an operational cockup that led to the victim's death. MBS's top advisor al-Qahtani had stressed at the beginning of the rendition that returning Khashoggi to Riyadh would be a 'significant achievement.'

Moreover, major-general al-Asiri had been lied to, the Saudi prosecutors claimed. The negotiation team headed by brigadier-general Mutreb and the leader of the operation major-general Abahussein confessed to filing a false report with their superior major-general al-Asiri that said 'the victim had left the consulate building after the failure of negotiating or forcing his return.'

It was a compelling story, except for the fact that, ostensibly, al-Asiri 'The Beast' had accepted that a fifty-nine-year old suffering from a severe cold and asthma seemed to have single-handedly outmanoeuvred the Tiger Team to walk away from the consulate, unharmed, wielding words that outsmarted his professionally trained extradition team.

King Salman duly praised the Saudi magistrates for exonerating his son.

On 16 November, however, the *Washington Post* reported as a riposte that the CIA had concluded that Crown Prince bin Salman 'ordered' the assassination of journalist Jamal Khashoggi. It was later leaked that MBS sent at least eleven messages to Saud al-Qahtani, who was overseeing the operation, in the hours surrounding the murder. Al-Qahtani was one of the officials who was sacked as part of the investigation by the Saudi prosecutor general and one of seventeen people sanctioned under the Magnitsky Act by the US treasury department for being linked to the killing. Al-Qahtani's last public tweet was on 22 October, twenty days after Khashoggi's last tweet.

Again Saudi officials repeatedly denied that MBS had any involvement. Unofficially, a CIA official, however, told the *Post*: 'The accepted position is there is no way this happened without his being aware or involved.'

The agency had reached its conclusions after examining multiple sources of intelligence, including a phone call that the prince's brother, Khalid bin Salman, the Saudi ambassador to the United States, had with Khashoggi. The CIA officer's implication was that Khashoggi and KBS had spoken about where to have the two marriage documents certified, and that KBS had said, not in DC but only in Istanbul or Ankara. But it didn't realise the text of the conversation.

Khalid tweeted back furiously: 'I never talked to him by phone and certainly never suggested he go to Turkey for any reason. I ask the US government to release any information regarding this claim.'

KBS also tweeted that a text on 26 October 2017 was his last contact with Khashoggi, nearly a year before the journalist's death. That assertion would have been easy to disprove. Was KBS playing with fire, or was he telling the truth? KBS would look like an idiot and his role in his brother's government would become untenable if the CIA had later intercepts with Khashoggi. Surprisingly, the CIA would leak more information on a discussion between MBS and KBS to AKP paper *Hürriyet*.

On the same day, the *Washington Post* published a bombshell from the Saudi side. A strikingly beautiful fifty-year-old Egyptian woman living in the UAE called Hanan Atr said that she was the fourth wife of Khashoggi's. She had pictures of the day of the 2 June marriage ceremony and text messages. He had been waiting for her at the airport arrivals hall where he presented her with her wedding ring. They got married straight away that day in Alexandria, Virginia, she told *Emirates Voice*.

She last saw him on 7 September in New York when Hanan Atr was again in the US on business. He last texted Hanan on 30 September for her birthday, and she said that she had contacted Saudi officials at the UAE consulate with the pictures. Under Sharia law, the wife with no issue is entitled to up to one-fourth of the estate. She 'explained that as a Muslim wife, I want my full right and to be recognised'.

Jamal Khashoggi and his fourth wife Hanan Atr on his birthday on 22 January in Tysons Corner.

The pictures of her as Khashoggi's fourth wife soon emerged on a Twitter feed loyal to Riyadh and showed a beaming Khashoggi kissing Ms Atr dressed in what looked like a white marriage gown with an expensive-looking necklace of ruby-red jewels surrounded by what looked like diamonds and matching long earrings dripping with matching stones – one photograph was a selfie of the necklace and part of their faces. Khashoggi himself was dressed in a casual light-blue blazer and oxford-striped shirt, grey trousers and black leather shoes.

In another picture he kissed Hanan tenderly on her cheek. The June day was warm and rainy but not yet hot. In a further picture taken earlier in the season they were both smiling full-size to the camera while she was dressed in a heavy sabre-style fur coat and Khashoggi wore a shearling sheepskin jacket with his arm around her while holding a debonair grey trilby in his right hand on her waist and an elegant gift bag in his left hand, another was taken on his birthday on 22 January.

Hatice Cengiz, who had been told about the previous three marriages, said she had 'never heard of the woman' in a repeat of what Dr Alaa Nasief had said about her.

Was this the kingdom publicity machine striking back with lies Hatice wondered? Later, in February 2019, when she gave an interview to *Sabah* in order to publicise the release of her book *Jamal Khashoggi,* she tempered her judgement and said 'I do not know the life Khashoggi had before me. I only know the part about me'. Although she did think it was wrong to claim money and for Khashoggi's fourth wife to seek publicity with photographs. 'It is not moral', she rebuked her predecessor in the Turkish paper.

The news of the fourth marriage that the Saudis had fed into the news cycle blotted Khashoggi's memory and, in order to regain the upper hand, Istanbul responded with a barrage of newly leaked facts that undermined the Saudi narrative that the murder decision was taken in Istanbul by Mutreb alone.

'Khashoggi's body injected with clotting agent,' yelled a *Yeni Şafak* headline on 17 November. Officials leaked to the paper that, after he was strangled, the drug the Saudi prosecutor had mentioned was meant 'to leave no blood trace' rather than cause his death by overdose. Like the bone-saw, bringing blood-clotting agent showed the degree to which his death had been anticipated during the Tiger Team's operational preparations in Riyadh – it was not a decision on the hoof in Istanbul, it implied.

Al-Madani (left, still in Jamal Khashoggi's clothes) at the Blue Mosque at 4.13pm, al-Qahtani (right) carrying a plastic bag with his clothes, and at the airport after 11.30pm (left in his own clothes).

The paper also said Turkish investigators claimed that 'hydrofluoric acid and other chemicals' were found in the water samples of the well of the consulate-general's garden, indicating that the body was dissolved. Again, the implication was that these chemicals had been brought in anticipation of Khashoggi's assassination. But no measurements that at least *prima facie* in a forensic way supported these anonymous leaks was provided.

There was also a new lugubrious audio snippet 'It is creepy to wear the clothes of a man whom we killed 20 minutes ago,' Khashoggi's body-double al-Madani said on the consulate audio. It was leaked on 19 November to *Haberturk*, part of the same media conglomerate as Bloomberg Turkey.

Al-Madani also complained that Khashoggi's shoes were too small and his feet got stuck. He asked the team leader for permission to wear his own sneakers, which led to the exterior CC-TV debacle. Before al-Madani left the consulate's backdoor at 2.52pm, he and Saif al-Qahtani were given instructions to 'first walk for four streets, take a taxi, go to Sultanahmet, get rid of the clothes, and meet us at the consulate-general's residence'.

They didn't execute the last instruction, likely an indication that Tiger-Team leader brigadier-general Abahussein gave the men new orders when Turkish authorities showed up at the private-jet terminal looking for Khashoggi. He obviously no longer wanted the look-alike on the jet. When Maher Mutreb gave al-Madani permission to wear his sneakers he must have realised this would in time be another clue to his real identity from the MoBeSe CC-TV surrounding the consulate. But he also knew that all al-Madani's disguise would temporarily create the impression that Khashoggi might still be alive and be enough to throw MİT off the scent so that the Tiger Team could get away.

To *Haberturk*'s Çetiner Çetin a story about the locations of the microphones in the consulate was leaked, including statements by Turkish investigators that some of the signal jamming by the Saudis had been successful.

Writing in *Hürriyet* – whose owner had wept in 2014, calling Erdoğan 'boss', when rebuked over a negative piece on the president – Khashoggi-conduit Abdulkadir Selvi also reported leaked information that the CIA had a recording of MBS giving instructions to 'silence Jamal Khashoggi as soon as possible'.

The recording had been made as the result of a US wiretap. The crown prince and his brother KBS were reportedly heard discussing the 'discomfort' created by Khashoggi's public criticism of the kingdom's administration.

How a Turkish paper would obtain privileged CIA information was not clear, unless perhaps the CIA had leaked this as a gesture of the new *détente* to the Turkish government and as an answer to KBS's furious tweet to show their evidence.

Selvi also introduced a new character, injecting more family drama into the affair.

'The hit-squad, which was composed of close aides of Crown Prince Mohammed, told Khashoggi to send a message to his son, otherwise he "would be brought to Saudi Arabia"... [whom they] had earlier contacted.'

Magnifying the mystery, *Hürriyet* did not spell out what that message might have been. Instead Selvi merely stated Khashoggi rejected the demand in order to protect his son, which in turn 'led to the quarrel that ended with his killing by strangulation with a rope or plastic bag.' Spelling out the finishing touch to the tragedy, Selvi wrote: 'The subsequent murder is the ultimate confirmation of this instruction [by MBS].'

President Trump still refused to accept that the crown prince knew anything about the murder, because he had himself talked to the man.

'He told me he had nothing to do with it,' Trump argued on 18 November. 'He told me that, I would say, maybe five times. He did certainly have people that were reasonably close to him and close to him that were probably involved.... But at the same time we do have an ally and I want to stick with an ally that in many ways has been very good.' This was presumably a reference to the $350bn and counting deal he was keen to bring in.

It was again argued that MBS must have known about it as Riyadh had conceded that a potentially fatal extraordinary rendition had been sanctioned by high Saudi officials close to the crown prince. A Western diplomat in Riyadh told the *Sunday Times*: 'He is the only real centre of power in the kingdom. There's no one that is seriously challenging him. And that also means there is no one else that could have ordered the murder.'

Mourners gathered in mosques in Mecca and Istanbul though still no body had been produced and there was nothing to bury.

The mystery concerning the body's whereabouts deepened when this time one of Turkey's most senior politicians, defence minister Hulusi Akar, went officially on the record as one of the few Turkish senior authorities apart from Erdoğan.

He once again speculated that the killers might have taken the body parts out of Turkey, even though this conflicted with statements from the criminal investigators working for the Istanbul chief prosecutor who seemed to have abandoned this idea days before Sheikh al-Mojeb's fact-finding tour in Istanbul, and also with statements that the luggage on both private jets had gone through airport X-ray. Was he saying that the leaked X-rays were of the second jet, and that Turkey had no X-ray records of Mutreb's team's luggage going through security to the first plane due to lax security at Atatürk private-jet terminal as reported by the Middle East Eye? Either way, his comments created a talking point that tied in with the news – this time the virtual burial ceremony in Istanbul's Fatih Mosque.

'One probability is that they left the country three to four hours [on the 'getaway' Gulfstream IV] after committing the murder. They may have taken out Khashoggi's dismembered corpse inside luggage without facing problems due to their diplomatic immunity,' Akar told the BBC in Halifax, Canada.

While the CIA said that MBS was behind the murder of Khashoggi, President Trump maintained this didn't mean that the jury wasn't still out on 20 November.

'Our intelligence agencies continue to assess all information, but it could very well be that the crown prince had knowledge of this tragic event,' he said. In a sideways move he equivocated not on the facts known to the CIA, but rather on their sum total. He doubted whether these facts merited the CIA's conclusion beyond reasonable doubt: 'Maybe he did and maybe he didn't!... We may never know all of the facts.'

Trump agreed to meet MBS at the upcoming G20 meeting in Buenos Aires, a city overlooked by a Trump hotel in Punta del Este. He was after the nuclear arms deal and was duly praised by MBS's friends in the Gulf States for his stead-fast loyalty to the crown prince.

However, two senior senators again wielded the 2012 Global Magnitsky Act in an attempt to order the president to determine whether the crown prince was responsible for Khashoggi's death.

'In light of recent developments, including the Saudi government's acknowledgement that Saudi officials killed Mr Khashoggi in its Istanbul consulate, we request that your determination specifically address whether Crown Prince Mohammed bin Salman is responsible,' they wrote.

'I disagree with the president's assessment. It's inconsistent… with the intelligence I've seen… The intelligence I've seen suggests that this was ordered by the crown prince,' Republican senator Mike Lee said on NBC's Meet the Press. Plainly he felt President Trump's assertion was at odds with the evidence.

'It is not in our national security interests to look the other way when it comes to the brutal murder of Mr Jamal Khashoggi,' Republican senator and former presidential rival Lindsey Graham concurred. 'Mr Trump has betrayed American values in service to what already was a bad bet on the thirty-three-year-old prince.'

Writing on Twitter, Bob Corker, chairman of the Senate foreign relations committee added witheringly: 'I never thought I'd see the day a White House would moonlight as a public relations firm for the crown prince of Saudi Arabia.'

While Donald Trump continued to insist that the CIA had not found MBS responsible and had come to no conclusion, Jack Reed, the senior Democrat on the senate armed services committee, put it more bluntly and said yes that the President was 'lying', foregoing the usual media euphemisms of 'false statements' or misspeaking.

'The CIA concluded that the crown prince of Saudi Arabia was directly involved in the assassination of Khashoggi,' he said. Not only that, Reed added the CIA had 'high confidence' in its assessment.

'It's based on facts, it's based on analysis,' he said. 'The notion that they didn't reach a conclusion is just unsubstantiated. The CIA has made that clear.'

The considerable pressure that was building up on Saudi Arabia to do something, and Trump's defence of his friend in the desert kingdom, did have one further result though.

In December 2016, with Trump a month away from moving into the White House, MBS as minister of defence had started discussing the purchase by the palace of the US THAAD air defence system designed to shoot down all types of hostile missiles. Lockheed had developed the system after the experience with Scud missiles in the first Iraq War.

On 28 November 2018 the kingdom signed a letter of offer and acceptance for a 'massive sale' of forty four THAAD launchers, missiles and related equipment. The deal was worth $15bn. On 1 April 2019 the Pentagon would announce the first step in rolling out the system to Saudi Arabia.

XXIII
High-five!

Before travelling to the G20 in Argentina on 30 November, MBS visited the United Arab Emirates, where he met his closest ally, Sheikh Mohammed bin Zayed crown prince of Abu Dhabi or MBZ, the federation's *de facto* ruler. He would go on to Gulf state Bahrain, Egypt and Tunisia – all friendly allies sponsored by the kingdom – on his way to Buenos Aires. The tour sent a message to the world that MBS's position remained unassailable in the kingdom. It was the diplomatic equivalent of saying there will be no change and it is safe for the crown prince to be out of the country.

Nonetheless, when MBS landed in Tunisia, the birthplace of the Arab Spring, there were demonstrations and popular protests. A large banner hanging from the headquarters of the Tunisian journalists' union showed the crown prince wielding a chain saw – a reference to the dismemberment of Khashoggi's corpse. Demonstrators carried placards saying, 'The murderer is not welcome' and 'Go away assassin', while some held up hacksaws.

'It's inhuman to see an Arab leader killing his brothers in Yemen, and the murder of a journalist is the icing on the cake,' said Basma Rezgui, a teacher brandishing a red-stained bone saw.

'He's a very dangerous person because he doesn't seem to understand politics or respect his own people or other people,' said Radwan Masmoudi, president of Tunisia's Centre for the Study of Islam and Democracy, who was among those protesting MBS's visit. 'There's no way he'll bring stability. His actions speak louder than his words.'

On the same day that MBS started his trip, the Istanbul chief prosecutor revisited defence minister Akar's words and decided to restart the search for Khashoggi's body in a new location.

This looked like a propaganda move as his officials had said before Sheikh al-Mojeb's Istanbul visit they considered the well in the consul-general's garden Khashoggi's last resting place. Turkish police, trailed by the media like MBS on his trip, publicly searched a palatial villa near the town of Termal in the Yalova province near Istanbul. This was the area where MİT had accidentally traced the consulate's secret service staff in the evening before the murder.

The villa belonged to Mohammed al-Fawzan, a Saudi businessman close to MBS. On 26 November, Istanbul's chief prosecutor duly added this name to the roster of the Saudi hit-squad.

Al-Fawzan, codenamed 'Ghozan', had been called by brigadier-general Abahussein, the leader of the hit-squad, when he arrived in Istanbul on the day before Khashoggi's assassination.

'The chief prosecutor's office believes that this phone call was about disappearing or hiding the body parts of the murdered journalist Jamal Khashoggi,' the official press statement said. Al-Fawzan was not in Turkey when Jamal Khashoggi was killed, but Turkish investigators believed he may have let the hit-squad use his property – though there was no suggestion that al-Fawzan personally knew of the assassination or that the hit-squad would try to hide Khashoggi at his property. Large photographs of King Salman and the crown prince adorned the walls inside the villa.

Investigators clad in familiar white suits with blue gloves and show covers took a particular interest in a well on the grounds of the villa, which they drained and in which they said they found traces of chemicals – though not which ones and what it signified. They used drones and dogs in the ten-hour search, which covered the grounds of a neighbouring property. The TV footage of their progress matched the progress of MBS's tour through the Middle East.

'Jamal Khashoggi's body was cut into pieces and dissolved after his murder in the Saudi consulate in Istanbul,' said the prosecutor's press release. 'As a part of the ongoing investigation, it has been detected that the day before suspect Mansour [Abahussein] got in touch with Saudi citizen Mohammed Ahmed [al-Fawzan] in Yalova. It is assumed that their conversation is connected to the Khashoggi murder, and the dissolving and hiding of his body.'

The prosecutor also noted that a man named Mohammed Ahmed al-Fawzan had been appointed head of a Saudi company shortly after the crown prince seized control of it from one of the rich Saudis he had imprisoned on corruption charges at the 2017 Riyadh Ritz Carlton shakedown.

In Buenos Aires, Human Rights Watch submitted papers calling on Argentina to use a clause in its constitution to prosecute MBS for the murder of Jamal Khashoggi and war crimes in Yemen if he attended the G20. A file containing details of Jamal Khashoggi's slaying and other cases of torture was sent to the Argentinian prosecutor's office. Argentina's constitution recognises universal jurisdiction for war crimes and torture. This meant the authorities can investigate and prosecute those crimes no matter where they were committed. The Argentine prosecutor did accept the request to prosecute Mohammed bin Salman, but when MBS arrived in Argentina, he was warmly received by government officials nonetheless.

When the G20 summit opened in Buenos Aires on 30 November, Prime Minister Theresa May said she would confront the crown prince about the killing of Jamal Khashoggi. They shook hands, at any rate. A Downing Street spokesman said: 'The Prime Minister stressed the importance of ensuring that those responsible for the appalling murder of Jamal Khashoggi are held to account, and that Saudi Arabia takes action to build confidence that such a deplorable incident could not happen again.'

French President Emmanuel Macron also had a word. MBS told him not to worry about Khashoggi's murder.

'I am worried,' Macron had replied. 'You never listen to me.'

'I will listen, of course,' MBS replied. 'It's OK. I can deal with it.'

But the most significant meeting was between President Putin and MBS.

Putin had grown up in Soviet Russia at the height of its power and had been stationed as Komissariat-5 KGB officer in East Germany where the Stasi, the German equivalent of the KGB, held files on over one third of the total population. MBS, unlike most Saudi royals, had never lived abroad or outside a Saudi palace. Both authoritarians (together with Erdoğan and, arguably, Trump) instinctively treated their national media as a power tool.

Putin was well-seasoned in flouting international opinion since his rule began in 2001 – it didn't penetrate the Russian media carapace. Like MBS he had started out being the darling of the Western media, hailed in his case as a breath of fresh air after dipsomaniac Boris Yeltsin. It had lasted until the excruciating death by poisoning on 23 November 2006 of his former colleague, FSB colonel Alexander Litvinenko, in London, with rare isotope Polonium 210 exclusively produced in a high-security Russian-government facility.

He had countered what was levelled at Russia with his own 'facts' and 'conclusions' in a precursor to what other governments called 'false news' and 'alternative facts'. Since then he had invaded and incorporated Crimea as part of Russia, fired on Ukrainian boats in the Kerch Strait, and violated the air space of other nations among other more insidious interference in local politics often through its superior understanding of cyber warfare.

Apart from Litvinenko, Putin had got away with the assassination of many inconvenient people outside of Russia. There were mysterious deaths, fifteen notable ones in Britain alone. There was Dr Matthew Puncher, the scientist who identified Polonium 210 and committed suicide after a visit to Russia, as did Putin's arch-opponent Boris Berezovsky, seemingly choosing a shower-curtain rail and a tie to hang himself. A lot of Putin opponents seemed to get terminally depressed. There were even some unexplained deaths of Russians once close to Putin in supposedly safe America, such as Putin aide Mikhael Lesin in 2015. Even collateral damage amongst civilians did not deter Russia.

When Putin launched his surprise attack on 'traitor' Sergei Skripal at the energy conference on 3 October, it was the day after Jamal Khashoggi had been assassinated. In the presence of MBS's right-hand man, energy minister Khalid al-Falih, he dismissed it as 'hubbub'. He advised his audience that opinions would always die down eventually. The brouhaha was not a real problem. The real challenge for a government, Putin observed, was that 'espionage, like prostitution, is one of the most important professions in the world. Nobody has managed to stop them and nobody is still able to do it.' When dealing with a traitor, as a government you ignore the talk and focus on what is really important – you lance the boil.

Two days before the G20, the Kremlin had promised a face-to-face meeting between MBS and Putin where they 'would discuss the killing last month of Saudi journalist Jamal Khashoggi... oil markets and the conflict in Syria'. Russia was the third largest oil producer in the world. Saudi Arabia was at the fulcrum of global chatter due to the assassination recordings. MBS, head of Aramco, was also the world's largest oil producer after the US.

Like a school boy Putin high-fived MBS and it was all smiles.

There was no publicity value in being seen with either and President Donald Trump appeared to snub them both. President Erdoğan didn't meet MBS after all. As Erdoğan had just started including MBS's name in his public calls for 'justice' it would create a mixed message.

In Washington, DC, protestors renamed the street outside the Royal Embassy of Saudi Arabia 'Khashoggi Way'. Their fake street sign was accompanied by an inflatable rat made to mimic Donald Trump.

Also shortly after the summit, a trove of private text messages between Khashoggi and Montreal-based activist Omar Abdulaziz surfaced. They revealed yet another part of Khashoggi's secretive side.

One read: 'Like Pac-Man... the more victims he [MBS] eats, the more he wants. I will not be surprised if the oppression will reach even those who are cheering him on.' Another called the ruler who had never lived outside the kingdom a 'beast' – also the nickname of the sacked major-general al-Asiri.

Donald Trump not speaking to MBS in public at the G20, Buenos Aires.

According to the *Independent*, Khashoggi's texts could have been accessed by

Saudi security officials, contributing to the execution.

Khashoggi's social-media friend Omar Abdulaziz sued NSO Group, an Israeli software company that provided a spyware package called Pegasus to the Saudis. The Israeli company was benefiting from the fact that selling such spy-technology to Israel's authoritarian neighbours was considered the avenue to neighbourly peace by the Israeli government. NSO conceded that both Saud al-Qahtani and major-general al-Asiri had been clients. On 1 October Canada-based Citizen Lab had reported Abdulaziz's phone had been infected by an infiltrator linked to Saudi Arabia. It allowed the kingdom's government to hack his messages which were conveyed via the normally securely-encrypted WhatsApp. The software also gave spy-access to his contacts, photos, text messages, online chat logs, emails, other personal files, camera as well as microphone to listen in on his conversations. On 1 August, Amnesty International had reported the same about the phone of UK-based former Saudi air-force officer Yahya Assiri.

This news mattered more than what might come of Abdulaziz's law suit. As did the surprise news that the kingdom Tiger Team members had been trained in intelligence work in the US by companies owned by Cerberus Capital Management, NY, whose co-CEO was on Trump's Intelligence Advisory Board.

In the US, government-to-government deals, 'foreign military sales' or 'direct commercial sales' require a government arms license reviewed by the senate. Furthermore, under 'Leahy vetting' the US state department has a federal duty to ensure no 'gross violations of human rights' (GVHRs) are committed by foreign entities, such as 'torture, extrajudicial killing, enforced disappearance, and rape under colour of law' its website clarifies.

Following the news of Khashoggi's assassination all licensing to Saudi Arabia had swiftly dried up. Weary of the unwanted attention, on 14 February 2019 the controversial NSO Group was sold by its owners for $1bn to the group's founders funded by 'ethical' London private equity firm Novalpina Capital. This firm with at least $1bn in investor money had been co-founded in 2014 by Stephen Peel, a visiting fellow at the Blavatnik School in Oxford and an advisory board member at Yale's Jackson Institute. How invasive NSO's products were became clear on 14 May 2019 when it was reported that all 1.5bn WhatsApp users were at risk from NSO's spyware after a security breach.

On 6 December an Istanbul court issued further arrest warrants for former deputy head of Saudi intelligence major-general Ahmad al-Asiri and Saudi royal minister Saud al-Qahtani for 'willful murder with monstrous sentiment'. This raised the total number to twenty – the two new ones, plus the fifteen Tiger Team members and the three secret-service staff at the consulate. Istanbul prosecutor Fidan would add another staff member later, bringing the number up to twenty one, the same as the Saudi prosecutor general.

'The prosecution's move to issue arrest warrants for Asiri and Qahtani reflects the view that the Saudi authorities won't take formal action against those individuals,' a Turkish official said. It also conceded in as many words that the arrest warrants were being used for political purposes.

Damagingly to the White House, it was reported in the *New York Times* that Jared Kushner had enquired during the first months of Trump's move into the White House, and before MBS took over crown prince on 21 June 2017, whether the US government could 'influence' the royal succession in MBS's favour. Kushner certainly did his best. In March 2017, when Trump and Saudi minister of defence MBS first met impromptu when Angela Merkel cancelled because of a snow storm, it was an unusual meeting. MBS was merely deputy crown prince then. Yet he received full head-of-state honours. The White House denied the first story as 'false'.

The US senate had had enough. It reached for a new measure to overrule President Trump's foreign policy regarding Saudi Arabia's war in Yemen and his response to the murder of Jamal Khashoggi. The move, significantly, was not partisan and had the support of both Republicans and Democrats. Following a briefing by CIA director Gina Haspel, leading senators also said relatively plainly that the Saudi crown prince was 'complicit' in the killing of Jamal Khashoggi.

Senator Lindsey Graham (R) told reporters: 'There's not a smoking gun, there's a smoking saw. You have to be willfully blind not to come to the conclusion that this was orchestrated and organised by people under the command of MBS and that he was intricately involved in the demise of Mr Khashoggi. I think he is complicit in the murder of Mr Khashoggi to the highest level possible. I cannot support arm sales to Saudi Arabia as long as he's in charge.'

Senate foreign relations committee chairperson Bob Corker (R) told reporters: 'I have zero questions in my mind that the crown prince directed the murder… If he was in front of a jury he would be convicted in 30 minutes. Guilty. So, the question is what do we do about that.'

The day before the Senate vote, *Haberturk* published new grisly information on cue. 'They opened Khashoggi's veins and drained his blood into the sink!' its headline shouted.

The consulate had also allegedly used three times as much water over the nine days leading up to the access of Turkish forensic investigators in order to dilute any forensic traces, according to the paper's leak-supremo Çetiner Çetin. High-pitched spinning noise of an autopsy saw and chopping and cleaving sounds could be heard on the audio, he also revealed.

'Eleven times that sound goes on for quite a long time', officials leaked in the article. The number of body parts may have been lower than fifteen, the paper speculated.

On 13 December, the US senate passed a unanimous resolution stating that

Saudi Crown Prince Mohammed bin Salman was responsible for Jamal Khashoggi's murder and in a separate resolution it formally voted to withdraw US support for the Saudi war in Yemen that MBS had started.

The Saudi foreign ministry released a statement saying: 'The recent position of the United States, which has been built on baseless allegations and accusations, includes blatant interference in its internal affairs and the role of the kingdom at the regional and international level. The kingdom has previously asserted that the murder of Saudi citizen Jamal Khashoggi is a deplorable crime that does not reflect the kingdom's policy, nor its institutions, and reaffirms its rejection of any attempts to take the case out of the path of justice in the kingdom.'

'The kingdom hopes that it is not drawn into domestic political debates in the United States to avoid any ramifications on the ties between the two countries that could have significant negative impacts on this important strategic relationship.'

Vladimir Putin couldn't have wished for greater discord in the Saudi-American relationship. Mevlüt Çavuşoğlu, the Turkish foreign minister, raked it over by saying that Trump was turning a blind eye to the murder. He then lashed out at the EU's response, which he complained was no more than 'cosmetic'. It was a change from having to defend Turkey's own record on free speech. Three weeks earlier, Australian BBC correspondent Yalda Hakim had observed to foreign minister Hulusi Akar that Turkey had more journalists in prison than China. He had curtly fielded semantics that could have come from Donald Trump, 'They are not journalists. They may have the title of journalist.'

Emboldened by the senate's accusation of MBS as the responsible king pin, Erdoğan said, 'We have learned this from the audio recordings: of those who arrive, those closest to the crown prince played the most active role,' said President. 'The perpetrators are clear to me.'

Citing Nikki Haley, outgoing US envoy to the United Nations, who took the same line as the US Senate, President Erdoğan said hopefully, 'She openly named people', and, 'This shows something. Now, the whole incident is fully resurfacing.' He added: 'It's clear where this business will end up.' Though it wasn't entirely clear where 'where' was.

XXIV
Diplomatik Vahşet

Time magazine named Khashoggi and three persecuted journalists as its 'Person of the Year'. The three were Maria Ressa who was the co-founder of Filipino news site *Rappler* and who had criticised President Duterte's anti-drug crackdown which had killed nearly five thousand people since 2016, and Reuters reporters Kyaw Soe Oo and Wa Lone who were arrested in Myanmar on 12 December 2017 while investigating the execution of ten Rohingya men. They had been sentenced to seven years in prison. Sean Penn, meanwhile, turned up in Istanbul to make a documentary on Jamal Khashoggi.

On 28 December *Sabah*'s investigative team Abdurrahman Şimşek, Ferhat Ünlü, and Nazif Karaman published their book *Diplomatik Vahşet* in Turkey. It was published by Turkuvaz Books, which, like *Sabah*, is owned by Çalik Holding the conglomerate previously headed by Erdoğan's son-in-law, Berat Albayrak, subsequently finance minister until his dismissal for Turkey's economic malaise.

The sources of the book were Turkish officials with first-hand knowledge of the top-secret recordings, the *Sabah* journalists wrote. The book revealed that the 7.5 minute clip given to foreign intelligence agencies was edited from recordings made before and after Khashoggi's arrival. The voices on the clip were predominantly 'negotiation-team' leader Maher Mutreb's and pathologist Salah Tubaigy's. It was the first time *Sabah*'s team returned to recording leaks since the Apple Watch debacle. Where indicated, the book's claims are set against the June 2019 UN report by Callamard's team which was given access to primary evidence, unlike the authors of *Diplomatik Vahşet*.

Their source leaked that the audio covered the hour before Khashoggi's arrival, and that a discussion had been taped between Mutreb, Tubaigy, and royal guard al-Harbi from MBS's personal security detail. Since the men spoke before his arrival, the book made clear why there was no doubt in the minds of Turkish investigators that Khashoggi's murder had been pre-meditated.

'We'll ask him to come back to Riyadh', said Mutreb. If he doesn't 'we will kill him here and get rid of the body.'

To this Tubaigy responds, 'I have never worked on a warm body until now, but I can handle that easily. Normally while working on a cadaver, I put on my headphones and listen to music. And I drink my coffee and smoke my cigarette.'

'Khashoggi is tall, around 1.80 meters,' he adds. 'The joints of a sacrificial animal are easily split, but dismembering still will take time.'

'After I dismember, you will wrap them in plastic bags and put them in the luggage and carry' the body parts out, Tubaigy instructed the others. Mutreb then orders his men to set out the tools and materials they brought. On the recording metal items can be heard, said the writers of the book.

In other words, Tubaigy had not, after all been salivating over Khashoggi's death. It was the way Turkey had initially edited the audio that had caused the revulsion around the world.

Though hard-boiled words by a pathologist, out of context they had made Tubaigy sound like a blood-thirsty Hannibal Lecter salivating over Khashoggi's body. It was the way it had put together that made the Saudi secret intelligence officer who listened to the clip speculate he was on 'heroin'. The facts were different. Turkey had intentionally manipulated the recording to turn it into Pulp Fiction.

As the objective had been achieved, the new point – unfolding in the December book of leaks – was to move away from Pulp Fiction and focus on buttressing the Turkish case that Riyadh's extraordinary rendition plan was meant to end with pre-meditated murder – a 'truth' that no more suited Erdoğan's plans.

In 2019, the UN rapporteur would also be given new material underlining this latest narrative.

Mutreb and Tubaigy had continued their conversation right until 1.02pm when Khashoggi was due to arrive any minute. 'Mutreb asked whether it will "be possible to put the trunk in a bag?" Dr. Tubaigy replied, 'No. Too heavy.' He expressed hope that it would "be easy. Joints will be separated. It is not a problem. The body is heavy. First time I cut on the ground. If we take plastic bags and cut it into pieces, it will be finished. We will wrap each of them." "Leather bags". There was a reference to cutting skin' (UN detail 91).

In fact, Turkey's officials even gave Tubaigy a human side in the material it chose to share in 2019. On the recording given to UN rapporteur Callamard the pathologist was heard worrying, 'My direct manager is not aware of what I am doing. There is nobody to protect me'.

When Khashoggi enters the consul-general's office around 1.20pm for tea and is grabbed by his arm, Mutreb says, 'Come, sit down. We came to take you to Riyadh.' Khashoggi immediately answers, 'I won't go to Riyadh.'

Mutreb says all will be 'forgiven' if he comes back and the men ask him to text his son Salah, 'My son, I am in Istanbul. Do not worry if you don't hear from me for a while'.

The recording that Callamard would hear underlined the story in the book about how the Saudis leveraged his son Salah to get to Khashoggi.

At 1.22pm, Mutreb asked for the brand of Khashoggi's phones to get him to type the message.

"'Send a message to your son.' 'Which son? What should I say to my son?'.' There was silence and it seemed as if Khashoggi briefly considered this option.

"'You will type a message – let's rehearse; show us.' 'What should I say? See you soon? I can't say kidnapping".'

'Cut it short', Mutreb pressured Khashoggi. "'Take off your jacket.' 'How could this happen in an embassy?' 'I will not write anything.' 'Cut it short.' 'I will not write anything.' 'Type it, Mr Jamal. Hurry up. Help us so that we can help you because at the end we will take you back to Saudi Arabia and if you don't help us you know what will happen at the end; let this issue find a good end".'

After 10 minutes of this, at 1.33pm, Khashoggi said 'There is a towel here. Are you going to give me drugs?' Mutreb responded, 'We will anaesthetise you' (UN detail 94, reconstructed from memory, as MİT blocked 'transparency' by prohibiting note-taking).

Mutreb orders his officers to grab Jamal. MBS's royal guard al-Harbi tries to cover Khashoggi's mouth, but is repelled by him. Finally the five men, including al-Harbi, al-Zahrani another royal guard in MBS's personal security detail, al-Madani, and Saif al-Qahtani, pull a plastic bag over his head, securing it with a piece of nylon.

It takes 5 minutes before the last sound of his rasping breath is heard. Jamal Khashoggi dies at 1.24pm in this new version, some 10 minutes after entering the consulate. But on the recording that the UN delegation will hear, the last word they hear Khashoggi speak is at 1.33pm. They then hear sounds of a struggle, and Tiger Team operatives say: 'Did he sleep?' 'He raises his head.' 'Keep pushing.' 'Push here; don't remove your hand; push it.' The delegation then hears 'movement', 'heavy panting' and 'plastic sheets'.

Khashoggi's body-double al-Madani and his travel companion Saif al-Qahtani (they entered the consulate together at 11.03am, possibly with Tubaigy) now take off his clothes for al-Madani to put on to leave through the consulate's back door an hour and a half later at 2.52pm.

In order to decrease spillage and creating a mess in the consulate, Tubaigy inserts a tube in Khashoggi's arm, which proved only effective in part. Turkish forensic experts later removed fresh paint from the walls of the consulate and found traces of Khashoggi's blood behind it. Officials leaked this to Qatar-based al-Jazeera in a documentary aired on 3 March 2019, but the actual forensic evidence was not shared.

Earlier officials had leaked to *Haberturk* that their investigation had revealed marble floors and skirting boards were cleaned with two types of chemicals. They had nonetheless found tissue there – mainly on the skirting boards though they did ultimately admit that the DNA could not be matched with Khashoggi's. Turkish investigators also said the three rooms where they found evidence of the plot had been repainted after 2 October.

As Tubaigy furiously begins dismembering the body, it is a race against time. Over half an hour, orders rain down on the other men present who are struggling with what they are witnessing – 'quickly bring the bags', 'what are you waiting for', 'why are you standing there!'

Five bags are then transported to the consul-general's residence in the Mercedes Vito minivan (number plate 34 CC 1865) that leaves after 3pm to drive the few hundred yards to his home address. They drive into his concealed garage port to unload and then park the van in front.

The Saudi's forensic cleaning of the consulate and residence, the book revealed, was executed in several stages. The assassins themselves did the first rough clean on the afternoon of 2 October, followed by a thorough one by Saudi consular staff. But the real detailing had been done by the 'wipers', the chemist al-Zahrani and toxicologist al-Janubi, who were part of the delegation of the governor of Mecca, Prince bin Faisal.

Diplomatik Vahşet now claimed, in yet another pivot back that there was really no evidence how or where the Tiger Team disposed of the body. Turkey's so-called investigation was like a wind vane on this point.

In Turkey, there were persistent rumours that Hatice Cengiz was a UAE spy and in on the plot to assassinate Jamal. The three journalists discounted this theory, as Cengiz did everything she could to expedite the involvement of the highest levels of government rather than merely alert the police.

On the vexed question where the recording came from, the *Sabah* journalists of *Diplomatik Vahşet* passed on yet another mixed bag of stories in the wake of their embarrassing Apple-Watch/iCloud blunder.

On the one hand, Ferhat Ünlü, said in an interview, 'There are a number of intelligence scenarios, forecasts and speculations about how [the] records are obtained. In order not to speculate, we left that part unclear.' But *Sabah,* reporting on the book, also leaked what was said at a meeting between Turkey's and Saudi Arabia's security chiefs – Hakan Fidan and Abdulaziz al-Howairini. The latter said Saudi Arabia found ten bugs in their consulate. Fidan had retorted that 'anybody could be listening'. Perhaps that was Fidan telling the truth.

In yet another variation of having one's cake and eating it, English-language website dailysabah.com.tr (edited by *Sabah*) claimed that the recordings weren't 'unlawfully achieved' by Turkey in its attempt to paint a picture of Turkey as a punctilious defender of 'human conscience'.

Instead it said, cryptically, that 'the recordings were automatically saved, meaning that Turkey did not deliberately listen to the consulate and save the recording.' This tortuous phrase implied a recording was made without the intention of making a recording inside the consulate.

As to the time line of events, *Diplomatik Vahşet* said – as mentioned earlier – that 'sound analysts… solved MİT's question within two hours' upon listening to the conversations in Arabic on 2 October.

This made sense if you had the recording. It contained, for example, an in-depth discussion about butchering the body between Tubaigi and Mutreb just before Khashoggi entered the consulate [revealed for the first time in the UN report]. Even if you didn't know who has speaking to whom, those words left little to the imagination in Arabic or in any language. Unless consulates were like slaughterhouses, one sentence of this conversation would have been enough for 20/20 vision of the situation.

Another 'accelerator' to MİT's understanding on 2 October would have been if their sound analysts heard brigadier-general al-Madani's words first. He said 'it is creepy to wear the clothes' of a man who has just been killed. On 17 November *Yeni Şafak* had also leaked to great effect that al-Madani had said 'a man whom we killed 20 minutes ago'. Al-Madani, it was leaked, was putting on Khashoggi's clothes while he spoke those words, complaining as he tried to squeeze into Khashoggi's smaller size shoes.

It wouldn't have required a genius to figure out who had uttered this sentence. Evidently this was the operative who was close in age to Khashoggi and looked like him. On both counts, there was only one who qualified.

The 7 passport scans Turkish officials leaked to the US media.

Indeed, MİT's MoBeSe staff was trained for this kind of old-school visual search. It 'quickly' (as leaked by MİT to the *Wall Street Journal* on 22 October) identified Khashoggi's body-double through its CC-TV footage. As it had also made the link between Khashoggi and the Gulfstream IV that had ferried al-Madani in at 3.29am that morning (after all MİT searched jet before its departure at night), MİT would have had his passport and barcode details. Both terminals at Atatürk airport checked travellers' ID's electronically – scans of seven of the operatives passports from both airports were leaked to the *Washington Post* on 17 October (it is unclear why they weren't given the scans of all fifteen). The brigadier-general had his leisurely dinner with Saif al-Qahtani went through Atatürk's passport control at night at 0.18am to board his plane to Riyadh at 1.20am at his leisure. This was over seven hours from the moment the Turkish investigations commenced and four to five hours from the moment the jet on which he had arrived was searched by specialist MİT agents disguised as airport staff.

The Turkish investigators who spoke to the UN delegation in 2019, didn't pick the 'within two hours' version that the readers of *Diplomatik Vahşet* were being told on 28 December, passing the light touch of its authors. For the UN team of professional investigators and criminal lawyers, they picked the version that the *Wall Street Journal* had been given on 22 October.

On 2 October (the 'same evening', so before midnight) MİT had its 'raw recordings', Turkey told Callamard's team. The first operative, Maher Mutreb, arrived at the consulate at 9.55am and the last operatives, including Tubaigy, left the consulate at 7.40pm. One would, therefore expect the raw data to cover almost ten hours, but the UN report mentions that they were given to understand that there were 'seven hours' (detail 108: their report also mentioned 'at least seven hours of recordings' under detail 41a, but there it may or at any rate seems to refer to recordings during a 'two-day period' before 2 October).

But, they told the UN team, the recordings were 'complex and it took them several days to reach a firm conclusion'. This was a slightly different issue from the one that the *Journal* was after on 22 October – when did you realise Khashoggi was assassinated by the fifteen – this is what the humble pie of 'missed chances' referred to. In the case of the UN investigation, 'complex' referred to the moment when MİT understood everything there was to understand about them.

Just listening to these audio recordings didn't 'divulge' their stories, the UN delegates were told. 'Background noises have to be interpreted; conversations thought to be insignificant initially can become meaningful once more information comes to light. In this instance, some of the available recordings were less clear acoustically than others, making identification of those speaking difficult and making interpretation of what was happening at any given time difficult too' (detail 41d).

Weirdly, MİT seemed to say to Callamard that they got the recordings spectacularly wrong. Their first assessment was that Khashoggi 'had been injected with something, passed out, and taken alive from the consulate in some box or container', they told her team [detail 108]. Having the recording seemed to have been no help at all for quite a long time [really? what about 'put the trunk in a bag', 'First time I cut on the ground', etc]. It took sound analysts 'several days' to rectify their mistake, they told the UN investigators.

Interestingly, the UN version was the first time Turkish authorities went on the record on the matter and, so, officially Turkey defended a position that they had no idea it was murder until Thursday 4 October or so. That is to say, the recording not withstanding, as a matter of understanding the basics of what had happened they were no better off than if they only had external evidence. It was ludicrous, but that is what they claimed as the truth.

Although the UN report passed no comment on the discrepancy between 'official' leaks – it had excluded them from on principle from its investigation as mentioned – to the Turkish or international press, nor on what brigadier-general al-Madani said on the recording the delegates listened to, it did observe, again, Turkey's lack of transparency and *bona fide* cooperation. 'Turkish authorities undoubtedly have more information and intelligence about events in the Saudi Consulate than they were willing or able to share with the inquiry' (detail 41d). The UN delegation, for example, did not record hearing Khashoggi's former colleague Mutreb say 'Traitor! This is what you deserve!' This memorable phrase was one of the earliest and most widely reported bits of the recordings. But it was a leak and the UN excluded these from its investigations. However, given al-Qahtani's instructions to the Tiger Team as disclosed by Saudi prosecutors, it seems pretty clear that Mutreb said those words even if its audio wasn't played to Callamard's team.

There was another curious fact passed on in *Diplomatik Vahşet*'s. If al-Madani got dressed in Khashoggi's 'still warm' clothes '20 minutes' after they had killed him at around 1.24pm, it looks as if he was walking around in them inside the consulate for close to an hour until 2.52pm, when he and Saif left the building through the back entrance and were caught on CC-TV. That meant almost an hour and a half of walking around in Khashoggi's clothes in the consulate. While possible, it didn't seem probable. More on this below.

Turkey now also claimed in the book that it had no recording on which consul-general al-Otaibi pleaded with Mutreb 'Don't do it here, I'll get into trouble'.

It was an odd thing to make a news item of *not* having a recording. If al-Otaibi did say those words, they implied prior knowledge and that Riyadh's orders relayed to the consul-general had included Khashoggi's execution. To confirm that al-Otaibi's words had indeed been uttered would invite an unwanted narrative in December. Clearly, MİT, while speaking to the authors of *Diplomatik Vahşet*, wanted to steer the reader away from the idea that the Khashoggi Operation had been pre-meditated murder.

On 22 October Erdoğan had claimed credit for the consul-general's sacking in his speech to the Turkish parliament and in his November *Washington Post* piece he had yet again made a point of singling out the consul-general – a minor figure in the plot – demanding al-Otaibi would be charged as he 'lied through his teeth to the media'. On the evidence so far, it looked as if his officials should be charged with the same..

Was there any chance that the key operatives would be punished, the authors wondered? They said professor lieutenant-colonel Tubaigy was in a luxury Jeddah villa with a pool. The consul-general's family was very well-connected, and al-Otaibi would likely receive immunity from prosecution in the kingdom. Nor was Mutreb under arrest, it was claimed separately in Middle East Eye, though the news site hadn't been able to verify this independently.

Although MBS's right hand man Saud al-Qahtani was relieved of his command of the Center for Studies and Media Affairs, he, like Michael Flynn at the time in the US, continued to brief his team members sources reported. He was for a while still in charge of the Saudi Federation for Cyber Security and in control of the extensive secret files he had compiled over the years.

The Center itself was folded under the leadership of Dr Nasir Al-Biqami, a Saudi official with a Master's from Loughborough University and a 2001 PhD from Nottingham University – both in 'information management'. His brief was very wide indeed and he had on 17 April 2018, met a Vatican delegation to discuss the 'moderation of extremism'. The UN inquiry report of 19 June 2019 said 'Subsequent reports, including official statements from Western governments, have suggested however, that at least Mr al-Qahtani is still in place, performing his advisory functions.'

Sabah also reported the book's surprising claim that Mutreb never said to al-Qahtani 'tell yours [boss] the deed is done' which first appeared in the *New York Times*. It was another case of MİT pedalling back from having a recording.

If MİT did have it, it would be the most direct piece of evidence linking Khashoggi's execution to MBS. But now *Diplomatik Vahşet* passed on MİT's opinion that it had been misreported by the *Times*.

It seemed that Erdoğan had also decided to drop his attempts to implicate MBS directly.

Another indication that Turkey was retreating from the high point of its narrative came months later in the UN report. Authorities now disowned the proof that instruments of torture had been brought into the country. To the UN team, the Istanbul prosecutor denied having the airport X-rays of the luggage of the Saudis involved (those travelling on the getaway jet, the sitting-duck, nor even of the officers travelling on commercial flights). The UN report noted without further comment that this denial was contradicted by what was written in

Diplomatik Vahşet (detail 87 footnote).

Whether *Sabah* journalists acted, in fact, as a serving-hatch for MİT and the Turkish government was addressed head on by Vice News/HBO. On 19 October, Andrew Potter of the news site visited *Sabah*'s Abdurrahman Şimşek and Ferhat Ünlü and challenged them on this point. Citing the fact that they had published most of the Khashoggi leaks, he challenged them whether they weren't being 'used' by 'unnamed sources inside the Turkish government' to do their bidding. Although *Sabah* had so far shown pitch-perfect timing, the two men rejected this charge and defended themselves to Vice News/HBO (reported on ahvalnews.com) by saying that they had published their leaks if anything 'a little early' for their government's liking.

***

On 1 January Arab-Spring online publication Rassdnews, or RNN – claiming to be a populist, independent network inspired by CNN – in Egypt, voted Erdoğan 'the world's most prominent president' at 72 per cent.

The news was enthusiastically reported by *Sabah* and other media in Turkey. Deposed Egyptian Muslim-Brotherhood ex-president Mohamed Morsi was second at 52 per cent, the oddball trio of Donald Trump, Vladimir Putin and King Salman brought up the rear for 2018, according to RNN.

XXV
Lies Ahead

On 30 January, UN special rapporteur Agnes Callamard was in Istanbul to investigate Jamal Khashoggi's murder. While Saudi Arabia had not agreed to give access to the consulate, Turkish authorities allowed Callamard to listen to the edited audio clip that MİT had distributed to intelligence agencies.

She presented a preliminary statement of her week-long fact finding mission on 6 February, saying that 'woefully inadequate time and access was granted to Turkish investigators to conduct a professional and effective crime-scene examination and search required by international standards for investigation.'

However, she also said that Turkey was guilty of the same charge with respect to her investigation, as investigators did not 'fulfil their pledge to provide access to forensic, scientific and police reports'. It was a damning conclusion for both countries.

Her charge of a lack of interest in the truth and cherry-picking through the evidence was equally true of Turkey's unofficial leaks to the media following 2 October. Apart from Erdoğan's personal press statements, spokespersons for Turkish government institutions rarely went on the record. Even these statements were contradictory. From the moment of access to the consulate even the investigations of the Istanbul chief prosecutor seemed to have more to do with optics and angling for headlines than a transparent process under the rule of law.

As for the unofficial, anonymous leaks of evidence to the press, these often provided suggestive imagery that fit into Turkey's 'Pulp Fiction' storyboard that prevailed in October. Turkey then dropped 'torture' from the story board from November after Saudi Arabia admitted to pre-meditated murder. Taken together, the second-hand leaks to the press created conflicting time lines, lacked detail, made unsubstantiated claims, provided words that were supposedly said on a recording but then apparently not said, and words that were presented to lead to a false impression as in the case of Tubaigy's being 'on heroin' or MİT's aggrandisement.

Instead of creating clarity, once it had released the information on Saturday 6 October that Khashoggi had been murdered, Turkey had used the leaks increasingly to show that Saudi Arabia acted in bad faith whereas Turkey supposedly acted in good faith.

But all it had done was chop and change the leaks to whatever point was needed at one time to embarrass Riyadh. While it had successfully forced the palace to admit high-ranking royal officials had assassinated Khashoggi during an extraordinary rendition, it was as cynical as Riyadh's in its use of releases to the international media. To Turkey's surprise it worked abroad because facts mattered in countries where the press was not on the government's leash. Regardless of the exact details surrounding it, Khashoggi's assassination by Saudi officials inside state offices had become undeniable.

Erdoğan claimed to 'have moved heaven and earth', but all that Turkey had done publicly was to issue arrest warrants while keeping forensic evidence a secret from everyone. Nor had it asked the UN to investigate or set up an independent inquiry in Turkey. In comparison, once Saudi authorities got started the usually taciturn country launched one investigation after another they almost seemed loquacious in their official statements and conclusions, ahead of the criminal case. In the month after the killing, the Saudi Press Agency (SPA) would issue no fewer than 148 releases (including 89 news items, 19 statements by minsters and princes, 11 phone calls and meetings by the king, 3 meetings by the crown prince, 2 statements by the consulate, 2 statements by attorney general Sheikh al Mojab, 1 statement by the minister of the interior, 2 statements by the foreign minister, 4 letters of condolences to the Khashoggi family, 1 letter by the supreme Wahhabi scholars *ulema* ('council'), 4 royal decrees).

Turkey's most public act was a furtive one – giving a severely edited audio clip to the secret services of Saudi Arabia, the United States, Germany, France and Britain that established only a minimum of bare facts in much the same way the short CC-TV clips did. The access given to UN rapporteur Callamard – who in particular thanks Istanbul chief prosecutor Irfan Fidan – for her report created the most official record of the 'crucial information' about the murder. But it was no more than partial access as the report carefully details.

Apart from its own facts with cracks, *Diplomatik Vahşet* (24 December) was the most comprehensive quasi-official catalogue of Turkey's leaks in one place and was important for that reason alone.

In the book the three *Sabah* journalists – Abdurrahman Şimşek, Ferhat Ünlü, Nazif Karaman (the first two with selfies with Erdoğan on their twitter masthead) – recreated a time line that matched what had been filtered to the media so far. Jamal Khashoggi dies some 10 minutes after entering the consulate at around 1.24pm and professor Tubaigy dismembers the body in about half an hour. He finishes around 1.54pm while the other operatives simultaneously pack the parts in the suitcases.

While that may well have been what happened, it meant that the majority of time spent in the consulate by the Tiger Team members remained unaccounted for. The Vito minivan with Khashoggi's remains left the consulate's backcourt at 3.08pm for the consul-general's residence. In a nutshell, it meant that for over 80 minutes ten people (UN detail 90, Table B) were doing what exactly?

Çetiner Çetin, *Haberturk*'s liaison with the Turkish Khashoggi investigators, did address this hiatus in his piece written in Turkish on 19 November. After the first minutes (11 according to his piece) of '*mêlée* and fight', followed 110 minutes of silence during which 'the Saudi team allegedly ran jammers'. These jammers explained the almost two hours of silence, as leaked by Turkish officials.

Then three men pierce the silence of the recording when they run downstairs. One of the three was an IT expert. He reset the nineteen internal CC-TV cameras that had been turned off before Khashoggi's arrival, and he wiped all data. One of the other two shouted he wanted the front-door of the consulate locked. This anonymous leak by security officials preceded the one described in *Diplomatik Vahşet*.

Çetin was also given detailed information about the location of the recording microphones. They were placed in 'Unit A', the consulate's section open to the public, and 'Unit B', the administrative offices behind it on the ground floor.

In Çetin's narrative, Khashoggi was apprehended by 'four voices' the moment he entered the door to the public section and was taken straight to the 'Unit B' offices behind it where the 11-minute '*mêlée* and fight' ensued with the cursing and shouting of 'seven voices', in addition to Jamal Khashoggi's. The three new voices included Maher Mutreb's, the negotiation-team leader, and Mohammed al-Otaibi's, as well as an unidentified third one.

After the *mêlée*, nineteen calls were made from 'Unit C', the consulate's upper-floor comms, encryption, and sound-sealed rooms. The reason why, Çetin writes, the microphones picked up nineteen calls despite the signal-jamming was because listening devices were placed at the bottom of the stairs of the consulate. They recorded talking voices and detected four calls to al-Qahtani by Mutreb. Their first call was 13 minutes after Khashoggi's arrival.

After some 2 hours, Çetin writes on 19 November, the crew left through Unit B and piled their luggage into the consular Vito van caught on MoBeSe CC-TV angled at the consulate's back entrance at 3.08pm. The van parked two hundred yards away at the consul-general's residence, together with the consular Audi with another group of Tiger Team operatives. (From '46 minutes' after the Tiger Team leaves the residence, Çetin writes, al-Otaibi did not leave his home until his departure back home days later, in a remarkably precise though seemingly irrelevant detail.)

The article went on to explain that 'Turkish authorities have no recording of the killing because there were no recording bugs in 'Unit C' itself. He then said that the three rooms that were repainted according to the Turkish forensic team were in Unit C upstairs, which was also where the marble floors were cleaned with two chemicals. They also found Tubaigy's finger-prints on two electrical outlets in these rooms.

Yet in *Diplomatik Vahşet*, the authors wrote that the recording heard everything, from Mutreb's decision to murder Khashoggi down to metal objects being put down in preparation for Tubaigy's dismemberment of the body well before Khashoggi's arrival.

Was what Çetin said about 1 hour and 50 minute 'silence' because of signal jamming nonsense, or was the detail based on the at least three hours of recordings in *Diplomatik Vahşet* the Apple-Watch story here?

If *Diplomatik Vahşet*'s new information was accurate then Jamal Khashoggi died about 30 minutes before Tubaigy got involved – dismember and have the body packed up in a frenzy. Al-Madani left the consulate's backdoor at 2.52pm on CC-TV. The Vito van with the suitcases would leave some 15 minutes later to head for the consul-general's residence. The five other cars dispersed at the same time. Bearing in mind that *Diplomatik Vahşet* claims Khashoggi died around 1.24pm, Jamal Khashoggi's time of death was at the latest between 2.15 and 2.30pm. Such a time would leave 60 to 75 minutes unaccounted during which Khashoggi was still able to talk.

On 13 October, Khashoggi's presumed birthday, *Sabah* had reported leaks by Turkish officials what was on the audio ahead of the transcripts that would follow the days ahead. In fact the reporters who also wrote *Diplomatik Vahşet*, wrote then that Khashoggi 'was interrogated, tortured'. Leaking to the Middle East Eye news site, Turkish officials had leaked this as early as 7 October and had added that Khashoggi was 'beaten'. Yet at the end of December, during the publication of *Diplomatik Vahşet*, this aspect of the Khashoggi affair lay fallow.

Whether one believes that Khashoggi was interrogated or not, and whether he was tortured in the process of extracting answers, depends on one's view of the balance of probabilities. What was the likely point of a nineteen-men operation equipped with torture tools? When Mutreb decided – on the section of the consulate audio recording shared with foreign intelligence agencies, if Khashoggi doesn't agree to come back 'we will kill him here' – did he mean injecting Khashoggi as quickly as possible with a killing drug? Or did he want to try to extract at least some of the answers Riyadh was hoping to get by interrogation in Saudi Arabia (if Khashoggi agreed to fly back 'voluntarily') or Yalova (if not)?

The affirmative seems inescapable. The one thing Khashoggi as a former intelligence official was certain of if Saudi authorities detained him at the consulate was that they would interrogate him. He just didn't think they would be heavy-handed or, for example, knew about his secret talks with al-Baghdadi and the US Muslim Brotherhood. There were a minimum of ten operatives in the consulate (six cars left at 3.08pm and seven men and two cars are seen at the consul-general's residence minutes later). Did they really only spend that time mopping the floor after pathologist Tubaigy dismembered Khashoggi from MİT's putative time of death – 1.24pm? The conclusion he was tortured seems inescapable, as that an *omertà* had been brokered between Turkey and the palace.

The UN report noted the absence proof here, too, but without further analysis: 'The exact time of Mr. Khashoggi's death could not be confirmed with certainty. The ten minutes reference is based on the fact that after ten minutes, Mr. Khashoggi voice was not heard' (detail 92 footnote 39). At 1.39pm in the recording Turkish intelligence told the UN delegation they heard a bone saw, but they 'could not make out the sources of the sounds they heard' (UN detail 96).

Nor was the access Turkey gave the UN very transparent. The UN rapporteur noted that they were 'prohibited from making notes' once the recording reached Khashoggi's voice (detail 94 footnote 40). The report gave no analysis of Turkey's reason for this obfuscation, but it also said that they were hampered in yet another way, in that they could not 'retain any transcript' (detail 41c). Though no journalist ever got to hear the recordings first-hand, otherwise the UN delegation was treated no different than members of the press and were fed a narrative rather than insight into the forensics by Turkish officials.

The UN rapporteur did, however, address the issue of obfuscation in respect of the select number of recordings the UN delegation were allowed to listen to. They were 'not allowed to have clones of the recordings'. The point of this was preventing access to metadata of the recording such as 'when, how the data were created, the time and date of creation and the source and the process used to create it' (UN detail 41b). In other words if the recordings that were played had been sliced together only Turkey would know it. In October, the 7-minute Pulp Fiction edit had been given to foreign secret-services; but, from the copy they had, none had realised that Tubaigy's words were spoken before the execution (which would at the time have weakened Turkey's leverage).

Officials told the UN delegation it had at least 7 hours of recording over a two-day period, but that they would only play seven phone calls totalling 45 minutes to them. The delegation also listened to 'a recording of the killing' and recordings dated from '28 September to 2 October'. There was 'much more recorded information than that made available'.

If Turkey made everything a matter of public record, as Western governments would be expected to do, Erdoğan's control over the story would be lost. Thus freedom of information requests in the West, for example, break Western governments' monopoly over the narrative, giving the media and others a means of doing their own fact finding. Like MBS, Erdoğan's officials were instructed to distribute and redistribute the facts in a flexible manner. For the Turkish (and the Saudi) media this movable feast was business as usual, too – asking good questions could have dangerous consequences.

As for the issue whether Khashoggi was interrogated and tortured during the unccounted hour and half in the consulate, this was leaked for the last time in the Affair by both a reliable Saudi and a reliable Turkish source to *Independent*'s respected journalist Borzou Daraghi on 30 October. This interrogation took either 1 hour (according to the Turkish source close to Turkish officials) or 2 hours (according to the Saudi source close to Saudi authorities, who were by that time moving to the 'gone rogue' story). Mutreb's five-strong 'negotiation team' (whose existence was disclosed by Saudi prosecutors) interrogated Khashoggi whether there was any record of his sensitive 9/11 work for Saudi intelligence under Prince Turki and the names of his associates after his self-exile.

Clearly, this part of the story was no longer welcome to the Erdoğan of June 2019. But was it true? Turkey had twisted facts (Tubaigy's music) and unfacted leaks (al-Otaibi's 'don't do it here' and MBS's 'boss') and denied them (the airport X-rays) and withheld them (unfettered UN access to forensics and audio). But it couldn't be accused of having invented them – Saudi Arabia would have a field day if they did (as per the iPhone's 'Turkish update' and Khashoggi's passport). As to this part of the Khashoggi story, Turkey's anonymous officials stopped using 'interrogation' and 'torture' in leaks after 19 October, the day on which Saudi Arabia admitted Khashoggi had died at the hands of palace operatives. Thus, the conclusion seems inescapable that Turkey had audio evidence that at least some interrogation, if not worse, of Khashoggi took place during the missing hour and a half on a balance of probabilities.

Before the affair, relations between Turkey and Saudi 'went down and suffered a lot, over Syria, over the Muslim Brotherhood, over the US, over Yemen', according to Vehbi Baysun, a history and literature scholar at Ibn Haldun University in Istanbul, cited by Daraghi in his piece. Erdoğan's leverage – the idea that there was more evidence in Turkey's possession – had the advantage of making MBS beholden to Turkey and turning Erdoğan's own pariah status around.

Apart from the seesaw beauty contest between MBS and Erdoğan, easing Saudi pressure on Qatar, the brotherhood, and US, support for rebellious Kurds in Syria, etc was a coup for Turkey. It would bring its own diplomatic and financial rewards for Turkey's listing economy. At his economic forum, for example, MBS made a conciliatory remark about Qatar and, on 25 April, the news broke that the US and Turkey were negotiating joint patrols in Kurdish safe zones in Manji, Northern Syria. The harvest from Erdoğan's Khashoggi campaign was plentiful.

***

Timed a few days after Agnes Callamard's press statement, Hatice Cengiz published her own book *Jamal Khashoggi* in Turkey. It was co-written with a Turkish war correspondent who did the last interview with Muammar Gaddafi and was now editor of the authoritative Turkish magazine *Foreign Policy* for which Cengiz had written, as well as a Turkish freelance journalist who had contributed

Turkish pieces to the BBC News Türkçe news site.

The book was published by Kopernik, a dual-language publisher with offices in Istanbul (kopernikkitap.com) and Gaithersburg, Maryland (kopernikpublishing.com). Among many rejections, it said on its website 'we reject double-standards', and promised the best of Turkish writing – including 'pulsating' thrillers and 'subliminal' poetry. On its publication board was Mehmet Erdoğan, a onetime civil servant in Turkey's Public Relations Directorate and a literary critic. An English language edition was announced but then withdrawn.

Contrary to what she had said on Turkish TV in October, Cengiz wrote in her book that Khashoggi considered the Saudi consulate very safe, much safer than the embassies in London and Washington, DC – where KBS had amiably invited him to and entertained him in his private office after embassy staff had recognised him during his December 2017 visit.

In a quick guide to the book on publication in Turkey on 7 February, *Sözcü* ('spokesman'), one of the few non-AKP papers left in Turkey, described Cengiz as a baker's daughter from Bursa. The *New York Times* added in an interview of 3 May 2019 that Cengiz had attended Bursa's *imam hatip*, a state-run religious secondary school and then the prestigious al-Azhar university in Cairo.

The *Times* also included the information that it was her father who paid for her three years in Cairo, as he was 'a wealthy kitchenware merchant in Istanbul'. The cost of tuition and living expenses would have been around $30,000 according to its website estimate. The family it seems moved away from Bursa at around the time she herself went to Cairo for her studies. It also seems that her father changed from owning a bakery to owning a kitchenware emporium in Bursa, and then Istanbul. Clearly that was a very fortuitous move as he was successful enough to cover the Cairo costs of six times Turkey's average wage.

Asked what advice Khashoggi would give her Cengiz thought he would say to her, 'Continue where you left off. You're a different person now. You'll be the prophet of Oman', referring to the Shia-Sunni divide. She planned to travel the Middle East by backpack to do research and write to get over the emotional emptiness she felt following Khashoggi's assassination.

Before backpacking, however, Hatice Cengiz started on a tour of human rights conferences – giving talks and taking part in discussions as Khashoggi once had. She would also on 16 May 2019 give testimony before the US House Foreign Affairs Committee at a hearing on 'the danger of reporting on human rights'. When she spoke, she was at times close to tears and spoke emotionally about the life they were going to have in DC. Chris Smith, a US congressman on the committee, said that her 'written testimony was really a love letter' to Jamal.

She said that here had been 'no truth', no one knew where the body was nor why he was killed. Furthermore, 'seven, eight months later we see nothing has been done and that is why I'm here today'. She regretted that 'the world' was pulling its punches. She hoped that Congress could initiate an 'international investigation' and thought that 'President Trump could initiate this as well'.

Asked by the chair of the committee, Democratic congresswoman Karen Bass, what she thought the US government should do, she angled her answer at Saudi Arabia:

'The legal process in Saudi Arabia was not transparent. We don't know why he was killed. We don't know where the body is. If congress, if it undertakes an international investigation to put pressure on Saudi Arabia to share its information with the public and the United States that could be one thing, there could also be sanctions against Saudi Arabia.'

In the book Cengiz also published her formal interviews with Khashoggi for the first time, whose recordings had brought them together from 6 May 2018.

Khashoggi addressed Saudi Arabia's structural problems, from 'skyrocketing numbers of guest workers to the diminishing oil income'. MBS 'needs to realise Vision 2030. Actually, it would be enough if he could realise one third of the things Erdoğan has achieved in Turkey', Khashoggi said from the grave. He praised his presidential friend for opening up Turkey to Syrian refugees and Egyptian exiles, though he also criticised the shrinking space for opinions in public in what was going to be his new host country.

Specifically Khashoggi's objection to MBS was that 'Mohammed bin Salman believes he is an extraordinary leader, like Atatürk.' 'He thinks he is the only one who can save us from radicalism and poverty.' MBS should be like his grandfather King ibn Saud the founder of the kingdom instead, Khashoggi argued. 'Even to him, people could go with different opinions', but instead 'the crown prince never listens to anyone'.

That rankled most with Khashoggi. It wasn't that he was necessarily convinced MBS's economic policies were wrong as such. In all honesty, 'He didn't really know whether he would consider MBS a failure in ten years' time', said Cengiz.

On 29 October, Kirsty Wark had asked Cengiz whether the fact of the two of them getting married could be seen by the Saudis as a 'provocation'. It was the key question considering al-Qahtani's briefing of the Tiger Team on 29 September that Khashoggi was a traitor.

'If he had ever expected that marrying a young Turkish woman would be seen as a political provocation, I would have thought he would not have allowed this relationship to move forward', she had responded to Wark's question.

In her own book, Cengiz gave the answer from her own point of view and said, 'I wouldn't have accepted the marriage proposal if I knew this would happen'. But, then, Jamal Khashoggi withheld information from her.

She had never had the same intensity of feeling for anyone else, though she also curiously admitted to the *New York Times* in May 2019 about their marriage,

'Let's not think of it as a romantic proposal'.

'We were not children – we were two adults, and we immediately had a very rational conversation about how we could share it, how we could make it work.'

In February specialist retrieval firm Kroll analysed the WhatsApp messages between Saud al-Qahtani and MBS, and, reviewing the report, the Saudi chief-prosecutor concluded non were connected with the Khashoggi rendition. In early March, the *Guardian* published news reports on MBS's position thought to be 'baseless' by Riyadh officials. Before and after his father's visits to Egypt that month, MBS was increasingly absent in public and at officials meetings. The king had also received the damning conclusions of an investigation into political prisoners, which MBS had resisted. MBS was relieved of some investment and governmental authority, and on a trip to Egypt the king replaced his royal personal security detail with thirty staunch loyalists.

A month and a half after King Salman's 'human-rights' interventions, thirty seven Saudis were beheaded by sword around the kingdom, however, 'for adopting terrorist and extremist thinking and for forming terrorist cells to corrupt and destabilise security'.

On 17 March, at the second trial hearing in Riyadh cultural attaché al-Muslih said he didn't know Khashoggi's body was in the minivan he drove to the consul-general's residence; al-Balawi said that Mutreb had ordered him to dissect Khashoggi's body. Earlier on 30 January, brigadier-general al-Madani argued that it was his duty to impersonate Jamal. Similarly, al-Balawi and the two al-Sehris said they were executing orders when they covered Khashoggi's mouth when he started screaming. The UN report noted later that no screaming was heard on the recording their delegation heard (UN 213), and called for the suspension of the trial because of it 'is held behind closed doors; the identity of those charged has not been released nor is the identity of those facing death penalty' (UN 16), noting that some statements by Saudi chief prosecutor al-Mojeb 'and the identity of 11 perpetrators currently on trial do not match' (UN 6).

On 30 March, Amazon and *Washington Post* owner Jeff Bezos's security advisor of 22 years wrote in the Daily Beast that 'the Saudis had access to Bezos's phone, and gained private information' which they then leaked to the *National Enquirer*, a tabloid run by a friend of Donald Trump's, David Pecker, and led to Bezos's divorce. This was part of a campaign of harassments against Amazon and Bezos since October 2018.

President Erdoğan, MBS fiend and the world's greatest imprisoner of journalists, was given opeds in Bezos's *Washington Post* print edition on 2 November and on 19 March. It was as often as Khashoggi's pieces had appeared in the main paper, including his posthumous one. On 19 March Erdoğan wrote, 'Western leaders must learn... to embrace Muslims living in their respective countries'. A report published around the same time by UK foreign secretary

Jeremy Hunt stated that the AKP portrayed Christians as a 'threat to the stability of the nation' and as 'not real Turks but as western collaborators'.

On 1 April, Erdoğan's party narrowly lost the mayoral elections against the opposition in both Ankara and Istanbul. The election board cancelled the outcome due to perceived irregularities on 7 May, ordering a rerun in both cities. 'Those who rely on the guns in their hands, those who rely on the power of the media cannot build democracy', Erdoğan had said after the coup in Egypt. 'Democracy can only be built at the ballot box'. Erdoğan's strong-man appeal was waning among Turkish metropolitan voters after the Khashoggi affair.

On 3 April, CNN revealed that Khashoggi's children received houses, a lump sum of 1 million riyals ($267,000) and $10,000 a-month stipends further to Riyadh's official admission that palace officials had killed their father. King Salman himself had approved these payments.

Depending on guilty verdicts against the eleven accused, the siblings could look forward to further compensation that would bring the total close to $70 million. Under Sharia law this would depend on the family accepting 'blood money', CNN reported, whereby the accused offered money to avoid the death penalty. In the past the palace had picked up the bill in similar circumstances and paid between 100-200 million riyals ($27 and $54 million).

Only Khashoggi's eldest son Salah still lived in Saudi Arabia, and had received a house worth $4 million, while his three siblings received more modest accommodations. As the three intended to remain in the US, where they had naturalised, they would not receive any of the benefits according to Saudi officials, CNN also reported.

On 10 April 2018, Salah posted on his twitter account 'no settlement discussion had been or is discussed', but, he continued, 'Acts of generosity and humanity come from the high moral grounds they possess, not admission of guilt... We... thank acts of good not disavow.' Callamard's UN inquiry team 'obtained information regarding a financial package offered to the children'.

On 23 December, after a trial behind closed doors a Saudi court sentenced five operatives – Mutreb, Tubaigy, al-Balawi, Turki al-Sehri, Waleed al-Sehri (UN detail 183) – to death (usually carried out by beheading) and three defendants received prison terms. These were Abahussain (as group leader, otherwise al-Zahrani who was at the consulate like the following two), al-Madani and Saif al-Qahtani presumably. The remaining three defendants were acquitted. Four of the Tiger Team were never charged.

Subsequently, on 22 May 2020, during Ramadan, traditionally a period of grace in Saudi Arabia, Salah tweeted, 'we, the sons of the martyr Jamal Khashoggi, announce that we forgive and pardon those who participated in the killing of our father'. On 7 September, the death penalty was commuted by the Saudi courts to 20 years in prison. Of the other three defendants, the two generals received a final sentence of 17 years each and al-Qahtani was given a 10-year sentence. Where and how the sentences were served exactly remained unclear.

Turkey started its own in-absentia trial against 20 Saudis, including MBS's associates al-Asiri and Saud al-Qahtani, on 3 July 2020. Prosecutors called seven employees at the consulate, apart from others. Callamard welcomed the trial as she thought Turkey would finally share its forensic evidence with the rest of the world.

A lawyer, she was in particular interested in the chain of command. She concluded in her 19 June UN report that there was 'credible evidence' of MBS's individual involvement and that it 'warranted further investigation'. Her verdict was followed on 29 September by MBS himself on CBS's 60 Minutes, where he had previously announced he wanted nuclear weapons if Iran had them. He said, 'I take full responsibility as a leader in Saudi Arabia', but he denied have given the assassination order or any direct involvement.

To what extent had US intelligence closed its eyes prior to 2 October so as not tangle with Trump administration priorities to sell nuclear technology? On 9 May 2019, *Time* magazine reported that the CIA issued public 'Duty-to-Warn' notices to Khashoggi's contacts Iyad el-Baghdadi, Omar Abdulaziz, and another who asked not to be part of the publicity. The first two lived in Norway and Canada, rather than the US, and were geographically beyond the scope of the duty-to-warn directive. The three men were told to 'avoid travel to a wide swath[e] of countries in Europe and Asia where Saudi Arabia has particular influence, and to move family members out of at least one particular country, Malaysia'.

There is one Middle Eastern country that has not been mentioned so far. It is the only one in the region that is suspected of already having nuclear weapons – Israel. It is also one of the four nations in the world that never signed the 1968 Non-Proliferation Treaty (India, Pakistan, and South Sudan, a country minted in 2011, are the others).

Israel's policy has been to ensure that none of its neighbours join the select club of nations with atomic weapons. It has effectively sabotaged nuclear power plants in Iran and Iraq to destroy facts on the ground establishing themselves in those nations. Yet its response to the Trump administration's plan to sell nuclear technology to Saudi Arabia was as mute as was its response to tearing up the 2015 Iran Treaty. It seems not to consider the Saudi royal family a threat to its existence and tacitly supported special envoy Jared Kushner's mission in this area.

Did a benefit materialise for Israel during this period? On 23 March 2019, Donald Trump said that it is time to recognise Israel's sovereignty over the strategically important Golan Heights that Israel has occupied since the 6-day war in 1967. On June 16, Netanyahu's cabinet inaugurated Ramat Trump (Trump Heights), a rebranded thirty-year-old settlement of ten people in the Golan

Heights.

On 3 April 2019, Bloomberg revealed footage of Saudi Arabia's first atomic facility.

'There's a very high probability these images show the country's first nuclear facility', Robert Kelley, a former IAEA director told the TV station. Argentina's state-owned INVAP SE sold the unit to Saudi Arabia, which planned to start later in the year.

Although this was merely a small training and research facility, Saudi Arabia had instructed a French firm to undertake a study for the tender of 2 reactors in the winter of 2018. Rosatom (Russia), Westinghouse Electric (IP3's troubled infant) China National Nuclear, Kepco (South Korea) and Électricité de France (EDF) were selected to bid for the $10bn tender. It was supposed to be announced in 2018, but the decision on the final contract was kicked into the long-grass after the Khashoggi Affair until at least 2022.

On 8 April, Erdoğan visited Putin in Russia to discuss the ongoing formalities to purchase the s-400 air-missile defence system and joint-efforts against the Kurds in Syria now that the US was withdrawing. It was his third visit in three months.

Conclusion
Erdoğan and Khashoggi

☙

The central unanswered question that remains is the one BBC journalist Kirsty Wark asked Hatice Cengiz on 29 October: why did Jamal Khashoggi take up his whirlwind plan to marry her and set up a life in Istanbul?

Khashoggi 'wanted to get married again' to fill the emptiness in his life, she said, and, indeed, so he did. In June, he married his fourth wife, the beautiful Egyptian Hanan Atr, in Washington DC after having wooed her since the beginning of the year. By the end of the Spring his life was settled again after his exile. He was officially a resident of the US and could freely and safely travel again. He was rebuilding his life, jetting around the world to conferences – including the 6 May one at which he met Cengiz – and had big plans to discuss with the *Washington Post* about setting up an Arabic online edition of the paper aimed at pan-Arabia. On a practical note, Riyadh hadn't interrupted his pension despite his critical pieces online in the *Post* and after the collapse of the Iran Nuclear Deal in May, and MBS even seemed to have come round that he needed Khashoggi to become his (honest) advisor – though Khashoggi had zero interest in that role after the Ritz Carlton putsch.

Khashoggi didn't tell Cengiz about his fourth marriage as they continued their post-conference 'conversations' (even as his fiancée, she didn't know many other things from his life). But from the moment he had mentioned his desire to get married, Cengiz saw him differently and started a 'special, direct dialogue'. He visited Turkey more often, meeting his friends President Erdoğan, Yasin Aktay and others. As their intimacy grew, Khashoggi floated the idea of marriage, saying 'no one has loved me like you do.' 'Let's not think of it as a romantic proposal', she told the *New York Times*, despite their obvious attraction. They discussed frankly how it might work.

It was a fateful move. Khashoggi's sudden change of plan in August to marry a Turkish foreign-affairs analyst and start a life in Istanbul reached Saudi Arabia and his extraordinary rendition was put on the agenda by palace intelligence. As MBS's right-hand man Saud al-Qahtani told the fifteen Tiger Team operatives on 29 September, his 'presence outside of Saudi Arabia represents a threat to national security'.

Not that Turkey was a notably safe place for writers. In fact, Erdoğan's record was far worse than that of Saudi Arabia. According to the Sweden-based advocacy group Stockholm Center for Freedom that tracks cases of prosecutions of Turkish journalists, Turkey had 245 journalists behind bars as of 24 January 2018, with another 140 journalists facing outstanding arrest warrants. 'Turkey jails more journalists than the rest of the world combined', its secretary general Levent Kenez said on 23 May 2019. Like Vladimir Putin after his election as Russian President in 2001, Erdoğan had increasingly throttled the relatively free Turkish press since his first rise to power in 2003 through popular Islam. Reporters without Borders said that between 25 and 30 professional and non-professional journalists were being detained in Saudi Arabia – a country where there had never been press freedom.

As with MBS, Khashoggi had a personal relationship with Erdoğan. 'There was some kind of bond there. In how he viewed Erdoğan, it was with an eye towards what he [Erdoğan] had been during his earlier political career. Khashoggi saw there was some of that still there', said Qatar Foundation's Maggie Salem Mitchell. Of roughly the same age, both men had flirted with the Muslim Brotherhood in their twenties. 'He felt real simpatico with Erdoğan'.

One major difference was that Khashoggi had no interest in Turkey's national politics, nor spoke Turkish. His obsession was with Saudi Arabia and the Arab world and the consequences of the Arab Spring. Turkey with its mix of religious and non-religious parties in a parliament was the best working model in the Arab Middle East in the way that Iran's democratic theocracy was certainly not. 'There can be no political reform and democracy in any Arab country without accepting that political Islam is a part of it. A significant number of citizens in any given Arab country will give their vote to Islamic political parties if some form of democracy is allowed'. This is what Khashoggi wrote in one of his last online pieces for the *Washington Post* Global Opinions section.

In any case, while the Turkish-language media were held in a vice by Erdoğan's government, there was greater breathing space for those writing in English and Arabic. Aktay flatteringly called his friend, the 'most intellectual person in Saudi Arabia'.

What bothered Khashoggi most about modern Saudi Arabia was that free-wheeling political discussions behind closed doors could land you in trouble. Though obedient in public when he lived in Saudi, he enjoyed those kind of private jousts. But, now, under MBS's rule, if you said something critical during a dinner party you could be arrested. Saudi friends told Khashoggi Khahoggi this had happened to a member on the Consultative Assembly of Saudi Arabia, the *Majlis ash-Shura*, an advisory council of one hundred and fifty wise men chosen by royal appointment. Optically, it functioned as the Saudi parliament as it theoretically had the ability to propose laws to the monarch. 'This really upset, Jamal' said Salem Mitchell.

But what exactly did Khashoggi talk about with President Erdoğan and top officials like Yasin Aktay, chief aide to the president and deputy chairman of AKP, when he and they met in the early summer of 2018?

Erdoğan and his lieutenants had a country to run. Did they discuss the Arab version of the *Washington Post* Global Opinions that Khashoggi was hoping to set up through his editor Karen Attiah? Or was that a way for Khashoggi to get the president interested in taking a meeting? What other proposals were on Ankara's agenda, and did the men comment on the fast-moving developments with Cengiz and Khashoggi's relocation to Istanbul? Yasin Aktay clearly knew of her because he already had her number in his iPhone under 'Kaşikçi' rather than her maiden name 'Cengiz'.

When Qatar Foundation Maggie Salem Mitchell sent back her mark-ups of Khashoggi's August piece for the *Washington Post* he went with them but wrote, 'They're going to hang me when it comes out'.

Khashoggi's meetings with Aktay and Erdoğan, however, were in a very different league from opinions filtered through a US newspaper. Khashoggi's X-ray vision of Saudi politics, Riyadh and the palace, not to mention his vast network of Saudi and global contacts could be harnessed to aide Erdoğan's geopolitical rivalry with MBS. There was also his thirty-years of refined knowledge of top-secret Saudi intelligence, including 9/11.

Needless to say, for anyone seeking to play, derail or understand the oil kingdom, the opportunity of getting Khashoggi on side would be worth his weight in gold several times over. It was as if a KGB general voluntarily tendered himself to the CIA, knocking at the door at Langley. When Erdoğan, briefed by Aktay, sat down to talk business with Khashoggi, he must have thought his visitor was a gift from god.

The Killer Prince?

∾

MBS and King Salman were Saudi reformers, but only to the extent that they realised that unrest could only be staved off by reforming the government. Neither had any intention of reforming the monarchy. Following in the footsteps of Salman's father ibn Saud, their style of government was based on a complex number of practical bargains. Like ibn Saud, foreign policy relied on allegiance to the world's superpower. Originally, this meant the British Empire and, after World War II, al-Saud fealty transferred to the US. MBS carried on that tradition, like Khashoggi had aided King Abdullah with the same. At the heart of this relationship were also deals: purchases of the latest weaponry to stay ahead of neighbouring countries. The overal result was not pretty, but it proved highly effective in a combustible part of the world for the al-Sauds.

The Khashoggi Affair did affect MBS and Salman's nuclear ambitions. In 2020, the Joe Biden White House was in no mood to continue the nuclear reactor deals promoted by Donald Trump's team. At the same time, these initiatives were not closed down. Nor did US arms sales to Saudi Arabia cease. King Salman, a senior Saudi statesman since 1964, knew that the most important thing in international relations was to mount real negotiations such those MBS started with Trump in 2017. Once formalised they are hard to hard to shut down and at some point they will bear fruit through either financial or strategic logic.

On 10 March 2020, Salman and MBS bolstered MBS's sucession when they arrested Salman's last-living Sudairi brother Prince Ahmed, former Sudairi crown prince bin Nayef and his younger brother, Prince Nawaf. The charge was treason. Prince Ahmed was the head of the Allegiance Council, a body made up of ibn Saud's sons and their male descendents. Though it was never ratified, King Abdullah had founded it in 2006 as the body that would determine royal succession, hitherto the prerogative of the king. The three princes were alleged to have had a discussion to use the council to block MBS's succession.

The million dollar question remained: why did Riyadh bother with the Khashoggi Operation in the first place? Something about him must have touched a vital nerve, like the three princes.

The Affair created many more negative headlines than Khashoggi could ever have created while alive. Even if one believes with the CIA that MBS gave the order, it remained odd that, once the information was out in the open, Riyadh seemed unphased by the negative media attention. If media containment was the objective, Riyadh could have shut down Turkey in the first week by announcing an internal investigation into the disappearance. Instead, Riyadh all but fanned the flames.

What the palace must surely also have regretted was the damage to Vision 2030 – for which MBS was courting foreign investors.

With the benefit of hindsight, would either MBS or King Salman have stopped the operation against Khashoggi had they known what would follow? Was there ever a real bargain that Khashoggi could accept at the consulate, or was it too a ruse to buy his cooperation and transfer him peacefully to the villa in Yalova, outside Istanbul? There is an Arab expression, *ana bayna yadaikum*, I am in your hands, that describes the position of a courtier to their lord. Surely it wasn't just that. What was worth the enormous risk and deployment of resources fit for a high-ranking prince to capture him – for example his knowledge of 9/11? Was torture part of the plan or indeed part of what happened at the consulate? Given Riyadh's lukewarm reaction when the Tiger Team's work in Istanbul became public knowledge, what would it say if the team had needed no formal approval from Saudi Arabia's top? For most of his life, Jamal Khashoggi held the view that, rooted in Sharia law interpreted by Wahhabi clerics, the al-Saud dynasty should govern Saudi Arabi. Towards the end of his life, he seemed to have changed his opinion at least with regards to MBS. Or was it not personal, and was he convinced that the Saudi media should be as free as it had been when King Abdullah ruled, or had he reached the conclusion that it should be freer in the wake of digital media. And which Khashoggi was right?

On 8 October 2021, PIF, a Saudi investment fund of $500 billion chaired by MBS bought Newcastle United, a British football club. The owners received $400 million to the delight of its fans and the dismay of human rights groups. On 9 October, the *Guardian* published a report on the reemergence of MBS's right-hand man and Khashoggi's nemesis at the consulate. In the words of an anonymous Gulf official, 'There is no question that [Saud al-]Qahtani is back'. MBS's Davos in the Desert in November 2021 was given a Bloomberg headline that said, 'Gets Its Timing Right'. Perhaps King Salman was right in trusting spycraft, the passage of time and the power of money in international affairs when planning ambitious deals?

Reader, over to you.

Lightning Source UK Ltd.
Milton Keynes UK
UKHW011539221021
392666UK00003B/42